LIBRARY OF NEW TESTAMENT STUDIES

363

formerly the Journal for the Study of the New Testament Supplement series

Editor
Mark Goodacre

RECONSTRUCTING THE FIRST-CENTURY SYNAGOGUE

A Critical Analysis of Current Research

STEPHEN K. CATTO

t&t clark

Published by T&T Clark International
A Continuum imprint
The Tower Building, 11 York Road, London SE1 7NX
80 Maiden Lane, Suite 704, New York, NY 10038

www.tandtclark.com

British Library Cataloguing-in-Publication Data
A catalogue record for this book is available from the British Library

ISBN-10: 0-567-04561-7 (hardback)
ISBN-13: 978-0-567-04561-4 (hardback)

Typeset by Data Standards Limited, Frome, Somerset, UK.
Printed on acid-free paper in Great Britain by Cromwell Press Ltd, Trowbridge,
Wiltshire.

This work is dedicated to
Mandy Lorna Catto

CONTENTS

LIST OF FIGURES

Full bibliographical information is given in the bibliography.

LIST OF TABLES

ACKNOWLEDGEMENTS

This work is based on my doctoral thesis accepted by the University of Aberdeen in 2005. I am extremely grateful to my supervisor, Dr Simon Gathercole, who made himself freely available, offering help, criticism and perceptive guidance and, more importantly, was a constant encourager as I progressed. I am also indebted to my examiners, Dr Andrew Clarke and Prof. Sean Freyne, whose comments were particularly helpful.

There are many people who have helped me during my research, and I am grateful. Drs Clint Arnold and Moyer Hubbard were a source of great encouragement, as were their families; Dr Steve Walton read an early version of Chapter 5 and offered valuable guidance; similarly, Dr Steve Brady commented on Chapters 1–3; and Dr Charles Crowther discussed the Theodotos inscription with me. In addition, various scholars have provided help in sourcing material, or providing up-to-date information about archaeological sites, and their assistance is noted in the text. My colleagues at Moorlands College are also a source of encouragement, and I am particularly grateful to one of my students, Tom Oldman, for his help in the preparation of this manuscript.

During the process of research and writing, I have had the joy of belonging to two church communities: Drumoak and Durris Church of Scotland, while in Aberdeen, and St John's Church in Wimborne. I am particularly grateful to my minister in Aberdeen, Rev. Jim Scott, who regularly read and commented on the text of my dissertation, and to Elizabeth Crowther, in Wimborne, who read through the final version.

The opportunity to spend three years focused on this subject was a great privilege. An additional bonus was that it often allowed me to be available to my children, Jenna, Scott and Gregor, when they came home from school; and twenty minutes of wrestling or football seemed to refocus my mind well! This book, however, is dedicated to my wife, Mandy: she is my closest friend, confidante and encourager – thanks!

Bibliographical

AB   Anchor Bible

ABD   David Noel Freedman (ed.), *The Anchor Bible Dictionary* (New York: Doubleday, 1992)

AGJU   Arbeiten zur Geschichte des antiken Judentums und des Urchristentums

AJA   *American Journal of Archaeology*

ANES   *Ancient Near Eastern Studies*

ANRW   Hildegard Temporini and Wolfgang Haase (eds), *Aufstieg und Niedergang der ro«mischen Welt: Geschichte und Kultur Roms im Spiegel der neueren Forschung* (Berlin: W. de Gruyter, 1972–)

AnSt   *Anatolian Studies*

ASHAAD D. Urman and P.V.M. Flesher (eds), *Ancient Synagogues: Historical Analysis and Archaeological Discovery* (SPB, 47; 2 vols; Leiden: Brill, 1995)

BA   *Biblical Archaeologist*

BARev   *Biblical Archaeology Review*

BASOR *Bulletin of the American Schools of Oriental Research*

BECNT   Baker Exegetical Commentary on the New Testament

BJS   Brown Judaic Studies

BNTC   Black's New Testament Commentaries

CHJ   W. Horbury, W.D. Davies and J. Sturdy (eds), *The Cambridge History of Judaism*, vol. 3, *The Early Roman Period* (Cambridge: Cambridge University Press, 1999).

CIG   *Corpus inscriptioneum graecarum* (ed. A. Boeckh; 4 vols; Berlin, 1828–77)

ConNT   *Coniectanea neotestamentica*

CPJ   *Corpus papyrum judaicorum* (ed. V. Tcherikover; 3 vols; Cambridge, 1957–64)

CRINT   Compendia rerum iudaicarum ad Novum Testamentum

DSD   *Dead Sea Discoveries*

EKKNT Evangelisch-Katholischer Kommentar zum Neuen Testament

EvQ   *Evangelical Quarterly*

GLAJJ   M. Stern (ed.), *Greek and Latin Authors on Jews and Judaism* (3

OSMAP   Ostia Synagogue-area Masonry Analysis Project. University of Texas

PEFQS   *Palestine Exploration Fund, Quarterly Statement*

RB   *Revue biblique*

RevQ   *Revue de Qumran*

RevScRel   *Revue des sciences religieuses*

SAIS   Studies in the Aramaic Interpretation of Scripture

SBLCP   Society of Biblical Literature Centennial Publications

SBLDS   SBL Dissertation Series

ScEs   *Science et esprit*

SEG   *Supplementum epigraphicum graecum*

SJ   Studia judaica

SJLA   Studies in Judaism in Late Antiquity

SNTSMS   Society for New Testament Studies Monograph Series

SPB   Studia postbiblica

STDJ   Studies on the Texts of the Desert of Judah

STK   *Svensk teologisk kvartalskrift*

Str-B   H.L. Strack and P. Billerbeck, *Kommentar zum Neuen Testament aus Talmud und Midrasch* (6 vols; Munich, 1922-61)

SUNT   Studien zur Umwelt des Neuen Testaments

TANZ   Texte und Arbeiten zum neutestamentlichen Zeitalter

TBAFCS   B.W. Winter *et al.* (eds), *The Book of Acts in its First Century Setting* (5 vols; Grand Rapids: Eerdmans, 1993–6).

TDNT   G. Kittell and G. Friedrich (eds), *Theological Dictionary of the New Testament* (trans. G.W. Bromiley; 10 vols; Grand Rapids, 1964–76)

TNTC   Tyndale New Testament Commentaries

TRENT   Traditions of the Rabbis from the Era of the New Testament

TSAJ   Texte und Studien zum antiken Judentum

TynBul   *Tyndale Bulletin*

WBC   Word Biblical Commentary

WUNT   Wissenschaftliche Untersuchungen zum Neuen Testament

ZNW   *Zeitschrift fu«r die neutestamentliche Wissenschaft*

Ancient Sources

Cicero

Flacc.   *Pro Flacco*

Josephus

Ant.   *Antiquities of the Jews*

Apion   *Against Apion*

Life   *Life of Josephus*

War   The Jewish War

Juvenal
Sat.   *Satires*

Mishnah, Talmud and Related Literature
Abot   *Avot*
Arak.   *Arakhin*
Ber.   *Berakhot*
Ket.   *Ketubbot*
Kil.   *Kil'ayim*
Mak.   *Makkot*
Meg.   *Megillah*
Miqw.   *Mikwa'ot*
Sanh.   *Sanhedrin*
Shabb.   *Shabbat*
Sotah   *Sotah*
Sukkah   *Sukkah*
Taan.   *Ta'anit*
Tamid   *Tamid*
Yad.   *Yadayim*

Philo
Abr.   *De Abrahamo*
Agr.   *De agricultura*
Dec.   *De decalogo*
Deus Imm.   *Quod Deus sit immutabilis*
Flacc.   *Against Flaccus*
Hypoth   *Hypothetica*
Leg. Gai.   *Legatio ad Gaium*
Omn. Prob.Lib. *Quod omnis probus liber sit*
Plant.   *De plantatione*
Praem. Poen.   *De praemiis et poenis*
Quaest. in Gen. *Quaestiones in Genesin*
Somn.   *De somniis*
Spec. Leg.   *De specialibus legibus*
Vit. Cont.   *De vita contemplativa*
Vit. Mos.   *De vita Mosis*

Pseudepigrapha
3 Macc.   *3 Maccabees*
Ep. Arist.   *Letter of Aristeas*
Jub.   *Jubilees*

Pss. Sol.	*Psalms of Solomon*
Sib. Or.	*Sibylline Oracles*

Tacitus
Hist.	*Histories*

Chapter 1

INTRODUCTION

1. *Theme*

In the recent past, if someone wrote about the 'first-century synagogue', scholars had a fairly clear picture of what was being described. It would be assumed to mean an architecturally defined public building which was used for religious purposes especially on the Sabbath. In the last two decades, however, many of the assumptions previously held regarding the ancient 'synagogue'[1] have been challenged, with scholars questioning such a presentation from a number of different perspectives. Indeed, in their work, Urman and Flesher suggest that describing 'synagogue' studies as going through a paradigm shift would be an understatement, and that in fact 'many paradigms are shifting'.[2]

In recent years the ongoing work of archaeologists, particularly within Israel, has produced new sites which have been identified as potential synagogue buildings, while buildings previously identified are being re-dug to clarify points of uncertainty.[3] At the same time, textual material has been re-examined in greater detail particularly in light of the questions being posed by archaeology. Areas of current debate include: the origin of the 'synagogue', with a wide variety of possibilities proposed; architectural development and adaptation of synagogue buildings and the models they may have used; the function of the 'synagogue'; and whether 'synagogues' should be understood to be buildings or gatherings. Often this work has been carried out by scholars of Judaism with some of it first appearing in articles in Hebrew, the result being that the work has been slow to make its way into the field of New Testament studies.

Within New Testament scholarship the increased focus on 'synagogue' studies has raised new questions over what the 'synagogue' was like, and

---

1   Throughout this work inverted commas around 'synagogue' will be used where either a building or community is meant. When a building is solely intended, it will be identified as a synagogue building. This will inevitably lead to a slightly awkward style but will aid a clearer discussion of the material.

2   *ASHAAD*, vol. 1, p. xvii.

3   E.g. the re-examination of the synagogue building at Ostia by the University of Texas. See http://www.utexas.edu/research/isac/projects/index.html (accessed 28 May 2007).

how it might inform our exegesis of New Testament texts. Also, as it undoubtedly played an important role in first-century Judaism, the 'synagogue' as an institution has a significant contribution to make in historical Jesus studies. In an excellent recent article, Mark Rapinchuk notes that the area of Galilee has become of great significance in historical Jesus research;[4] an accurate understanding of the situation that existed in the region, and indeed in wider Palestine, will help bring a fuller understanding of Jesus and his social milieu.[5] Within such an assessment a clear presentation of the role that the 'synagogue' played in local communities will be important background material for Jesus research. Similarly, a more accurate understanding of the Jewish cultural background in areas such as Asia Minor or the city of Rome will provide a more nuanced and comprehensive understanding of the early Christian communities and their interaction with Jewry.

The purpose of this work is to enter into this debate, assessing both the primary sources and recent scholarship on the first-century 'synagogue'. Specifically, we will, first, examine the literary and archaeological material available which can inform our understanding of the first-century 'synagogue'; second, assess the practices that might be defined as 'sacred' and which were associated with 'synagogues' during this period; and third, compare the evidence gathered to the presentation of the 'synagogue' in Luke-Acts, identifying possible anachronism as well as highlighting how this material can better inform our exegesis of passages.

In order to carry out this task, and in light of the recent debate over whether synagogue buildings existed in the first century CE, it will be helpful to re-examine the literary evidence available to us. This will be the focus of Chapter 2, which will show that in the first-century period, and before, buildings were used by the Jews for Sabbath gatherings. Against the arguments of the minimalists in the debate, it will be shown that συναγωγή could be used of these buildings in the first half of the first century CE; however, a variety of other terms were also used for these meeting-places and these will be identified. The geographical spread of the various terms will be noted and it will be argued that their use is likely to reflect the understanding of the function of a meeting place within a particular locality.

While the literary material will be re-assessed in light of the new debate, by far the most fluid area of research has come in archaeology, and this will be the focus of Chapter 3. Within the last ten years possible new synagogue-building sites have been proposed at Jericho, Qiryat Sefer and

4   M. Rapinchuk, 'The Galilee and Jesus in Recent Research', *Currents in Biblical Research* 2 (2004), pp. 197–222, esp. 214–15.

5   See for example the work of Peter Richardson on how the archaeology of towns such as Cana and Capernaum can assist such an endeavour, *Building Jewish in the Roman East* (Waco: Baylor University Press, 2004).

Khirbet Qana. These architectural remains can be assessed in light of other sites previously proposed in Palestine. Further, new light may also be shed on these earlier sites, in relation to architectural style and structure, by such comparisons. In the Diaspora a great deal of scholarly debate has revolved around the building at Ostia. This has culminated in a five-year project to re-dig the site, which is being carried out by a team from the University of Texas. It will be argued that this complex and the one at Delos were first-century synagogue buildings and as such offer insight into possible differences in practice in these Diaspora communities. The integration of this material will allow a more accurate presentation of synagogue buildings in the first century CE.

In order to combat the overly sceptical stance of the minimalists, throughout Chapters 2 and 3 the focus of the discussion will be on the 'synagogue' as a building. This does not, however, preclude the possibility that in some communities assemblies would have taken place in locations other than purpose-built structures, that is, in domestic settings or in other public buildings. Therefore, we will steer a middle course between the maximalists and minimalists: it will be shown that in this period the 'synagogue' should not be seen as a monolithic institution; rather, we need to take account of the geographical location and socio-economic environment of particular Jewish communities in order to understand better how the first-century 'synagogue' may have looked in any particular location.

Chapter 4 will focus on the 'worship' of the 'synagogue'. The possible problems of using words such as 'worship' to identify sacred practice in the first-century period will be noted, and it will be argued that twenty-first-century distinctions between sacred and secular practice ought not to be used of the earlier period. Following the pattern of Chapters 2 and 3, the geographical location of any practice will be highlighted and possible local distinctions noted. While the connection of Scripture reading with the 'synagogue' is not disputed by anyone, whether it should be regarded as a sacred act is more contentious. Here it will be argued that such reading and teaching were more than a didactic activity and should be seen as worship. Against the arguments of McKay, Levine and Fleischer, prayer will be shown to have existed both in Palestine and the Diaspora, although potential differences in practice between Palestine and the Diaspora will be noted.

Two further areas will be addressed which will shed light on the use of the 'synagogue'. First, issues of sanctity, both of the place and the person, will be explored: geographical variations in practice will be identified and it will be argued that Jewish groups were influenced by the cultural environment in which they lived. Second, the influence of voluntary associations in relation to dining will be examined. The synagogue building at Ostia with its *triclinium* will be used as a case study, comparing it to the design and function of other guild buildings in the city in the first century CE. In addition, other sites, along with references to communal dining, will be examined. Again, a comparison with the cultural milieu within which Judaism existed will show that these communal meals would have had a sacred element to them.

While the homogeneous nature of the 'synagogue' has been assumed in much New Testament scholarship, it will be shown that greater distinction between 'synagogues' of various locations needs to be incorporated into New Testament studies. It is wrong to take for granted that a 'synagogue' in Galilee should be perceived as exactly the same, either in architecture or in function, as that in a Diaspora city. Unlike a modern franchise operator such as McDonald's, there was, as far as we know, no central authority which had control over how a 'synagogue' should look or function in a particular locality. Individual Jewish groups would assimilate into their new communities to a greater or lesser extent; similarly, local styles of gathering, worship and architectural form were incorporated in differing measures within these communities. This is not to say that there were no similarities, only that they should not be assumed.

In the penultimate chapter the presentation of the 'synagogue' in Luke-Acts will be addressed. In 1997 Kenneth Atkinson wrote:

> Although Luke-Acts is not in all respects historically accurate, it does remain an important witness to the existence of pre-70 CE synagogues as distinctive architectural edifices. The only anachronisms remaining are those scholars who, in the face of overwhelming evidence, continue to doubt the existence of pre-70 synagogues. *Cadit quaestio*, let us move on to other matters.[6]

It would appear that this was misguided optimism. Clearly the debate was not over, as can be seen from the number of monographs and essays which have been published in the years subsequent to his article appearing.[7] Rather than the debate being over, it has in fact become

---

6 K. Atkinson, 'On Further Defining the First-Century CE Synagogue: Fact or Fiction? A Rejoinder to H.C. Kee', *NTS* 43 (1997), pp. 491–502 (502).

7 E.g., H.A. McKay, 'Ancient Synagogues: The Continuing Dialectic Between Two Major Views', *Currents in Research: Biblical Studies* 6 (1998), pp. 103–42; D.D. Binder, *Into the Temple Courts: The Place of the Synagogues in the Second Temple Period* (SBLDS, 169; Atlanta: SBL, 1999); P.W. van der Horst, 'Was the Synagogue a Place of Sabbath Worship Before 70 CE?', in S. Fine (ed.), *Jews, Christians, and Polytheists in the Ancient Synagogue* (New York: Routledge, 1999), pp. 18–43; J.F. Strange, 'Ancient Texts, Archaeology as Text, and the Problem of the First-Century Synagogue', in H.C. Kee and L.H. Cohick (eds), *Evolution of the Synagogue: Problems and Progress* (Harrisburg: Trinity Press, 1999), pp. 27–45; R.A. Horsley, 'Synagogues in Galilee and the Gospels', in Kee and Cohick, *Evolution of the Synagogue*, pp. 46–69; C. Claußen, *Versammlung, Gemeinde, Synagoge: Das hellenistisch-jüdische Umfeld der frühchristlichen Gemeinde* (SUNT, 27; Göttingen: Vandenhoeck & Ruprecht, 2002).

more finely tuned, or nuanced. Luke-Acts provides more references to 'synagogues' than the rest of the New Testament combined. It also provides the most detailed accounts we have in any source of the Sabbath Torah reading and activities related to it. However, these New Testament books have come under the greatest scrutiny by scholars who suggest that much of the material presented reflects the time and place of the author, that is, the late first century in the Diaspora. In Chapter 5 we will clearly identify the various positions in this debate, identifying potential weaknesses. It will be shown that the discussion has become overly polarized so that New Testament scholars seeking to apply this discussion to their exegesis often refer to one side of the debate without fully appreciating the other. We will draw on the material gathered in the earlier chapters in order to compare it with the accounts in Luke-Acts, both to assess the presentation of Luke, and to aid our understanding of particular texts. It will be argued that Luke is not anachronistic in his historical presentation of the 'synagogue'; however, in his consistent use of the term συναγωγή he does indeed fail to reflect geographical differences in terminology. It will be argued that generally Luke's material fits well with our other sources, but that scholars have often used later rabbinic material to build on a layer of formality which would not have existed within first-century 'synagogues' and which Luke does not provide. Further, a comparison with the archaeological data will highlight the differences in character of purpose-built facilities.

Although the focus of this work is to highlight areas where current research on the first-century 'synagogue' will better inform New Testament scholarship on Luke-Acts, the work in Chapters 2, 3 and 4 will not be limited by such a goal. Therefore, we will not pre-judge the issue and only include such references that are directly relevant to the New Testament. Rather the work will be holistic, gathering all the material relevant to first-century 'synagogues'. From the perspective of Luke-Acts studies, this will inevitably lead to some 'wastage' in these earlier chapters; however, the dangers associated with pre-judging our sources are much greater.

2. Methodology

2.1. Terminology

At the beginning of this study it will be useful to identify certain methodological parameters that will be followed throughout. As mentioned above, previous generations of scholars had a clear idea of what was meant by the term 'synagogue'. However, in more recent research, how the first-century 'synagogue' is defined can have a major impact on how research is undertaken, and which sources are ruled in or out as bearers of legitimate information. To give one example: Marilyn Chiat's *Handbook of Synagogue Architecture*, published in 1982, made a very useful contribution to the identification of synagogue buildings. Surveying all the available archaeological material relating to synagogue buildings within Palestine, Chiat first had to have a method of identifying such structures:

> To qualify as a synagogue a building or its architectural/decorative fragments must be decorated with common motifs, such as the image of the Torah Shrine, menorah, lulab, ethrog, and shofar, or contain inscriptions that establish its identity as having been constructed and used by a Jewish community for a form of assembly. Neither a building's plan nor its location within a presumed Jewish village can qualify a ruin as a synagogue. Only rarely is it possible to identify a building as a synagogue solely on the basis of its architectural form or location.[8]

While this was, in many ways, a good way to proceed, the necessity of certain characteristics being present in order to identifying a synagogue building gives rise to a particular definition, with other possible buildings excluded. Such identification has ruled out virtually all of the first-century examples suggested, as few of them contain the elements that Chiat sought. Burtchaell's critique of this kind of view is valuable. Discussing the many theories for the origin of the 'synagogue', and those who propose them, he writes:

> Each of them identifies the synagogue with some component and then looks to find that one component in full and mature form...[he lists some of the elements sought]. One might as well look for priests and church buildings among Christians, and conclude that Christianity did not originate until the fourth century after Christ.[9]

It is understandable why such definitions and terms are sought: it allows clear theories to be forwarded. But is Chiat's definition really an accurate representation of what might have been considered a synagogue building by a first-century Jew? Further, the choice of identifying features clearly indicates that she understands a synagogue building as a place used principally for religious functions. Whether we perceive the central role of the 'synagogue' as communal or religious will again have some bearing on how we examine the evidence. Our sources can highlight one particular function of the 'synagogue' with other areas being downplayed.[10] Sources,

---

8   M.J.S. Chiat, *Handbook of Synagogue Architecture* (BJS, 29; Chico: Scholars Press, 1982), pp. 2–3.

9   J.T. Burtchaell, *From Synagogue to Church: Public Services and Offices in the Earliest Christian Communities* (Cambridge: Cambridge University Press, 1992), p. 204. See also Strange, 'Ancient Texts', p. 34.

10   E.g., T. Rajak betrays her bias when she writes, 'when it comes to the life of those synagogues, the most important source is inscriptions' ('The Synagogue within the Greco-Roman City', in Fine, *Jews, Christians, and Polytheists*, pp. 161–73 [161]). For Rajak this

such as Philo and Josephus, often used by New Testament scholars, as well as the New Testament documents themselves, tend to focus on the religious dimension of the 'synagogue' as well as portraying them as similar from one location to another. However, other sources, not so readily accessed in New Testament scholarship, such as archaeological material, tend to emphasize the communal nature and the diversity of 'synagogues'.[11] It is no accident that in the last 10 years a number of new potential synagogue buildings have been proposed, as the wider role of the 'synagogue' and the lack of identifying features in this period have been recognized. The problem then becomes, by what criteria do we identify these as synagogue buildings?

As will be shown in the following chapters, the first-century 'synagogue' fulfilled a variety of functions and this must be recognized if an accurate picture is to be obtained. There is no doubt that at some point 'synagogue' came to mean a building used principally for religious functions, but understanding what might constitute a 'synagogue' in the first century CE needs to be more flexible and wide-ranging. Here 'synagogue' will be used to refer both to the gathered community and the building, and it will be recognized that activities carried out within such 'synagogues' were not confined to the clearly sacred.[12]

2.2. *Sources*

A second major problem within scholarship is the misuse of sources. Too often New Testament scholars writing on the subject of the 'synagogue' incorporate in their analysis material from synagogue buildings or literary sources of a much later period. Although this problem has been clearly identified and those writing in the area of 'synagogue' research recognize it, often non-specialists go to well-respected reference works for their information where anachronism is present.[13] In his recent study of the 'synagogue' Donald Binder has identified these problems as architectural

---

then leads to an over-emphasis on this source in an article with David Noy on the role of the archisynagogos, where literary testimony is not given sufficient weight, 'Archisynagogoi: Office, Title and Social Status in the Greco-Jewish Synagogue', *JRS* 83 (1993), pp. 75–93.

11   See L.I. Levine, 'The First Century C.E. Synagogue in Historical Perspective', in B. Olsson and M. Zetterholm (eds), *The Ancient Synagogue: From its Origins to 200 C.E.* (*ConNT*, 39; Stockholm: Almquist and Wiksell, 2003), pp. 1–24 (9–10).

12   Cf. B. Olsson, 'The Origins of the Synagogue: An Evaluation', in Olsson and Zetterholm, *The Ancient Synagogue*, pp. 132–38 (133). See also A. Runesson, *The Origins of the Synagogue: A Socio-Historical Study* (*ConNT*, 37; Stockholm: Almqvist & Wiksell, 2001), pp. 30–35.

13   E.g., W. Schrage, 'συναγωγή', *TDNT*, vol. 7, pp. 797–841; Schürer, *HJP*, 2.423-54; Str-B, vol. 4, pp. 153–276; and, although clearer, E. Meyers 'Synagogues,' *ABD*, vol. 6, pp. 251–60.

anachronism and literary anachronism.[14] To these we should add a third kind of error which should perhaps be labelled anatopism. While scholars may be careful in their use of literary evidence, clearly identifying material from the relevant period, and may also judiciously avoid using architectural evidence from a later period to inform their understanding of the first-century 'synagogue', it is still possible to fall into this third category of error where evidence from one site, perhaps in Palestine, is seen as equivalent to another, possibly somewhere in the Diaspora. So a scholar writing in detail on the subject of the first-century 'synagogue' can make the sweeping remark: 'When Luke-Acts records Jesus or Paul as entering a synagogue, an edifice similar or identical to the Gamla synagogue is being described'.[15] It should not be assumed that architectural features or styles found in one place existed in another. It is certainly important to recognize characteristics that may be common to different geographical areas as these may highlight important functions carried out in both, but these should not be assumed.

One final point should be made on the use of sources. In the past, the rabbinic material of the Mishnah, Tosefta and Talmuds would have been used as primary sources and incorporated into a discussion of first-century Jewish practice with little hesitation. However, during the 1970s and 80s, due particularly to the work of Jacob Neusner, the problems of using these sources were highlighted.[16] The practices of previous generations of scholars who used rabbinic sources to recreate first-century practice have correctly been criticized in more recent research. Although, it may be that the pendulum of suspicion has now swung too far in relation to rabbinic texts,[17] and work such as that of Jacob Neusner and David Instone-Brewer may mean that scholars can use them again, this time with an

---

14 Binder, *Temple Courts*, pp. 4–13; see also, R. Hachlili, 'The Origin of the Synagogue: A Re-assessment', *JSJ* 28 (1997), pp. 34–47 (45); M.J. Martin, 'Interpreting the Theodotos Inscription: Some Reflections on a First Century Jerusalem Synagogue Inscription and E.P. Sanders' "Common Judaism"', *ANES* 39 (2002), pp. 160–81 (176).

15 Atkinson, 'Further Defining', p. 499.

16 For a discussion of the problem of using these texts in New Testament studies generally, see P.S. Alexander, 'Rabbinic Judaism and the New Testament', *ZNW* 74 (1983), pp. 237–46. More specifically in relation to 'synagogue' studies see, Binder, *Temple Courts*, pp. 10–13; P.V.M. Flesher, 'Palestinian Synagogues Before 70 C.E.: A Review of the Evidence', in *ASHAAD*, vol. 1, pp. 29–30 n. 8. Neusner highlighted the problems associated with the use of rabbinic texts in, 'The Use of the Later Rabbinic Evidence for the Study of First-Century Pharisaism', in W.S. Green (ed.), *Approaches to Ancient Judaism: Theory and Practice* (BJS, 1; Missoula: Scholars Press, 1978), pp. 215–25.

17 See the comments of S.C. Reif, *Judaism and Hebrew Prayer: New Perspectives on Jewish Liturgical History* (Cambridge: Cambridge University Press, 1993), p. 54; *idem*, 'The Early Liturgy of the Synagogue,' in *CHJ*, p. 328 n. 4.

appropriate framework for reference.[18] For our purposes, rabbinic material will not be used as an independent source; however, it will occasionally be referred to where parallels are found in first-century material or to highlight possible trends in 'synagogue' practice originating in the first century that carried on into the tannaitic period.

So too, the evidence of the New Testament has been used as a single source without enough recognition of the different times and communities in which any particular gospel or letter may have been written. Some scholars argue that many of the documents of the New Testament should not be accepted as an accurate representation of what was going on in Palestine in the early part of the first century; rather, things that existed in the Diaspora towards the end of the first century are projected back into Jesus' ministry.[19] These arguments mainly come from New Testament scholars, and it is interesting to note that others, working outside of this discipline, are often far happier to accept the evidence that it brings.[20] Here, New Testament material will be included but, in view of the debate, it will be used carefully, providing supporting evidence of other sources rather than as a source of unique information. In Chapter 5, Luke-Acts will be compared with the material gathered in the earlier chapters and only at this point will items unique to this corpus be discussed. Here we should also note that too often scholars who are highly critical of the documents of the New Testament or rabbinic material are happy to accept the testimony of Josephus or Philo uncritically. The particular social or political bias of these authors also needs to be borne in mind, and their apologetic agenda will be addressed as each is used as a source.

18   J. Neusner gives a clear presentation of his research in relation to the first-century figure Hillel and how rabbinic texts relating to him should be perceived, *Formative Judaism: Religious, Historical, and Literary Studies* (BJS, 37; Chico: Scholars Press, 1982), esp. pp. 87–97. David Instone-Brewer's TRENT project builds on the work of Neusner. While acknowledging himself that such work is more an art than a science, nevertheless he lays out a clear framework for dating the rabbinic texts, see *Traditions of the Rabbis from the Era of the New Testament* (6 vols.; Grand Rapids: Eerdmans, 2004–), vol. 1, pp. 28–40.

19   E.g., Flesher, 'Palestinian Synagogues Before 70 C.E.', p. 32. See also H.C. Kee, 'The Transformation of the Synagogue after 70 C.E.: Its Import for Early Christianity', *NTS* 36 (1990), pp. 1–24 (14–19); S.B. Hoenig, 'The Ancient City Square: The Forerunner of the Synagogue', *ANRW* II.19.1, p. 453; R.A. Horsley, *Archaeology, History, and Society in Galilee: The Social Context of Jesus and the Rabbis* (Valley Forge: Trinity, 1996), p. 147; McKay, 'Ancient Synagogues', p. 121.

20   In some cases this may just be a lack of knowledge of the details of current arguments relating to the New Testament; however, this is not always the case, e.g., Lee I. Levine is aware of the debate but argues that the information that we are given in the New Testament is of value, *The Ancient Synagogue: The First Thousand Years* (New Haven and London: Yale University Press, 2000), p. 45, n. 11.

3. *Overview of Research*

Archaeologists have been examining the evidence for early synagogue buildings for many years. However, it is fair to say that such research received considerable fresh impetus with the creation of the state of Israel in 1948. From this date, numerous sites have been explored allowing more detailed research to be carried out. This, combined with methodologically more refined study in related disciplines, opened up new areas of 'synagogue' research both in Palestine and the Diaspora. Before going on to look at the first-century archaeological evidence on a site-by-site basis, it will be useful to give a brief survey of previous scholarship in this area.

Prior to the twentieth century, little had been done to synthesize the early history of the 'synagogue'. With the discovery of archaeological sites at the end of the nineteenth and beginning of the twentieth centuries, scholars began to formulate theories regarding the origin of the 'synagogue' and the subsequent architectural changes that may have taken place. Although a Diaspora synagogue building was identified by André Plassart in Delos this was an exception,[21] the bulk of discoveries coming in Palestine, and particularly in the area of Galilee. In their *Antike Synagogen in Galiläa*, Kohl and Watzinger first identified a basilica style they had discovered in Galilee.[22] With the identification of further synagogue buildings, Eliezer Sukenik added a second 'type' dating to the Byzantine period,[23] after which Avi-Yonah proposed a third category and arranged them chronologically.[24]

1. Early – Galilean. A building with its ornamental façade facing Jerusalem in which there were three entrances. Internally there were three rows of columns, and the floor was paved with stone slabs. Worship was focused towards Jerusalem through the open doors.
2. Transitional – Broadhouse. The entrance and the direction of prayer were no longer on the same wall, with one of the long walls now being in the direction of Jerusalem, and a niche for the Torah shrine made in this wall.
3. Fifth century – Byzantine. Built as a basilica, similar to that found in contemporaneous church structures. Two rows of columns divided nave and aisles, with a semicircular apse at one end to house the Torah shrine. There was also a raised area in front of the Torah shrine, called a *bema*. The entrances to the building were on the wall opposite the apse, and the floors were decorated with mosaics

---

21 See below, Chapter 3, 2.2.1.

22 H. Kohl and C. Watzinger, *Antike Synagogen in Galiläa* (Leipzig: Heinrichs, 1916).

23 E.L. Sukenik, *Ancient Synagogues in Palestine and Greece* (London: Oxford University Press, 1934), pp. 27–28, 68–69.

24 For a more detailed analysis see, Chiat, *Handbook of Synagogue Architecture*, pp. 4–5. Also, A.R. Seager, 'Ancient Synagogue Architecture: An Overview', in J. Gutmann (ed.), *Ancient Synagogues: The State of Research* (BJS, 22; Chico: Scholars Press, 1981), pp. 39–47 (39).

featuring biblical stories and, in some, the signs of the zodiac. Other symbols common in Judaism were also found in these buildings.[25]

One of the problems with this arrangement was that discoveries that did not fit into the styles outlined were too often labelled 'transitional,' and in one of his latter writings Avi-Yonah himself cautioned against too rigid an interpretation of these types.[26] As more finds were made which did not fit the pattern, the three-stage theory came under attack. Synagogue buildings were found close to each other dating to the same period but which had different architectural patterns.[27] Such diversity of chronology and style has now also been recognized for the first-century period, and potential synagogue buildings have been identified with some diversity. However, as will be shown in Chapter 3, there are common elements, particularly within Palestinian synagogue buildings, and the recognition of areas of similarity and difference will assist us in our understanding of the function of such buildings. Further discoveries were made in the middle part of the twentieth century including important Diaspora sites at Dura Europos, Sardis and Stobi and the analysis of these buildings added greatly to our understanding of the status of Jewry in Diaspora cities. Two further potential first-century synagogue buildings in the Diaspora were also discovered in the twentieth century and these will be discussed in detail below.[28]

Another major contributor to the area of 'synagogue' research was E.R. Goodenough.[29] His massive 13-volume work focused on Jewish artistic works and included a detailed analysis of synagogue buildings; indeed his discussion of the synagogue building and art found at Dura Europos occupies three volumes! With the increase in archaeological discovery, many reports on the progress of excavation at particular sites were published during the second half of the twentieth century. Interacting with these reports, Marilyn Chiat, in 1982, produced a *Handbook of Synagogue Architecture* in which she noted all the proposed sites in Palestine, assessed

25 M. Avi-Yonah, 'Ancient Synagogues', in J. Gutmann, *The Synagogue: Studies in Origins, Archaeology and Architecture* (The Library of Biblical Studies; New York: KTAV, 1975), pp. 95–109 (98–99), published originally as, 'Ancient Synagogues', *Ariel* 32 (1973), pp. 29–43.

26 Avi-Yonah, 'Ancient Synagogues' (1975), pp. 104–108.

27 See L.I. Levine, 'Ancient Synagogues – A Historical Introduction', in L.I. Levine (ed.), *Ancient Synagogues Revealed* (Jerusalem: Israel Exploration Society, 1981), pp. 1–10 (10); E.M. Meyers and J.F. Strange, *Archaeology, the Rabbis and Early Christianity* (London: SCM, 1981), pp. 145–46; E.M. Meyers and A.T. Kraabel, 'Archaeology, Iconography, and Nonliterary Written Remains', in R.A. Kraft and G.W.E. Nickelsburg (eds.), *Early Judaism and its Modern Interpreters* (SBLCP; Philadelphia; Fortress Press;, 1986), pp. 177–78; Seager, 'Ancient Synagogue Architecture', pp. 39–43.

28 See the discussion in Chapter 3 of Ostia (2.1.2) and Delos (2.2.1).

29 E.R. Goodenough, *Jewish Symbols in the Greco-Roman Period* (13 vols.; New York: Pantheon Books, 1953–68).

the arguments for their identification, and provided a bibliography for each. In the latter part of the twentieth century various collections of essays have added to these discussions, most notably those of Gutmann,[30] Levine,[31] Urman and Flesher,[32] and Fine.[33]

In the 1990s, Howard Kee, through a series of articles, focused scholarly attention on the 'synagogue' of the New Testament period.[34] He challenged the prevailing view that 'synagogues' were purpose-built structures, pointing out that συναγωγή simply meant 'gathering'. He argued that Luke's use of the term and his portrayal of what went on within the 'synagogue' reflected the time and place of Luke rather than Jesus. The articles of Kee have triggered a deluge of scholarship on the early 'synagogue' and related subjects. Heather McKay took a similarly minimal stance on the worship practices of the early 'synagogue', while Richard Horsley incorporated these ideas into his analysis of the Galilee region: 'Once the first-century landscape has been cleared of the synagogue buildings so desperately sought by modern scholars we can more readily catch sight of the community assemblies that had almost certainly been there for centuries'.[35] Again building on the work of Kee, Carsten Claußen published a monograph on the 'synagogue': while accepting that some communities would have had synagogue buildings, he argued that many gatherings would have taken place in house-synagogues.[36]

As the debate continued, archaeological remains which had previously been identified as synagogue buildings were re-examined and their chronological development questioned by scholars such as Michael White who argues that Christianity and Judaism developed their meeting places from domestic settings to purpose-built structures at around the same time. In his monumental work, *The Ancient Synagogue*, Lee Levine covers the period from the origin of the 'synagogue' to around 700 CE. He deals only briefly with the arguments of Kee and, as will be shown later,

30   Gutmann, *The Synagogue: Studies in Origins*; idem, *Ancient Synagogues: The State of Research*.

31   L.I. Levine, *Ancient Synagogues Revealed*; idem (ed.), *The Synagogue in Late Antiquity* (Philadelphia: The American Schools of Oriental Research, 1987).

32   *ASHAAD*.

33   Fine, *Jews, Christians and Polytheists*; idem (ed.), *Sacred Realm: The Emergence of the Synagogue in the Ancient World* (New York: Yeshiva University Museum, 1996).

34   H.C. Kee, 'Transformation', pp. 1–24; idem, 'The Changing Meaning of Synagogue: A Response to Richard Oster', *NTS* 40 (1994), pp. 281–83; idem, 'Defining the First-Century CE Synagogue: Problems and Progress', *NTS* 41 (1995), pp. 481–500, reprinted in Kee and Cohick, *Evolution of the Synagogue*, pp. 7–26.

35   Horsley, *Archaeology, History, and Society in Galilee*, p. 145. See also, idem, *Galilee: History, Politics, People* (Valley Forge: Trinity, 1995), pp. 222–37; H.A. McKay, *Sabbath and Synagogue: The Question of Sabbath Worship in Ancient Judaism* (Religion in the Graeco-Roman World, 122; Leiden: Brill, 1994); eadem, 'Ancient Synagogues: The Continuing Dialectic', pp. 103–42.

36   Claußen, *Versammlung, passim*.

wrongly accepts White's analysis that the first-century Diaspora synagogue buildings at Ostia and Delos were originally domestic spaces which
were later renovated to form synagogue buildings.

Since 1997, the building at Ostia has been the focus of a multi-
disciplinary investigation of the early 'synagogue' by a group at Lund
University. This has added greatly to the debate on 'synagogues' generally
and Ostia in particular, first producing a series of essays by those involved
in the project,[37] then, in October 2001, hosting an international
conference, the papers from which have been recently published.[38] In
addition, individual scholars have produced their own work, with that of
Anders Runesson's most pertinent to the present study.[39] One other major
monograph has appeared in the last few years: Donald Binder's *Into the
Temple Courts* covers all the available material from the Second Temple
period and argues that the 'synagogue' was effectively an extension of the
Jerusalem temple. He proposes that many of the features of the
architecture and practice of the 'synagogue' were based on those of the
Jerusalem temple. Binder tends towards a maximal view of the evidence
and, at times, assumes too much from the primary material he cites.

Given that there have been four recent monographs, as well as a
number of other works on the early 'synagogue', how can a further study
be justified? Although many of the books and articles written have
interacted with the texts of the New Testament, often the focus of the
material is elsewhere, for example, tracing a wide history of the
'synagogue' from its origin to 700 CE as in Levine, or focusing on the
origin of the 'synagogue' as in Runesson. The particular focus of this
work will be its application to New Testament studies. It will be shown in
Chapter 5 that often the recent debate over the first-century 'synagogue'
has been inappropriately or inconsistently applied to the field of New
Testament studies. As noted above, scholars seeking information on the
'synagogue' of the New Testament era will often use reference works
which pre-date the recent debate on this subject. Where current
scholarship is cited, the works of a few, which are more accessible, may
be overly influential. Here, then, we will re-examine all relevant material
incorporating the most recent archaeological evidence.[40]

---

37 B. Olsson, D. Mitternacht and O. Brandt (eds), *The Synagogue of Ancient Ostia and
the Jews of Rome: Interdisciplinary Studies* (Stockholm: Paul Åströms Förlag, 2001).

38 Olsson and Zetterholm, *The Ancient Synagogue*. In addition, a source book will
shortly be published, A. Runesson, B. Olsson and D.D. Binder, *The Ancient Synagogue: A
Sourcebook* (Leiden: Brill, 2007: forthcoming).

39 Runesson, *Origins*.

40 A further survey of recent scholarship on the 'synagogue', particularly relating to
Luke-Acts, will be given in Chapter 5.

Chapter 2

LITERARY EVIDENCE FOR THE 'SYNAGOGUE'

1. *Introduction*

The purpose of this chapter will be to evaluate the written evidence that exists, and which may relate to the 'synagogue' of the first-century period; examining the extant works of those who were writing around this time for any evidence that will shed light on the debate. The major sources will be Josephus, Philo and the New Testament, but it will be helpful to make reference to some rabbinic material as well as other sources which can help gain a picture of this period. One interesting phenomenon is the lack of references to 'synagogues' in Jewish writing before the turn of the era. Levine comments:

> Had the synagogue been a known and recognized institution in Palestinian Jewish life, one might well have expected it to be mentioned at least once in the many literary works of the third and second centuries B.C.E. Yet, despite the numerous references to Jewish elites and religious institutions of the day, Ben Sira takes no note of it. We also might have expected I and II Maccabees to note the impact of Antiochus' persecutions on the functioning of the synagogue, had it existed; they do not. Purity laws, circumcision, the Sabbath, festivals, kashrut, and, of course, the Temple are all mentioned, but not a word is said about the synagogue.[1]

Such omissions in Ben Sira are perhaps understandable as it is so focused on the temple.[2] The lack of references in Maccabees is more surprising, although it should be noted that while there is significant archaeological evidence of προσευχαί in Egypt there is no literary evidence before the first century CE.

---

1 L.I. Levine, *The Ancient Synagogue: The First Thousand Years* (New Haven and London: Yale University Press), p. 38.

2 But see M. Hengel, *Judaism and Hellenism: Studies in their Encounter in Palestine During the Early Hellenistic Period* (2 vols.; London: SCM Press, 1974), vol. 1, p. 79; J.G. Griffiths, 'Egypt and the Rise of the Synagogue', *JTS* 38 (1987), pp. 1–15 (5).

1.1. *Vocabulary Potentially Associated with 'Synagogues'*
There are a number of words that are associated with the meeting places
of the Jews. The two most common are συναγωγή and προσευχή, but in
literary sources we also find διδασκαλεῖον, ἱερός, περίβολος, οἴκημα,
προσευκτήριον, σαββατεῖον and ἱερόν.[3] The earliest use of any of these
words is προσευχή, which comes in inscriptions from Egypt dating to the
third century BCE.[4] Because of the widespread use of this word it is worth
noting that there is some debate about whether it was purely used in a
Jewish context. Hachlili argues that προσευχή was used to describe pagan
loyalty shrines in the Hellenistic world, in contrast to συναγωγή which
was used only by Jews to describe buildings.[5] However, in a thorough
examination of this word, in the context of classifying inscriptions as
Jewish, Levinskaya argues convincingly that 'there is no clear evidence
that the Gentiles ever borrowed this specifically Jewish term for their
places of worship'.[6]

There have been a number of suggestions regarding the use of
συναγωγή and προσευχή. Hengel proposes that one was used in the
Diaspora, and the other in Palestine. The temple in Jerusalem was central
to Jewish faith and practice and was described as the 'House of Prayer'
(οἶκος προσευχῆς).[7] It is suggested that the use of προσευχή would
therefore have been inappropriate: in order to protect the centrality of the
temple, the meeting places of Jews in Palestine were described as
συναγωγαί rather than prayer houses.[8] Levine points out that there are
problems with most suggestions, however, he comes down in favour of
Hengel's solution: 'thus, Egyptian Jewish sources (both epigraphic and

3 See R.E. Oster for a list of all the words used with their references, 'Supposed
Anachronism in Luke-Acts' Use of ΣΥΝΑΓ ΩΓΗ', *NTS* 39 (1993), pp. 178–208 (186); also A.
Runesson, *The Origins of the Synagogue: A Socio-Historical Study* (*ConNT*, 37; Stockholm:
Almqvist & Wiksell, 2001), pp. 171–73. But see the criticisms of Oster's table by H.A.
McKay, 'Ancient Synagogues: The Continuing Dialectic Between Two Major Views',
Currents in Research: Biblical Studies 6 (1998), p. 119.
4 See Chapter 3, 2.5.
5 R. Hachlili, 'The Origin of the Synagogue: A Re-assessment', *JSJ* 28 (1997), pp. 34–47
(39).
6 I. Levinskaya, 'A Jewish or Gentile Prayer House? The Meaning of ΠΡΟΣΕΥΧΗ',
TynBul 41 (1990), pp. 154–59; *eadem*, *The Book of Acts in its Diaspora Setting* (*TBAFCS*, vol.
5), pp. 207–25. See also D. Noy, 'A Jewish Place of Prayer in Roman Egypt', *JTS* 43 (1992),
pp. 118–22 (119).
7 Isa. 56.7, cf. Mt. 21.13; Mk 11.17; Lk. 19.46.
8 M. Hengel, 'Proseuche und Synagoge: Jüdische Gemeinde, Gotteshaus und
Gottesdienst in der Diaspora und in Palästina', originally published in G. Jeremias, H.W.
Kuhn and H. Stegemann (eds), *Tradition und Glaube. Das frühe Christentum in seiner
Umwelt. Festgabe für Karl Georg Kuhn zum 65. Geburtstag* (Göttingen: Vandenhoeck &
Ruprecht, 1971), pp. 157–83, reprinted in J. Gutmann (ed.), *The Synagogue: Studies in
Origins, Archaeology and Architecture* (The Library of Biblical Studies; New York: KTAV,
1975), pp. 27–54.

literary) as well as Greco-Roman authors employ the term *proseuche*, while Josephus, the New Testament, and rabbinic sources almost always use the term *synagoge* when referring to a Judean context'.[9] For these scholars, and others, προσευχή and συναγωγή are virtually synonymous,[10] and often προσευχή is translated with the English synagogue.[11]

It is only recent scholarship that has suggested that the use of different terms might suggest different 'institutions'.[12] Kee argues that a change of language took place suggesting that the συναγωγή was originally the group of people who met in the προσευχή: over time, however, this changed so that προσευχή died out leaving συναγωγή to describe the meeting place as well as the communal group. Kee acknowledges that Josephus does occasionally use συναγωγή to refer to the gathering places but this reflects his position of writing at the end of the first century, the time at which this change in language is happening. Similarly, Luke writing at around the same time uses both terms.[13] Anders Runesson takes this discussion one stage further proposing that the same word could be used of different institutions:

> Why, then, is the same term used for different institutions? The obvious explanation is that συναγωγή was not a technical term in the first century CE. Not only were different terms applied to the same institutions, but the same term (συναγωγή) also designated different institutions.[14]

With this background we can now go on to look at a variety of first-century writers to see how these terms were used. Possible reasons for their use will be explored and potential areas of influence discussed. As well as dealing with authors separately, it will be helpful to note the geographical location of the author or of the place being described.

---

9   L.I. Levine, 'The Second Temple Synagogue: The Formative Years', in L.I. Levine (ed.), *The Synagogue in Late Antiquity* (Philadelphia: The American Schools of Oriental Research, 1987), pp. 7–31 (21).

10   See S. Fine, *This Holy Place: On the Sanctity of the Synagogue During the Greco-Roman Period* (Notre Dame: Notre Dame Press, 1997), p. 26; Schürer, *HJP*, vol. 2, p. 445.

11   E.g., D.D. Binder, *Into the Temple Courts: The Place of the Synagogues in the Second Temple Period* (SBLDS, 169; Atlanta: Society of Biblical Literature, 1999), p. 303.

12   For an excellent discussion of the use of terminology see McKay, 'Ancient Synagogues: The Continuing Dialectic', pp. 103–42.

13   H.C. Kee cites *Ant.*, 19.300-305, *War*, 2.289; 7.44, 'The Changing Meaning of Synagogue: A Response to Richard Oster', *NTS* 40 (1994), pp. 281–83 (282). However, it should be noted that the language has, to some extent, already changed in order for these authors to use it.

14   Runesson, *Origins*, p. 316.

2. *Philo*

2.1. *Introduction*

There are a number of references in Philo that are useful to the discussion of the 'synagogue' of the first-century period, in Alexandria, the wider Diaspora and in Palestine. Philo writes in detail about the Jews in Alexandria and the surrounding areas, mentions Rome, but also knows at first hand about Palestinian Jewish practices: in a description of the city of Ascalon in Syria he notes, in passing, that he was on his way to the temple,[15] and elsewhere describes the events in Jerusalem during the great festivals.[16] Most of the relevant references come from events that happened within the lifetime of Philo rather than looking back to some period in the past; thus we have an author writing around the period of Jesus' ministry describing the situation at that time. Indeed, in recalling the events surrounding the pogroms in Alexandria in 38 CE, Philo had an intimate knowledge as he subsequently led a delegation to the emperor in Rome to plead on behalf of his fellow Jews. Even in the reference to the Sabbath in *De vita Mosis* 2, in which he links the establishment of the προσευχαί with Moses, the point is explicitly made that the practices described are ones that are going on currently within Jewish communities.[17]

In keeping with other Diaspora sources, particularly the Egyptian inscriptions and papyrus,[18] Philo most often uses the word προσευχή when describing the gathering places of the Jewish communities. Kee states that Philo uses προσευχή 18 times 'in contrast to *synagoge* which appears only twice in the surviving Philonic corpus, and refers to the gathered community rather than to the place of meeting'.[19] Προσευχή, in fact, appears 19 times, προσευκτήριον once, συναγωγή 7 times and συναγωγίον twice.[20] It should be noted that in five of the seven uses of συναγωγή, Philo is following the LXX translation of the Old Testament.[21]

Defining συναγωγή as the gathered community and not as a place is the central point of Kee's argument. He acknowledges that at times the term προσευχή was used to describe a place in which the Jews came together for some purpose; however, it was the gathered group that was

---

15 Philo, *Omn. Prob. Lib.*, 2.64.

16 Philo, *Spec. Leg.*, 1.68-79; cf. Josephus, *Ant.*, 4.203-04.

17 Philo, *Vit. Mos.*, 2.216.

18 See following chapter.

19 H.C. Kee, 'The Transformation of the Synagogue after 70 C.E.: Its Import for Early Christianity', *NTS* 36 (1990), pp. 1–24 (5).

20 See P. Borgen, K. Fuglseth and R. Skarsten (eds), *The Philo Index* (Grand Rapids: Eerdmans, 2000).

21 Συναγωγή appears twice in the translation of Num. 27.16-17 in *Poster. C.*, 67, twice in *Agr.*, 44, and once in the translation of Gen. 1.9 in *Quaest. in Gen.*, 2.66.

then described as a συναγωγή and not the building in which they met. I am happy to accept that συναγωγή can indeed have this meaning; nevertheless, Kee goes too far as it can also refer to a building. If we examine Philo's use of the word, it can refer to the gathering of the waters at creation or to the whole people of Israel, as noted above, all following the LXX; however, as will be shown below, on one occasion Philo uses the word of a meeting place.

2.2. *Diaspora*
2.2.1. *Egypt*
2.2.1.1. *Alexandria*

First we will examine the reports of the pogroms of Alexandria in 38 CE.[22] Here we can establish that among the acts committed against the Jews was the removal or desecration of buildings in which they met for sacred purposes. In his *In Flaccum* Philo recounts that when Herod Agrippa visited Alexandria he was welcomed and treated well by Aulus Avilius Flaccus, the local Roman Prefect. The Alexandrians were not pleased with the way in which this Jewish king had been so well received; therefore, they took 'a certain lunatic named Carabas' and, in the gymnasium, acted as though he were king.[23] Flaccus, we are told, saw this but did nothing to stop it. The crowds then emboldened went much further and called out for 'installing images in the meeting houses' (ἐν ταῖς προσευχαῖς).[24] Philo is concerned that people everywhere would take their cue from Alexandria and riot 'against their synagogues (προσευχάς)',[25] pointing out that the Jews would fight for their 'institutions':

> Because they are the only people under the sun who by losing their meeting-houses (προσευχαί) were losing also what they would have valued as worth dying many thousand deaths, namely, their means of showing reverence to their benefactors, since they no longer had the sacred buildings (ἱεροί περίβολοι) where they could set forth their thankfulness.[26]

22   For a description of the period of Flaccus' rule, see J.M. Modrzejewski, *The Jews of Egypt from Rameses II to Emperor Hadrian* (trans. R. Cornman; Edinburgh: T&T Clark, 1995), pp. 165–73.

23   The Jews then had their citizenship removed by Flaccus, and the people drove the Jews out of their quarters of Alexandria, into a small area in the eastern section of the city. The disturbances took place in the months of August and September, reaching their zenith during the feast of Tabernacles, see *Flacc.*, 116ff.

24   Philo, *Flacc.*, 41. Cf. Josephus' account of events in Dora, *Ant.*, 19.300-11, see below, section 3.2.2.1.

25   Philo, *Flacc.*, 47.

26   *Ibid.*, 48. Cf. *JIGRE*, 9. Here some of Philo's apologetic can be seen: he seeks to show that the Jews are no longer able to show reverence to those who had shown them favour.

He also points out that if those acting against the Jews were truly doing so out of a wish to honour the emperor then there were many temples in which they could have erected a statue,[27] and observes that during three hundred years no ruler of Egypt had seen necessary to have an image of themselves erected in the Jewish meeting houses.[28] Philo reports that the meeting houses were destroyed to the point that not even their names remained and that there were many meeting houses in each area of the city.[29] From the description we have here and the comparison of pagan temples with the προσευχαί, what appears to be certain is that buildings are described. Further, their association with pagan temples and the description of them as 'sacred' suggests that they were used for some form of ritual acts.

A second reference to Alexandria comes in *De somniis*, where Philo alludes to an unnamed ruler who tries to persuade the Alexandrian Jews to abandon their Sabbath practices:

> 'Suppose,' he said, 'there was a sudden inroad of the enemy or an inundation caused by the river rising and breaking through the dam, or plague or earthquake, or any other trouble either of human or divine agency, will you stay at home perfectly quiet? Or will you appear in public in your usual guise, with your right hand tucked inside and the left held close to the flank under the cloak lest you should even unconsciously do anything that might help to save you? And will you sit in your conventicles (ἐν τοῖς συναγωγίοις ὑμῶν) and assemble your regular company (τὸν εἰωθότα θίασον ἀγείροντες) and read in security your holy books, expounding any obscure point and in leisurely comfort discussing at length your ancestral philosophy?[30]

It is difficult to be conclusive on whether συναγωγίον should be understood here to refer to the gathered community or the place where they met. If we assume that συναγωγίον is referring to the gathered community of the Jews then it does appear a little strange that Philo also uses θίασος. We would then appear to have two 'technical' terms for a religious gathering: 'and will you sit in your gatherings and assemble your regular company'.[31]

Elsewhere he describes the 'tributes to the emperors which were pulled down or burnt at the same time, the shields and gilded crowns and the slabs and inscriptions, consideration for which should have made them spare the rest', *Leg. Gai.*, 133. Cf. *JIGRE*, 22, 24, 25, 27, 117 and 125.

27 Philo, *Flacc.*, 51.

28 Idem, *Leg. Gai.*, 132–38.

29 Idem, *Flacc.*, 53. The inscriptions from the προσευχαί in Egypt often bear the name of the kings, queens and benefactors of the buildings and this may be what Philo is describing. In Rome, 'synagogues' were named after prominent officials (see the later discussion in Chapter 3, 2.1.1).

30 Idem, *Somn.*, 2.125-27.

31 See 'Θίασος', *LSJ*, p. 801.

Kee himself, citing White,[32] argues that the synagogue building found at Delos indicates that 'synagogues' were a kind of guild or association: 'It is an instance of this pattern that the "synagogue" at Delos began as a *thiasos* or *koinon*, which then expanded under the patronage of a benefactor'.[33] It appears more likely that συναγωγίον here refers to the place in which, or at which, the θίασος met, but we cannot be certain.[34]

On two occasions Philo uses ἱερόν of Jewish assembly buildings. We will deal with one of these in Chapter 4;[35] in the other, Philo writes about behaviour befitting a woman:

> She should not shew herself off like a vagrant in the streets before the eyes of other men, except when she has to go to the temple (εἰς ἱερόν), and even then she should take pains to go not when the market is full, but when most people have gone home, and so like a free-born lady worthy of the name, with everything quiet around her, make her oblations and offer her prayers (θυσίας καὶ εὐχάς) to avert the evil and gain the good.[36]

Colson recognized that this may refer to a synagogue building, but in view of the reference to sacrifice concluded that this must be advice to the female population generally.[37] Binder, however, argues convincingly that this refers to a Jew and that ἱερόν refers to a synagogue building.[38] He also proposes that θυσίας should not be understood as a reference to sacrifices but to religious rituals more generally.[39] Runesson agrees that this refers to a building but points out that a more natural reading of θυσίας should render this as 'sacrifices'. Indeed his conclusions more generally are that the προσευχαί of Egypt were modelled on the pagan temples of the country and that in the first century, sacrifices of vegetables and incense continued.[40]

There is no doubt that this is a puzzling reference; although similar to the reference from Sardis, the statement here is made by a Jew making it

32   L.M. White, *The Social Origins of Christian Architecture*, vol. 1, *Building God's House in the Roman World: Architectural Adaption among Pagans, Jews, and Christians* (HTS, 42; Valley Forge: Trinity Press, 1990), pp. 11–14. Cf. *idem*, 'The Delos Synagogue Revisited: Recent Fieldwork in the Graeco-Roman Diaspora', *HTR* 80 (1987), pp. 133–60 (153).

33   Kee, 'Transformation', p. 11.

34   Contra Schürer, *HJP*, vol. 2, p. 440.

35   See Chapter 4, 2.3.2.1.

36   Philo, *Spec. Leg.*, 3.171.

37   Philo, LCL, vol. 7, p. 582, n. a.

38   Binder, *Temple Courts*, pp. 129–30. This is also the position of Levine, *Ancient Synagogue*, p. 84, n. 69, while C. Claußen is uncertain, *Versammlung, Gemeinde, Synagoge: Das hellenistisch-jüdische Umfeld der frühchristlichen Gemeinde* (SUNT, 27; Göttingen: Vandenhoeck & Ruprecht, 2002), pp. 137–38.

39   Binder, *Temple Courts*, pp. 129–30.

40   Runesson, *Origins*, pp. 446–54.

more difficult to explain.[41] While Runesson points out that the more natural reading here would seem to have θυσίας as sacrifice, it should be noted that elsewhere in *Special Laws* Philo clearly articulates that the Jerusalem temple is the only place which can be legitimately used for sacrifice.[42] It seems unlikely that he would have expressed such a view while at the same time encouraging women to carry out sacrifices locally. Therefore, with Binder we should conclude that this refers to other religious rituals in a synagogue building.

2.2.1.2. *Elsewhere in Egypt*

In *De vita contemplativa* Philo writes about the Therapeutic community from south of Alexandria. They are described as living in solitude, isolated from each other, in quiet contemplation and study.[43] We are told that on every seventh day they meet together and the description of the place at which they met appears to indicate a central building. It is a 'common sanctuary' (κοινὸν σεμνεῖον) and the architectural description suggests a building set apart for the purpose:[44]

> But every seventh day they meet together as for a general assembly and sit in order according to their age in the proper attitude, with their hands inside the robe, the right hand between the breast and the chin and the left withdrawn along the flank. Then the senior among them who also has the fullest knowledge of the doctrines which they profess comes forward and with visage and voice alike quiet and composed gives a well-reasoned and wise discourse... This common sanctuary in which they meet every seventh day is a double enclosure, one portion set apart for the use of the men, the other for the women. For women too regularly make part of the audience with the same ardour and the same sense of their calling. The wall between the two chambers rises up from the ground to three or four cubits built in the form of a breast work, while the space above up to the roof is left open.[45]

There is considerable debate about how the Therapeutic community should be identified. Are they an Egyptian branch of the Essene community of Palestine, or should they be seen as a small isolated group within Judaism?[46] Whatever their identity, there are clearly similarities in the description of their practices and those described

---

41 On Sardis see below Chapter 4, 4.2.1.1.
42 Philo, *Spec. Leg.*, 1.67-68.
43 Philo, *Vit. Cont.*, 28–30.
44 *Ibid.*, 32. See Binder, *Temple Courts*, pp. 149–51.
45 Philo, *Vit. Cont.*, 30–32.
46 J.E. Taylor and P.R. Davies have suggested that some of the assumptions made regarding the Therapeutic community need to be questioned and that this was in fact a very small group, 'The So-Called Therapeutae of De Vita Contemplativa', *HTR* 91 (1998), pp. 3–24.

elsewhere in Philo, for example, meeting every seventh day; 'their hands inside the robe' (cf. *Somn.*, 2.126); the seating according to age (cf. *Omn. Prob. Lib.*, 81); and the senior person teaching (cf. *Spec. Leg.*, 2.62; *Omn. Prob. Lib.*, 81).[47] The additional information regarding the partition wall, which protects the modesty of the women while at the same time allowing them to hear clearly what went on in the main assembly, is intriguing. Whether Philo remarks on the presence of women because they were not normally expected to attend such an assembly is not clear. Certainly there is little evidence elsewhere to indicate clear segregation by means of architecture.

2.2.1.3. *Conclusion on Egypt*

In the above references it appears that Philo is describing actual physical structures in Egypt. The word used most frequently to describe these buildings is προσευχή, but others can also be used to describe what appears to be the same institution. Within these buildings the Jews gathered to receive instruction on the Torah, and to enter into discussions about it. The Sabbath is highlighted as a time for this gathering, although this does not necessarily preclude it being used at other times and for other functions.

2.2.2. *Asia Minor*

In a letter purportedly from Agrippa I to Emperor Gaius in 40 CE, Philo again uses the term συναγωγίον. Arguing for the freedoms of Alexandrian Jews he points to those which had been enjoyed by the Jews of Asia Minor under Augustus:

> He ordered that the Jews alone should be permitted by them to assemble in synagogues (τοῖς Ἰουδαίοις μόνοις εἰς τὰ συναγώγια συνέρχεσθαι). These gatherings (συνόδους), he said, were not based on drunkenness and carousing to promote conspiracy and so to do grave injury to the cause of peace, but were schools (διδασκαλεῖα) of temperance and justice where men while practising virtue subscribed the annual first-fruits to pay for the sacrifices which they offer and commissioned sacred envoys to take them to the temple in Jerusalem.[48]

Here again συναγωγίον refers to the meeting places used by the Jews. The gatherings of the Jews are compared directly with the voluntary associations of the empire, but the Jewish meetings are portrayed as much more sober and learned gatherings than those of their pagan counterparts. It may be that apologetic reasons lie behind this termin-

---

47   Cf. the description of the Qumran community: 'This is the rule for the session of the many. Each one by his rank: the priests will sit down first, the elders next and the remainder of all the people will sit down in order of rank', 1QS 6.8-9.

48   Philo, *Leg. Gai.*, 311–12.

ology with Philo seeking to compare the 'synagogue' with Hellenistic philosophical schools and so raise the perception of them in the prevailing culture. The gatherings were places where money was collected for onward transmission to Jerusalem and it is likely that these would have been kept in the building.[49]

2.2.3. *Rome*

Another interesting reference in Philo comes when he mentions that there were προσευχαί in Rome which had been favourably treated by Augustus.[50] Here the Jews met together, 'particularly on the sacred Sabbaths when they receive as a body a training in their ancestral philosophy'.[51] It is difficult to corroborate this claim as little archaeological evidence has been found as yet to substantiate it. However, inscriptions from the Roman catacombs point to the existence of at least 11 'synagogues' in Rome; a Roman author refers to a *proseucha* in the city; an inscription dating to the first century also mentions a *proseucha*; and there is a first-century synagogue building in nearby Ostia. These references, inscriptions and archaeological remains will all be discussed below.[52]

2.3. *Palestine*

In *Quod omnis probus liber sit*, Philo describes the Sabbath practices of the Essenes as the study of ethics by means of the law. He says that they are instructed in these matters at other times:

> But particularly on the seventh days. For that day has been set apart to be kept holy and on it they abstain from all other work and proceed to sacred spots which they call synagogues (εἰς ἱεροὺς ἀφικνούμενοι τόπους οἳ καλοῦνται συναγωγαί). There, arranged in rows according to their ages, the younger below the elder, they sit decorously as befits the occasion with attentive ears. Then one takes the books and reads aloud and another of especial proficiency comes forward and expounds what is not understood. For most of their philosophical study takes the form of allegory, and in this they emulate the tradition of the past.[53]

Here the sacred spots (ἱεροὺς τόπους) are equated with the συναγωγαί.[54] It is the place where the Jews gather for their Sabbath activities and not the community that meets that are described as συναγωγαί. I accept that

---

49 Cf. Josephus, *Ant.*, 16.163-64.
50 Philo, *Leg. Gai.*, 155–57.
51 *Ibid.*, 156.
52 See section 4.1 below and Chapter 3, 2.1.
53 Philo, *Omn. Prob. Lib.*, 81. Cf. 1QS 6.8-9.
54 It is worth noting that this is plural.

this does not of necessity need to be a building, but merely point out that it goes further than the gathered community which Kee suggests. Elsewhere in Philo the connection of ἱερός with τόπος often does relate to a building,[55] and also specifically to προσευχαί.[56] Indeed Riesner can write: 'It cannot be denied that Philo once calls a Jewish place of worship συναγωγή'.[57] On Philo's use of συναγωγή here, Schürer suggests that it is a term used by Palestinian Jews and that he appears to be unfamiliar with it,[58] a suggestion which would fit well with Hengel's theory of geographical distinction in nomenclature.

2.4. References with no Geographical Connection

As mentioned above, as well as the two regular words for the place of gathering, Philo also uses a number of others. In De vita Mosis 2 he describes a man who is caught gathering firewood on the Sabbath:

> They arrested him, and took him before the ruler beside whom the priests were seated, while the whole multitude stood around to listen; for it was customary on every day when opportunity offered, and pre-eminently on the seventh day, as I have explained above, to pursue the study of wisdom with the ruler expounding and instructing the people ... Even now this practice is retained, and the Jews every seventh day occupy themselves with the philosophy of their fathers, dedicating that time to the acquiring of knowledge and the study of the truths of nature. For what are our places of prayer (προσευκτήριον) throughout the cities but schools (διδασκαλεῖα) of prudence and courage and temperance and justice and also of piety, holiness and every virtue by which duties to God and men are discerned and rightly performed?[59]

Here again, the gathering places are associated with schools, although here προσευκτήριον is used. The teaching is described as the 'acquiring of knowledge and the study of the truths of nature' which, as before, might indicate Philo's wish to elevate the activities of the Jews. It is interesting to note that meeting on every possible occasion appears to be the ideal.

---

55   Temples: Philo, Plant., 162; the Jerusalem temple: Spec. Leg., 1.115; 1.231; Leg. Gai., 318.

56   Philo, Flacc., 48–49.

57   R. Riesner, 'Synagogues in Jerusalem', in R. Bauckham (ed.), The Book of Acts in its Palestinian Setting (TBAFCS, vol. 4), p. 182.

58   Schürer, HJP, vol. 2, p. 440.

59   Philo, Vit. Mos., 2.214-16. Διδασκαλεῖα are also mentioned in Dec., 40, while it is not clear from this reference that these are the prayer houses that are being talked of, the study of Scripture certainly seems to be something carried out within the διδασκαλεῖα. In Spec. Leg., 2.62 Philo suggests that there are thousands of these schools, that they are in every city and are used every seventh day. This is doubtless an exaggeration, but it gives us a feel for Philo's sense of their ubiquity. Similar is Philo's claim that they can be traced back to Jacob, Praem. Poen., 66.

Again, we get the impression that these prayer houses are common features in many of the cities, although it is difficult to know what Philo means by this and what sort of a geographical spread he has in mind.

2.5. *Conclusion*

Within the writings of Philo we have a variety of terms being used for the meeting places of the Jews and it will be helpful to summarize them:

- προσευχή
  Alexandria: the meeting places were destroyed in the pogroms. They are described as sacred buildings and compared with local temples.
  Rome: the meeting places of the Jews which are used particularly on the Sabbath, presumably indicating that they were also used at other times.
- προσευκτήριον
  No specific location: gathering on the Sabbath is the usual practice; however, more regular meeting is encouraged.
- διδασκαλεῖα
  No specific location: Philo compares the προσευκτήριον with schools. Although used principally on the Sabbath, they are also used on other days.
  Asia Minor: Philo compares the συναγωγίον with schools and contrasts the behaviour of the Jews with that of the voluntary associations.
- συναγωγή
  Palestine: used in connection with the Essenes. The συναγωγαί are referred to as sacred spots which must refer to a place rather than the community and these are used on the Sabbath.
- συναγωγίον
  Alexandria: connected with Sabbath activity and referring to a place.
  Asia Minor: refers to the Jewish meeting places which are compared favourably to voluntary associations. Money was collected for the Jerusalem Temple.
- κοινὸν σεμνεῖον
  South of Alexandria: the communal building used by the Therapeutae.
- ἱερόν
  Alexandria: referring to buildings used by Jews for ritual activities which required some form of purification.

Although recognizing Philo's importance as a source of information on Alexandrian 'synagogues', Levine cautions that we must be careful how we use his works.[60] Certainly given his close involvement in the pogroms

---

60 Levine, *Ancient Synagogue*, p. 82.

of 38 CE it is perhaps to be expected that Philo's accounts will not be without some bias or apologetic nature. Similarly, with the emphasis on schools (nowhere else called these), Philo's description of study as 'philosophy' and the long periods of time set apart for study may reflect the Alexandrian elite, rather than the everyday Jew, or may be aimed at raising Judaism's standing in the Hellenistic world.[61] However, there is no reason to think that Philo invented buildings. Although Levine's caution ought to be heeded, we should recognize that the picture of the practices of Jews which Philo provides appears to coincide with much of the other evidence of the period.

Richard Horsley states: 'Philo's usage and other Egyptian evidence suggests that Egyptian Jewish communities did not yet use 'synagogue' even for the congregation'.[62] It has been shown that although Philo does normally use προσευχή to describe the Jewish meeting places, other words are also used, including συναγωγή. Indeed Kee seems to accept this by the time he writes, in 1994:

> In the first half of the first century CE, Philo does use the term for the places where the Jews gather to study the scriptures ('places called synagogues'), although he also uses the diminutive form, συναγωγία for the gathering places. When he is describing the Jewish practice of meeting to receive instruction in their 'paternal philosophy,' however, he identifies their meeting places not as synagogues but as προσευχαί. It is in his description of the Essenes that he notes how they gather in holy places which they call συναγωγαί. The process of change of terminology for places of Jewish study and worship has begun.[63]

It is unclear what Kee is trying to do here. He appears to want to draw what can only be described as an artificial line between the study of the Scriptures and 'paternal philosophy'. However, it should be noted that in the description of the Essenes, which Kee accepts, we are told that those gathered were engaged in 'philosophical study'. On Philo's use of συναγωγή in his description of the Essenes, Riesner, drawing on the arguments made by Hengel, suggests that it may be possible that he has

---

61   This is especially true of the two historical treatises from which we gain most of our information, *Legatio ad Gaium* and *In Flaccum*, see M.J. Martin, 'Philo's Interest in the Synagogue', *ANES* 37 (2000), pp. 215–23 (217–18).

62   R.A. Horsley, 'Synagogues in Galilee and the Gospels', in H.C. Kee and L.H. Cohick (eds), *Evolution of the Synagogue* (Harrisburg: Trinity Press, 1999), p. 51.

63   Kee, 'Changing Meaning', p. 282. Cf. H.A. McKay, 'From Evidence to Edifice: Four Fallacies about the Sabbath', in R.P. Carroll (ed.), *Text as Pretext: Essays in Honour of Robert Davidson* (JSOTSup, 138; Sheffield: JSOT Press, 1992), pp. 179–99 (194); R.A. Horsley, 'Synagogues in Galilee and the Gospels', in Kee and Cohick (eds), *Evolution of the Synagogue* pp. 46–69 (53–54).

got the terminology exactly right because in *Quod omnis probus liber sit* Philo is describing the Palestinian community of the Essenes.[64]

It appears that in Philo we have evidence of an educated and travelled Jew writing in the first half of the first century CE who knew of places at which his fellow Jews met. These places had a variety of terms which identified them, the most common, for Philo, being προσευχή; however, other terms including συναγωγή were also used. What also appears to be clear is that some of these places were buildings.

3. *Josephus*

3.1. *Introduction*

In *Against Apion* Josephus, quoting Apion, describes the meeting places of the Jews and assumes that they had been in existence from the time of Moses, a belief shared by other writers of this period:

> Moses, as I have heard from old people in Egypt, was a native of Heliopolis, who, being pledged to the customs of his country, erected prayer-houses (προσευχὰς ἀνῆγεν), open to the air, in the various precincts of the city, all facing eastwards; such being the orientation also of Heliopolis.[65]

As in Philo, a number of words are used by Josephus in connection with the meeting places, and geographically these cover both the Diaspora and Palestine. Josephus preserves many decrees and letters issued to protect the 'sacred rites' of the Jews in cities throughout the empire, and relevant references are found both in these and in Josephus' own writing.

Before going on to examine some of these references it is worth noting that there is some debate regarding the accuracy of the documents cited by Josephus, particularly those in *Antiquities* 14.190-264 and 16.162-73.[66] Josephus himself claimed that he was using public documents from the library in Rome which could be checked.[67] Smallwood, while accepting that problems exist in these documents, argues: 'The authenticity of the documents is hardly in doubt. Though some are mutilated, the style and terminology are those of genuine Roman and municipal enactments, and those originally issued from Rome contain recognizable Greek transla-

---

64 Riesner, 'Synagogues in Jerusalem', p. 182.

65 Josephus, *Apion*, 2.10. Cf. Acts 15.21.

66 See E.M. Smallwood, *The Jews under Roman Rule: From Pompey to Diocletian* (Leiden: Brill, 1976), p. 558.

67 Josephus, *Ant.*, 14.188; 14.265-67. Schürer notes that this library was destroyed in the fires of 69 CE and that although restored under Vespasian, would have held only some of the documents cited by Josephus, it being highly unlikely that decrees originating in Asia Minor, many of which are used by Josephus, would have been kept in Rome, *HJP*, vol. 1, p. 52, n. 19.

tions of Latin phrases.'[68] However, Moehring is very sceptical of Josephus' reliability. He dismisses his claim that the documents he uses could be checked, as a literary device of Josephus who, he argues, knew that it would be virtually impossible for someone to carry out such checks: 'It is wrong to read Josephus without always keeping his apologetic purpose in mind. That means, however, that the documents in Josephus must first and foremost be read as part of his apologetic scheme. Their direct use as historical evidence is impossible.'[69] In the last quarter of the twentieth century the historical value of these documents has been viewed more positively.[70] Pucci Ben Zeev compares Josephus' decrees with inscriptions recently found in Syria and notes the similarities both in content and form: 'These similarities allow us to conclude that Josephus' documents can be regarded as reliable, and can safely be used for the reconstruction of Caesar's attitude towards Jewish law'.[71]

3.2. *Diaspora*
3.2.1. *Asia Minor*

In a letter from Augustus to the Jews of Asia Minor, in 12 BCE, the emperor provides protection for the Jews:

> That their sacred monies shall be inviolable and may be sent up to Jerusalem and be delivered to the treasuries in Jerusalem, and that they need not give bond (to appear in court) on the Sabbath or on the day of preparation for it (Sabbath Eve) after the ninth hour. And if anyone is caught stealing their sacred books or their sacred monies from a synagogue or an ark (ἔκ τε σαββατείου ἔκ τε ἀαρῶνος), he shall be regarded as sacrilegious, and his property shall be confiscated to the public treasury of the Romans.[72]

Although this is the only use of σαββατεῖον to describe a 'synagogue' in the Second Temple period, the use of it is perhaps understandable coming in an imperial edict. Sabbathaios or Sambathaios was a very common personal name in this period within the Jewish communities, but, as

---

68   Smallwood, *Jews under Roman Rule*, p. 558.

69   H.R. Moehring, 'The *Acta Pro Judaeis* in the Antiquities of Flavius Josephus: A Study in Hellenistic and Modern Apologetic Historiography', in J. Neusner (ed.), *Christianity, Judaism and other Greco-Roman Cults* (SJLA, 12; 4 vols.; Leiden: Brill, 1975), vol. 3, pp. 133–57 (156). For a fuller bibliography on the documents quoted in *Antiquities* 14 see L.H. Feldman, *Josephus and Modern Scholarship (1937–1980)* (Berlin: Walter de Gruyter, 1984), pp. 273–76.

70   M. Pucci Ben Zeev points out that the work of Moehring is a solitary exception to this general consensus, 'Caesar and Jewish Law', *RB* 102 (1995), pp. 28–37 (29). See her bibliography, p. 29, n. 2.

71   *Ibid.*, pp. 29–30.

72   Josephus, *Ant.*, 16.163-64.

Tcherikover points out, there is also evidence of it in the wider Graeco-Roman world, and, they argue, this shows the influence that Jewish Sabbath-observance had on wider society.[73] There is also an inscription from the time of Hadrian where a similar word is used: 'Fabius Zosimos has built this sarcophagus and erected it on a pure place which is before the city near the Sambatheion in the precincts of Khaldaios on the public road'.[74] Given this acceptance of Sabbath related terminology it is not surprising to find a meeting place being termed a σαββατεῖον.[75]

We should also note that Augustus views the removal of money or the Torah scrolls as an act of sacrilege endowing them with the same level of sanctity as a pagan temple.[76] This is similar to Josephus' account of a soldier who removed the Torah from a village around one hundred furlongs from Jerusalem. He tore up the scroll in front of the inhabitants which is received with such shock and anger by the citizens that the soldier is beheaded.[77] One other point is worth noting: the LCL here uses ἀαρῶνος and translates this as 'an ark (of the Law)'. However, Cohen points out that 'the unanimous testimony of all the manuscripts' indicates that this should be ἀνδρῶνος.[78] While Hengel takes this as a separate room used for men,[79] it is more likely that this does not indicate a separation of the sexes, but rather was a room used as a dining-room attached to the main synagogue building as ἀνδρών has this meaning elsewhere.[80] As well as this function, it appears that the room could also be used for storing the Torah scrolls and money. This fits well with our other evidence, as we have details of additional rooms attached to synagogue buildings in a variety of places, and communal dining functions are attested in both archaeological and literary evidence.[81]

---

73 *CPJ* 3, 43. See 'The Sambathions', in *CPJ* 3, 43–56 and the related papyri, 56–87.

74 *CPJ* 3, 46. Tcherikover *et al.* correctly point out that the sarcophagus was erected after the 'synagogue' and therefore the argument that a synagogue would not be found next to a burial site does not stand. See also *CIG*, 3509 which details a σαμβαθεῖον outside the city of Thyatira in the second century CE.

75 Griffiths, 'Egypt and the Rise of the Synagogue', p. 7; Schürer, *HJP*, vol. 2, p. 440, n. 63.

76 E.P. Sanders, 'Common Judaism and the Synagogue in the First Century', in S. Fine (ed.), *Jews, Christians, and Polytheists in the Ancient Synagogue* (New York: Routledge, 1999), pp. 1–17 (7).

77 Josephus, *Ant.*, 20.115.

78 He also notes that *aaron* was not used of a 'synagogue' ark until the third century CE, S.J.D. Cohen, 'Pagan and Christian Evidence on the Ancient Synagogue', in Levine, *The Synagogue in Late Antiquity*, pp. 159–81 (176, n. 18). This possibility is also noted by R. Marcus and A. Wikgren, *Josephus*, LCL, vol. 8, p. 272, n. 6.

79 Hengel, 'Proseuche und Synagoge', p. 176.

80 See Cohen, 'Pagan and Christian Evidence', pp. 164–65; W. Horbury, 'Women in the Synagogue', in *CHJ*, pp. 384–86; Binder, *Temple Courts*, p. 148.

81 See further below.

3.2.1.1. *Halicarnassus*

Another decree, dated mid-first-century BCE, comes from the city of Halicarnassus which lay on the coast around 100 km south of Ephesus. The people passed a decree in which they say that they are following the example of the people of Rome:

> Their sacred services to God and their customary festivals and religious gatherings shall be carried on, we have also decreed that those Jewish men and women who so wish may observe their Sabbaths and perform their sacred rites in accordance with the Jewish laws, and may build places of prayer near the sea (τὰς προσευχὰς ποιεῖσθαι πρὸς τῆ θαλάττη), in accordance with their native custom. And if anyone, whether magistrate or private citizen, prevents them, he shall be liable to the following fine and owe it to the city.[82]

Here Marcus' translation of προσευχὰς ποιεῖσθαι πρὸς τῆ θαλάττη has been much discussed. Generally scholars have followed the translation given, with some noting the possibility that this could refer to 'prayers' rather than 'places of prayer'. Elsewhere I have argued that this decree in fact allows the Jews to 'offer prayers' in Halicarnassus and should not be understood as a reference to buildings.[83]

3.2.1.2. *Sardis*

The next decree quoted by Josephus concerns the people of Sardis. In *Antiquities* 14.235 Josephus tells us that the people of Sardis, from the earliest times, had an 'association of their own' (σύνοδον ἰδίαν) and a 'place of their own' (τόπον ἴδιον). In *Antiquities* 16.171 he preserves another decree ensuring that the Jewish population of Sardis are allowed to pay the temple tax. Below is a third decree, this time from the people of Sardis, probably dating to the same period as the decree from Halicarnassus, that is, around the middle of the first century BCE:[84]

> Whereas the Jewish citizens living in our city have continually received many great privileges from the people and have now come before the council and the people and have pleaded that as their laws and freedom

---

82 Josephus, *Ant.*, 14.257-58.

83 S.K. Catto, 'Does προσευχὰς ποιεῖσθαι, in Josephus' *Antiquities of the Jews* 14.257-8, Mean "Build Places of Prayer"?', *JSJ* 35 (2004), pp. 159–68.

84 P.R. Trebilco, *Jewish Communities in Asia Minor* (SNTSMS, 69; Cambridge: Cambridge University Press, 1991), p. 38; M. Pucci Ben Zeev, *Jewish Rights in the Roman World: The Greek and Roman Documents Quoted by Josephus Flavius* (TSAJ, 74; Tübingen: Mohr Siebeck, 1998), p. 217. Binder notes some difficulty over the order of these decrees: *Ant.* 14.235, which assumes that the people of Sardis had a τόπος, comes before the decree which commands the magistrates to build such a place. He suggests that Josephus is not using a chronological order, and that *Ant.* 14.235 could date to 104 BCE, *Temple Courts*, pp. 128–29.

have been restored to them by the Roman Senate and people, they may, in accordance with their accepted customs, come together and have a communal life and adjudicate suits among themselves, and that a place (τόπος) be given them in which they may gather together with their wives and children and offer their ancestral prayers and sacrifices to God, it has therefore been decreed by the council and people that permission shall be given them to come together on stated days to do those things which are in accordance with their laws, and also that a place (τόπον) shall be set apart by the magistrates for them to build and inhabit (οἰκοδομίαν καὶ οἴκησιν) such as they may consider suitable for this purpose, and that the market-officials of the city shall be charged with the duty of having suitable food for them brought in.[85]

It seems clear here from the use of τόπος and οἰκοδομέω that the Jewish population of Sardis was being granted permission by the βουλή to build a physical structure in which they would, among other things, meet to carry out religious functions.[86] In 17 CE, Asia Minor was affected by an earthquake, Tacitus recording that Sardis was more badly affected than any other city in the region.[87] The remains of a huge synagogue building has been discovered in Sardis dating from around the third century, and Seager and Kraabel think that it is likely that, 'the present synagogue must have had at least two predecessors, one before the earthquake and one sometime thereafter'.[88]

3.2.2. Syria
3.2.2.1. Dora

We now move to an incident that took place in Dora, a coastal city just north of Caesarea. We are able to date this event very accurately from the details of those involved. The decree was issued during the reign of Claudius, which began in 41 CE, and when Publius Petronius was the governor of Syria, 39–42 CE,[89] putting the date at either 41 or 42 CE. After the death of Gaius, Emperor Claudius renewed many of the freedoms that the Jews had previously enjoyed and issued edicts to

---

85   Josephus, *Ant.*, 14.259-61.

86   But see Pucci Ben Zeev, *Jewish Rights in the Roman World*, p. 222. Runesson incorrectly incorporates τόπος into his list of terms for buildings. Rather it refers to a place on which a building was to be erected, *Origins*, p. 172.

87   Tacitus, *Ann.*, 2.47.

88   A.R. Seager and A.T. Kraabel, 'The Synagogue and the Jewish Community', in G.M.A. Hanfmann (ed.), *Sardis from Prehistoric to Roman Times: Results of the Archaeological Exploration of Sardis 1958–1975* (Massachusetts: Harvard University Press, 1983), pp. 168–90 (179).

89   K. Ziegler and W. Sontheimer, *Der Kleine Pauly: Lexikon der Antike* (5 vols.; Munich: Alfred Druckenmüller, 1972), vol. 4, p. 672.

Alexandria[90] and to the rest of the empire[91] to ensure that these freedoms
were upheld. It appears to be as a reaction against these measures that
some young men of Dora did in a synagogue building what Gaius had
threatened to do in the temple in Jerusalem:

> Certain young men of Dora, who set a higher value on audacity than on
> holiness and were by nature recklessly bold, brought an image of Caesar
> into the synagogue of the Jews (εἰς τὴν τῶν Ἰουδαίων συναγωγήν) and
> set it up. This provoked Agrippa exceedingly, for it was tantamount to
> an overthrow of the laws of his fathers. Without delay he went to see
> Publius Petronius, the governor of Syria, and denounced the people of
> Dora. Petronius was no less angry at the deed, for he too regarded the
> breach of law as sacrilege. He wrote in anger to the leaders of Dora as
> follows: 'Publius Petronius legate of Tiberius Claudius Caesar Augustus
> Germanicus, to the leading men of Dora speaks: Inasmuch as certain of
> you have had such mad audacity, notwithstanding the issuance of an
> edict of Claudius Caesar Augustus Germanicus pertaining to the
> permission granted the Jews to observe the customs of their fathers, not
> to obey this edict, but to do the very reverse, in that you have prevented
> the Jews from having a synagogue (συναγωγὴν Ἰουδαίων κωλύοντας
> εἶναι) by transferring to it an image of Caesar, you have thereby sinned
> not only against the law of the Jews, but also against the emperor,
> whose image was better placed in his own shrine (ἐν τῷ ἰδίῳ ναῷ) than
> in that of another, especially in the synagogue (συναγωγῆς); for by
> natural law each must be lord over his own places (ἰδίων τόπων), in
> accordance with Caesar's decree.'[92]

Kee notes on one occasion that the letter from Petronius actually says that
the Jews were prevented from 'being' (εἶναι) a 'synagogue'.[93] But a literal
translation would be: 'preventing there being a synagogue of the Jews'.
Further, in context it appears that ναός and τόπος are associated with
συναγωγή. The correlation between the shrine of Caesar and the
'synagogue' makes it clear that here what is being referred to is a
building. Indeed, Kee is willing to accept that this does refer to the place
of gathering rather than just the gathered community itself, but that this
reflects his writing 'around and after the turn of the second century when
terminology is changing.' [94] However, on this dating three points need to
be made. First, to ascribe any of Josephus' works to the second century

90   Josephus, *Ant.*, 19.280-85, *CPJ* 2, No. 153.
91   Josephus, *Ant.*, 19.287-91.
92   Josephus, *Ant.*, 19.300-305.
93   H.C. Kee, 'Defining the First-Century CE Synagogue: Problems and Progress', *NTS*
41 (1995), pp. 481–500 (487).
94   Kee, 'Changing Meaning', p. 282.

appears to be going against the consensus of scholarly opinion.[95] Second, two of the other references that Kee accepts as meaning a place, come from *The JewishWar*,[96] generally held to have been written in the 70s.[97] Kee points out that Thackeray, in the Loeb translation, accepts that Josephus may well have continued to alter and add to his works. While such alterations may have been made, to assume that one of these additions would have been the use of the word συναγωγή appears to be pushing the evidence.[98] Third, Josephus is quoting a decree that was issued in the early 40s. While I accept, as noted above, that there are problems associated with Josephus' use of decrees, most scholars accept their general accuracy. It is possible that Josephus' source was written in Latin rather than Greek and so the use of συναγωγή here is Josephus' translation of a Latin term. However, it is also possible that his source could have been in Greek and Josephus is just reproducing the term that was used in the city of Dora. It appears that the minimalists are influenced by their general assumption that the term συναγωγή could not have been used for a building in the mid-first century; from the evidence presented elsewhere, this has been shown to be a false assumption. In this decree we have another example of συναγωγή being used of a building, and it is at least possible that this term was used for the building in the 40s CE.

3.2.2.2. *Antioch*

One other reference to Syria is worthy of note. Josephus' accounts of when the Jews became inhabitants of Antioch are a little confusing;[99] however, at the latest they were present from the time of Antiochus I who reigned from 280 to 261 BCE.[100] Here Josephus recounts the events that transpired in the city after Antiochus IV:

> For, although Antiochus surnamed Epiphanes sacked Jerusalem and plundered the temple, his successors on the throne restored to the Jews of Antioch all such votive offerings as were made of brass, to be laid up in their synagogue (εἰς τὴν συναγωγὴν αὐτῶν), and, moreover, granted them citizen rights on an equality with the Greeks. Continuing to receive similar treatment from later monarchs, the Jewish colony grew in numbers, and their richly designed and costly offerings formed a splendid ornament to the temple (ἱερόν). Moreover,

---

95   See Per Bilde, *Flavius Josephus between Jerusalem and Rome: His Life, his Works, and their Importance* (JSPSup, 2; Sheffield: JSOT Press, 1988), pp. 61–122; T. Rajak, *Josephus: The Historian and His Society* (London: Duckworth, 1983), pp. 237–38.

96   Josephus, *War*, 2.289; 7.44.

97   See H.St.J. Thackeray's introduction to *War* (LCL), p. xii; Bilde, *Flavius Josephus between Jerusalem and Rome*, pp. 61–122.

98   See Binder, *Temple Courts*, p. 102, n. 26.

99   See Josephus, *Ant.*, 12.119; *Apion*, 2.39; *War*, 7.43-45.

100   See the notes of Thackeray in LCL, vol. 3, p. 517, n. c.

they were constantly attracting to their religious ceremonies multitudes of Greeks, and these they had in some measure incorporated with themselves.[101]

This would have to have taken place between 163 and 65 BCE,[102] and if Josephus is correct when he says that later Seleucid kings gave further benefits, then the original gifts must have come towards the beginning of the period. Contra Thackeray, ἱερόν here does not refer to the temple in Jerusalem, but to the 'synagogue' in Antioch,[103] with συναγωγή and ἱερόν used of the same entity. The fact that these 'treasures' were being returned to the people to be kept 'in their synagogue' would indicate that a building is meant; the further description of their use of these gifts to create an ornate building, here called a ἱερόν, confirms this. Why the Seleucid kings chose to return these items to Antioch is not clear; Dion suggests that it was to create a rival sanctuary to Jerusalem, and this may have some merit.[104]

3.3. *Palestine*
3.3.1. *Caesarea*

We now move to some references from Palestine. In the first, Josephus recalls the event that, in his view, started the revolt of 66 CE, describing the situation in Caesarea where the Jews had a 'synagogue'.[105] Here they tried to buy a piece of land adjoining the 'synagogue', but the owner, a Greek of the city, refused to sell to them. Rather, he erected some workshops on the ground which meant that the Jews had only a small passageway to get to the 'synagogue'. Josephus then recalls an incident where another resident of the city had blocked this small passageway:

> On the following day, which was a Sabbath, when the Jews assembled at the synagogue (εἰς τὴν συναγωγήν), they found that one of the Caesarean mischief-makers had placed beside the entrance a pot, turned bottom upwards, upon which he was sacrificing birds. This spectacle of what they considered an outrage upon their laws and a desecration of the spot enraged the Jews beyond endurance.[106]

---

101 Josephus, *War*, 7.44-45.

102 Between the death of Antiochus and the taking of Syria by Pompey, see Levine, *Ancient Synagogue*, p. 116.

103 Thackeray, LCL, vol. 3, p. 519, n. b. Josephus uses ἱερόν on six other occasions possibly referring to 'synagogues', *Apion*, 1.209 (see below 4.1); *War*, 1.277, 4.408, 7.144; *Ant.*, 13.66-67, 14.374. See the detailed and persuasive discussion of Binder, *Temple Courts*, pp. 122–30, 234–36. However, Levine thinks it is unlikely that *War*, 1.277, 4.408 and *Ant.*, 14.374 refer to 'synagogues', *Ancient Synagogue*, p. 43 n. 4.

104 P.E. Dion, 'Synagogues et Temples dans L'Égypte Hellénistique', *ScEs* 29 (1977), pp. 45–75 (52).

105 Josephus, *War*, 2.284-90.

106 Josephus, *War*, 2.289.

These actions meant that the area was ritually unclean and led the Jews to remove their Torah scrolls and depart for the nearby village of Narbata. Kee remarks that in this passage εἰς τὴν συναγωγήν almost certainly means 'into the meeting, but it cannot be completely excluded that, following the destruction of the Temple in 70 CE, the term συναγωγή, which earlier had been used with reference to the Jewish group meetings, began to be used to refer as well to the structure where they met'.[107] No reason is given for the assumption that it means 'into the meeting', other than Kee's general view that this is what συναγωγή must mean. Again, in the context of the description of this event it would be better to accept that here a place, most probably a building, is in mind.

3.3.2. *Tiberias*

Josephus recalls another event that took place in Palestine, this time one of which he has first-hand knowledge. He describes a 'huge prayer-house' in Tiberias (τὴν προσευχὴν μέγιστον οἴκημα)[108] visited by Josephus during the revolt of 66 CE. The city was built by Herod Antipas, probably between the years 17 and 22 CE,[109] and Avi-Yonah suggests that because of the problems of impurity associated with Tiberias, many Jews would have been reluctant to move to this new city.[110] He argues that those who would have been prepared to move were:

> From the more well-to-do classes that looked less to the letter of the law and more to their personal profit. They were attracted to the new city, since, on the declaration of its being the capital of Galilee, government offices, including the royal bank, were transferred there. The other group of people who would have been willing to move were those at the other end of the economic scale who would have been attracted by the offer of land and houses.[111]

---

107 Kee, 'Defining', p. 488.

108 Josephus, *Life*, 277. It could accommodate the city boule, some 600 men (*War*, 2.641). This is the only occasion that a meeting place in Judaea is described as a προσευχή. It is not clear why Josephus uses this term here, although it has been suggested that the Hellenistic character of the city may be the reason, see, Hengel, 'Proseuche und Synagoge', p. 177; Levine, *Ancient Synagogue*, p. 50. See also Binder, *Temple Courts*, p. 117; S. Mason, *Flavius Josephus: Life of Josephus* (Leiden: Brill, 2001), p. 122, n. 1165.

109 M. Avi-Yonah argues that Herod started its construction on the ascension of Tiberius and that it was founded 4 years later in 18 CE, 'The Foundation of Tiberias', *IEJ* 1 (1950–51), pp. 160–69 (169). See also the discussion in Schürer, *HJP*, vol. 2, p. 179.

110 Avi-Yonah notes that the city was impure because its foundations had encroached on a cemetery, 'Foundation', p. 162. On account of this, E.P. Sanders writes: 'If there was a large building for prayer and study in Tiberius – a city that was permanently impure – we may assume that there were such buildings elsewhere in Palestine', *Judaism: Practice and Belief 63 BCE – 66CE* (London: SCM Press, 1992), p. 199.

111 Avi-Yonah, 'Foundation', p. 163.

As part of the construction we are told that Herod built a stadium[112] and a palace for himself.[113] Josephus recalls:

> The arrival of the sixth hour, at which it is our custom on the Sabbath to take our midday meal, broke off the meeting. Jonathan and his friends, accordingly, adjourned the council (βουλή) to the following day and retired without effecting their object. These proceedings being at once reported to me, I decided to visit Tiberias early on the morrow. Arriving there about the first hour next day, I found the people already assembling in the Prayer-house (εἰς τὴν προσευχήν), although they had no idea why they were being convened.[114]

Horsley argues that they met here for civic not religious purposes; therefore, 'this "prayer-house" was thus certainly not one of several "synagogues" in the city (which appeared only in late antiquity)'.[115] It should be noted, however, that here Josephus' aim is not to outline for us the normal proceedings that went on in this προσευχή, but rather to recall the political intrigue surrounding his visit to this city. Further, we are told that in order to trap Josephus, a certain Ananias called a fast the following day and requested that the people should return to the προσευχή 'in order to attest before God their conviction that without his aid no armour could avail them'.[116] Contra Horsley, the προσευχή is clearly being used for religious purposes. Here the προσευχή was used both as a place where the community gathered to worship and to decide on civic matters. It is described as a large structure and perhaps this should not surprise us given the city's origins and population.

3.4. Conclusion

As in Philo above, Josephus uses a variety of terms for the meeting places of the Jews:

- συναγωγή
  Dora: the taking of an image of Caesar into the συναγωγή is perceived as an act of sacrilege. That a more appropriate place for this would be Caesar's own ναός indicates that a building should be understood.
  Antioch: again used of a building, as booty is returned and used to adorn it.

---

112   Josephus, *War*, 2.618, 3.539; *Life*, 331.

113   Josephus, *Life*, 65.

114   Josephus, *Life*, 279–80.

115   Horsley, 'Synagogues in Galilee and the Gospels', p. 52; see also McKay, 'Ancient Synagogues', p. 122. On references to 'synagogues' in Tiberias in rabbinic literature, see the discussion in S.S. Miller, 'On the Number of Synagogues in the Cities of 'Erez Israel', *JJS* 49 (1998), pp. 51–66 (55–58).

116   Josephus, *Life*, 290.

Caesarea: that the συναγωγή lay next to a piece of land clearly indicates a place, in all probability a building.

- προσευχή
Tiberias: the large building in the city was used for a variety of purposes including political debate.
Heliopolis: referring to the belief that the places of prayer date back to Moses.

- σαββατεῖον
Asia Minor: this building is used to store sacred money and books, the stealing of which is an act of sacrilege. The books or money could also be stored in an additional building which may also have been used for dining. The name indicates a connection with the Sabbath.

- ἱερόν
Antioch: the συναγωγή is also referred to as a ἱερόν.
Jerusalem: this term is used of the 'synagogues' in the city.[117]

- τόπος
Sardis: the Jews of the city are allowed a place on which to build where they may come together as families to pray and make sacrifices.

Certain scholars want to carve up these terms and isolate them from one another. So Horsley notes that Josephus uses συναγωγή in reference to Dora, Caesarea and Antioch: 'all of these cases are from diaspora Jewish communities in Hellenistic cities on the nearer or farther fringes of Palestine, however, no conclusions can be drawn for the possible existence of "synagogue" buildings in Judean or Galilean villages and towns'.[118] In Chapter 4 we will show that many of the practices associated with the meeting places of the Jews are common to gatherings/places/buildings of which different terminology is used. Is this just a difference in vocabulary for what was the same institution, or should we understand these to be distinct 'institutions'? There are problems with both approaches; because of the similarities in function we should not drive too great a wedge between them, but the different terms might also suggest some distinction in practice between them on a local level.

As mentioned, Josephus preserves a large number of decrees concerning the Jews. Only a few of them actually mention meeting places. However, we conclude that the protection afforded the Jews in many other locations to 'come together for sacred and holy rites' would often have taken place within such places and that these would often be buildings of some sort.[119]

---

117 See below section 4.1. Josephus possibly also uses it of 'synagogues' on other occasions, see n. 103 above.

118 R.A. Horsley, *Galilee: History, Politics, People* (Valley Forge: Trinity, 1995), p. 225.

119 I am not presuming that these were of necessity specialized buildings; the place where the Jews met would to a large extent be governed by location and population.

4. *Other Literary Sources*

4.1. *Non-Jewish Authors*

Other writers commenting on the Jews around the turn of the era were generally negative. The Jews are often ridiculed for their religious practices, beliefs, dietary regulations[120] and, because of their observance of the Sabbath, accused of being lazy.[121] In some instances these regulations kept them at a distance from other religious or ethnic groups and perhaps inevitably led to suspicion; however, this was not always the case as they were also accused of proselytising.[122]

In a long passage describing the lifestyle of the Jews, Tacitus, writing in the first decade of the second century, describes their aversion to images of God: 'Therefore they set up no statues in their cities, still less in their temples (*nedum templis*)'.[123] In this analysis of the Jews, their land, and their practices, it would appear likely that Tacitus is unable to differentiate between the buildings that the Jews use for religious purposes and pagan temples, thus these 'temples' were in fact synagogue buildings. The same phenomenon can be seen in Agatharchides, quoted in Josephus:

> The people known as the Jews, who inhabit the most strongly fortified of cities, called by the natives Jerusalem, have a custom of abstaining from work every seventh day; on those occasions they neither bear arms nor take any agricultural operations in hand, nor engage in any other form of public service, but pray with outstretched hands in the temples (ἐν τοῖς ἱεροῖς) until the evening. Consequently, because the inhabitants, instead of protecting their city, persevered in their folly, Ptolemy, son of Lagus, was allowed to enter with his army.[124]

Agatharchides (mid to late second-century BCE) here discusses an event that took place in the fourth-century BCE; however, it is likely that he is describing practices that he was familiar with from his own time. The plural, 'in the temples', could refer to the temple in Jerusalem with Agatharchides, a pagan author, assuming that there must have been more than one.[125] The more likely solution is that he, like Tacitus, used the term

---

120   Cicero, *Flacc.*, 69; Tacitus, *Hist.*, 5.1-13; Juvenal, *Sat.*, 3.10-16, 296; 6.153-60; 14.96-106.

121   Seneca, *De Superstitone*, cited in Augustine, *De Civitate*, 6.11.

122   Valerius Maximus, writing at the beginning of the first century CE, gives us the first reference to Jews in Rome in the year 139 BCE. The *praetor* has them banished from the city because, 'they attempted to transmit their sacred rites to the Romans, and he cast down their private altars from public places', *Facta et Dicta Memorabilia*, 1, 3.3. Cassius Dio gives a similar reason for the expulsion of the Jews from Rome in 19 CE, *Historia Romana*, 57.18.5a.

123   Tacitus, *Hist.*, 5.5.

124   Josephus, *Apion*, 1.209, cf. *3 Macc.* 2.28.

125   See Levine, *Ancient Synagogue*, p. 25.

he was familiar with for an institution such as the Jewish synagogue buildings.[126]

Juvenal (ca. 60–130 CE), a Roman satirist, also disliked the influence that those from the east were having on Rome, and among those he mentions are the Jews. He shows that he is aware of the Jewish practice of Sabbath observance and their dietary rules in connection with pigs.[127] In a satire showing the bad influence of parents on children he mentions those whose fathers appear to have been God-fearers (although they could have been full Jews[128]) and had assumed some of the Jewish practices concerning Sabbath observance; they, 'gave up every seventh day to idleness, keeping it apart from all the concerns of life'.[129] In another of his satires he says that, 'the holy fount and grove and shrine are let out to Jews'.[130] Courtney acknowledges that this may mean that the Jews have rented a grove in Rome in order to build a synagogue building, but thinks that it is more likely to mean that the Jews had been allowed to settle in this particular place.[131] Of most interest is Juvenal's account of the dangers of travelling the streets of Rome at night. He describes an affray in which a beggar is assaulted, and asked, 'Where is your stand? In what prayer-shop (*proseucha*) shall I find you?'[132] Elsewhere Juvenal portrays Jews as indigents and beggars[133] and here *proseucha*, in Latin, is obviously loaned from the Greek.[134]

4.2. *Septuagint*

In the Septuagint, συναγωγή is used to translate 19 different Hebrew words.[135] It can describe the gathering of the waters, crops and rocks, [136] a

---

126 Dion, 'Synagogues et Temples', p. 55; Cohen, 'Pagan and Christian Evidence', p. 162; Hengel, 'Proseuche und Synagoge', p. 163. That this does not refer to 'synagogues' see Levine, *Ancient Synagogue*, p. 153 n. 149; I. von Görtz-Wrisberg, 'A Sabbath Service in Ostia: What Do We Know about the Ancient Synagogal Service?', in B. Olsson, D. Mitternacht and O. Brandt (eds), *The Synagogue of Ancient Ostia and the Jews of Rome: Interdisciplinary Studies* (Stockholm: Paul Åströms Förlag, 2001), pp. 167–202 (171, n. 64).

127 Juvenal, *Sat.*, 6.153f.

128 For a discussion of this see *GLAJJ*, vol. 2, pp. 103–106.

129 Juvenal, *Sat.*, 14.96f.

130 *Ibid.*, 3.13f.

131 E. Courtney, *A Commentary on the Satires of Juvenal* (London: The Athlone Press, 1980), p. 158.

132 Juvenal, *Sat.*, 3.296.

133 Cf. *Sat.*, 6.542-47. See also *GLAJJ*, vol. 2, p. 95.

134 Cf. Philo, *Leg. Gai.*, 155–57; *JIWE*, 2.602.

135 E. Hatch and H.A. Redpath, 'συναγωγή', in *A Concordance to the Septuagint and the Other Greek Versions of the Old Testament* (Grand Rapids: Baker, 2nd edn, 1998), pp. 1309–40.

136 Gen. 1.9; Exod. 23.16; Job 8.17.

swarm of bees,[137] a herd of bulls,[138] a band of ruffians,[139] the assembly of the dead,[140] and a group of scribes.[141] But by far the most common meaning is a group of people or nations[142] or the whole people of Israel.[143] In the Old Testament Apocrypha there is a move from using συναγωγή to refer to the whole community of Israel to it being used of local groups,[144] with the whole of Jewry then described as the συναγωγαί Ἰσραήλ.[145]

The only use of συναγωγή for a building comes in the Old Greek version of Susannah.[146] When the townspeople and the elders of the community gather in order to adjudicate in the case of Susannah,[147] the Greek reads: καὶ ἐλθόντες ἐπὶ τὴν συναγωγὴν τῆς πόλεως, which Collins translates as, 'they came to the synagogue of the city'.[148] The following part of the sentence, which states that all the Israelites were assembled there, would seem to make more sense if συναγωγή here referred to a building rather than to the 'gathering'.[149]

Προσευχή is used most commonly in the Septuagint to denote prayer, although on two occasions it may indicate a place of prayer. In the first, Judas Maccabeus, having gathered his troops, 'went to Mizpah, opposite Jerusalem, because Israel formerly had a place of prayer (τόπος προσευχῆς) in Mizpah'.[150] Runesson describes this as an 'earlier Jewish Shrine',[151] while Bartlett points out that Samuel gathered the people in this place to fast and confess their sin before meeting the Philistine

---

137   Judg. 14.8.

138   Ps. 68.30.

139   Ps. 86.14.

140   Prov. 21.16.

141   1 Macc. 7.12.

142   E.g., Gen. 28.3; 35.11.

143   Exod. 12.3.

144   Sir. 4.7; 16.6; 21.9; Sus. 41, 52, 60; 1 Macc. 2.42; 7.12.

145   *Pss. Sol.* 10.7.

146   See J.J. Collins, *Daniel: A Commentary on the Book of Daniel* (Hermeneia; Minneapolis: Fortress Press, 1993), p. 426.

147   The Theodotion version states only that 'the people gathered at the house of her husband Joakim'. Kee appears to refer only to this version, 'Defining', p. 485, n. 13.

148   Sus. 28. Collins, *Daniel*, p. 420.

149   καὶ συνήδρευσαν οἱ ὄντες ἐκεῖ πάντες οἱ υἱοὶ Ἰσραήλ. See Binder, *Temple Courts*, p. 93, n. 4; L.I. Levine, 'The Nature and Origin of the Palestinian Synagogue', *JBL* 115 (1996), pp. 425–48 (441). As well as Sus. 28, Claußen regards Num. 16.24 as a reference to a building, but this is certainly not the case, 'Meeting, Community, Synagogue – Different Frameworks of Ancient Jewish Congregations in the Diaspora', in B. Olsson and M. Zetterholm (eds), *The Ancient Synagogue: From its Origins to 200 C.E.: Papers Presented at an International Conference at Lund University, October 14–17, 2001* (ConNT, 39; Stockholm: Almqvist & Wiksell, 2003), pp. 144–67 (151).

150   1 Macc. 3.46.

151   Runesson, *Origins*, p. 429.

army.[152] Similarly, Judges 20 records that Mizpah was where the tribes of Israel gathered before the Lord prior to their battle with Benjamin.[153] It seems likely that the site was perceived as somewhere that prayers should be carried out before battle, hence the actions of Judas. Whether a building should be understood is less clear; it may be that the site was simply seen as an appropriate place to pray.

The second reference appears in *3 Maccabees* 7.20, although before dealing with this we will first examine another which occurs earlier in the book. *3 Maccabees* narrates the oppression of Jews in Alexandria: Ptolemy IV, having been refused entry to the sanctuary of the Jerusalem temple, returned to Egypt and erected a stele with the inscription: 'None of those who do not sacrifice shall enter their sanctuaries (εἰς τὰ ἱερὰ αὐτῶν εἰσιέναι), and all Jews shall be subjected to a registration involving poll tax and to the status of slaves'.[154] This must refer to the meeting places of the Jews in Egypt, here termed ἱερά.[155] After further threatened persecution, God comes to the aid of the Jews and they are freed, Ptolemy granting that they should be provided with food to celebrate. The festival takes place in Ptolemais and its importance is recognized in another inscription:

> Then, after inscribing them as holy on a pillar and dedicating a place of prayer (τόπον προσευχῆς) at the site of the festival, they departed unharmed, free, and overjoyed, since at the king's command they had all of them been brought safely by land and sea and river to their own homes.[156]

Clearly something physical must be meant here as it was possible either to inscribe directly onto it or to attach an inscribed stone to it, but should this be understood as a building?[157] Runesson incisively asks: if this is a synagogue building to be used weekly for Sabbath meetings and the reading of the Torah, for whom is it built?[158] We are told that following the festival the Jews dispersed by land, sea and river to their own homes so presumably it could not have been for them. While we should not entirely dismiss the possibility that here there is a reference to a synagogue

---

152   J.R. Bartlett, *The First and Second Books of the Maccabees* (Cambridge: Cambridge University Press, 1973), pp. 54–55.

153   See P. Davies, 'A Note on I Macc. III. 46', *JTS* 23 (1972), pp. 117–21.

154   *3 Macc.* 2.28.

155   Whether this was an accurate recording of an actual decree or not is difficult to know, see the comments of Dion, 'Synagogues et Temples', pp. 48–49.

156   *3 Macc.* 7.20.

157   Binder thinks so, *Temple Courts*, p. 46, as does Levine, *Ancient Synagogue*, p. 79, n. 35 and N.C. Croy, *3 Maccabees* (Septuagint Commentary Series, Leiden: Brill, 2006), pp. 117–18. Cf. Claußen, 'Meeting, Community, Synagogue', p. 151, n. 30.

158   Runesson, *Origins*, pp. 434–35.

building, it seems more likely that some form of monument is constructed to commemorate their liberation.

So, in the Septuagint, συναγωγή most often referred to the gathered community of Israel rather than meeting places. Similarly, προσευχή commonly referred to prayer, although it may also have been used of places of prayer, but these should not be assumed to be equivalent to the προσευχαί of the Egyptian inscriptions. Nonetheless, that the Jews had places of meeting is confirmed, and, as in our other sources, to pagans these were similar to their ἱερά.

4.3. *Rabbinic Authors*

As mentioned previously, when we turn to rabbinic literature, we need to be very careful how it is used. Some of the rabbinic material clearly focuses on Jerusalem, although the portrayal may be skewed by its distance in time from the events it is recording or by painting an idealized picture, particularly of the city of Jerusalem and the temple precincts. At times scholars are too willing to accept references to Jewish practices, in the Mishnah for example, and assume that they would also have been practices in the first century.[159]

There are a number of interesting references to 'synagogues' in Jerusalem during the time that the second temple was standing. The problem with these accounts is that they are from fairly late compilations, give differing numbers of 'synagogues', use different terminology and appear to be greatly exaggerated accounts.[160] Of these Levine writes: 'What these traditions do evidence, however, is the assumption by later generations that late Second Temple Jerusalem abounded in such institutions'.[161] This may be the case, but the assumptions of a later generation cannot be used here as particularly strong evidence for their actual existence.[162] Nonetheless, it will be useful to survey potential references.

In the Tosefta, the second-century rabbi Simeon b. Gamaliel mentions a discussion between the house of Hillel and the house of Shammai, who date to the first century CE, over charity being announced in the 'synagogue' on the Sabbath.[163] If this is accurately reported, then it seems

---

159   See my discussion in Chapter 1, 2.2.

160   E.g., *y. Meg.* 3,1,73d records 480; *b. Ket.* 105a, 394. The Talmuds also report that there were 13 'synagogues' in Tiberias (*b. Ber.* 8a), and 18 in Sepphoris (*y. Kil.* 9, 32b). See the discussion in S.S. Miller, 'Number of Synagogues', pp. 51–53.

161   Levine, *Ancient Synagogue*, p. 58.

162   There is also some patristic evidence for 'synagogues' in Jerusalem, but this is equally difficult to accept as evidence, see the discussion in Claußen, *Versammlung*, p. 96.

163   *T. Shabb.* 16.22 .

likely to reflect contemporaneous Palestinian practice.[164] There are also more difficult references to synagogue buildings on the Temple Mount itself,[165] where other major pieces on the temple, for example, Josephus and the Mishnah, do not mention synagogue buildings there. Perhaps of more value are the reports of a first-century 'synagogue' of the Alexandrians in Jerusalem[166] as there does at least seem to be some corroborating evidence for the existence of 'synagogues' in Jerusalem used by Diaspora communities.[167]

The Babylonian Talmud discusses what should happen to a man who had mistakenly shown reverence for a pagan temple thinking it to be a synagogue building.[168] This suggests that there may have been similarities between the architecture of synagogue buildings and the temples that existed in most of the Diaspora cities. Although this comes from a period some distance from the first century, as has been noted above, a similar inability to differentiate between pagan temples and synagogue buildings is attested in other authors who wrote nearer to the time.[169]

One very interesting potential piece of evidence comes from an early third-century Tosefta. Rabbi Judah, who dates to the end of the second century, gives a description of a very large synagogue building in Alexandria:

> Whoever has never seen the double colonnade (the basilica-synagogue) of Alexandria in Egypt has never seen Israel's glory in his entire life. It was a kind of large basilica, one colonnade inside another. Sometimes there were twice as many people there as those who went forth from Egypt. Now there were seventy-one golden thrones set up there, one for each of the seventy-one elders, each one worth twenty-five talents of gold, with a wooden platform in the middle. The minister of the synagogue stands on it, with flags in his hand. When one began to read, the other would wave the flags so the people would answer, 'Amen,' for each and every blessing. Then that one would wave the flags, and they would answer, 'Amen.' They did not sit in a jumble, but the goldsmiths sat by themselves, the silversmiths by themselves, the weavers by themselves, the bronze-workers by themselves, and the blacksmiths by themselves. All this why? So that when a traveller came along, he could find his fellow craftsmen, and on that basis he could gain a living.[170]

---

164   See Levine, *Ancient Synagogue*, p. 57.

165   *T. Sukjah* 4.5.

166   *T. Meg.* 2.17, y. *Meg.* 3,1,73d , b. *Meg.* 26a. (Note that in the Babylonian Talmud it is described as a synagogue of the coppersmiths or perhaps the Tarsians, see Riesner, 'Synagogues in Jerusalem', p. 189.)

167   E.g., the Theodotos inscription and Acts 6.9.

168   *B. Shabb.* 72b. As he passed, he turned and bowed down before the building.

169   E.g., see the discussion on Tacitus and Agatharchides in section 4.1. above.

170   *T. Sukkah* 4.6.

To what extent can this be seen as a historically accurate description of such a synagogue building? First, it should be noted that there are clear exaggerations in this account; the suggestion that twice as many people as had left Egypt could be accommodated is clearly one. There are also similarities, both in the language used to describe the building and in the physical features portrayed, to the temple in Jerusalem. This could either be seen as further evidence of literary invention or as a deliberate copying of the temple in a Diaspora synagogue building. Philo reports of one synagogue building in Alexandria that was 'the largest and most notable', into which the Alexandrians had brought a statue of a man being pulled in a chariot.[171] Similarly, the προσευχή in Tiberias described by Josephus was also a large building.[172] Levine asks why someone in Palestine would invent a description of such a synagogue building, and if it had been invented, why it would have been reported by Rabbi Judah.[173] It is certainly possible that the Alexandrian Jews had the economic ability to construct such a building, and the temple built by Onias IV in Leontopolis copied many of the features of the Jerusalem temple. Although it is inevitably difficult to be conclusive about this piece of evidence, and, as noted, some details have clearly been exaggerated, in light of what has gone before it is by no means inconceivable that such a building did exist.

Overall the information to be gleaned from rabbinic material is very limited. The mention of synagogue buildings in Jerusalem finds corroboration from the synagogue building of Theodotos, although some of the numbers given appear to be clear exaggerations or they have other significance. Philo's report of a large προσευχή in Egypt, combined with the archaeological evidence of the region, suggests that some of the details may be accurate.

4.4. *New Testament*

Having examined the other literary sources, we now turn to the New Testament to see if the picture that we have there is significantly different. Chapter 5 will focus on the presentation of the 'synagogue' in Luke-Acts, so it will only be necessary here briefly to highlight other important references. The word συναγωγή appears 56 times in the New Testament, all but three of which are found in the Gospels and Acts.[174] Προσευχή appears 37 times and usually just refers to the act of prayer; the two possible exceptions to this occur in connection with Paul's visit to the city

---

171   Philo, *Leg. Gai.*, 134.
172   See the discussion above in 3.3.2.
173   Levine, *Ancient Synagogue*, pp. 84–89.
174   H. Bachmann and W.A. Slaby, 'συναγωγή', in *Computer-Konkordanz Zum Novum Testamentum Graece* (Berlin: Walter De Gruyter, 1980), p. 1743.

of Philippi.[175] The close connection we have seen in other sources between 'synagogues' and the Sabbath continues when we examine the New Testament,[176] and in the Gospels Jesus is portrayed teaching in the 'synagogue' on the Sabbath.[177]

Two references would seem to indicate that συναγωγή refers to a place rather than to a gathering. In Jn 18.20 Jesus highlights the fact that his teaching has been done in the open: 'I have spoken openly to the world; I have always taught in a synagogue and in the temple (ἐγὼ πάντοτε ἐδίδαξα ἐν συναγωγῇ καὶ ἐν τῷ ἱερῷ), where all the Jews come together.' The pairing of a 'synagogue' with the temple makes it likely that a building is being referred to, but as John is a late first-century source this may reflect his time of writing. Similar cautions are appropriate for Matthew where the 'synagogues' are on this occasion paired with the street corners: 'And whenever you pray, do not be like the hypocrites; for they love to stand and pray in the synagogues (ἐν ταῖς συναγωγαῖς) and at the street corners, so that they may be seen by others'.[178] Presumably such ostentatious behaviour would have taken place at a time other than the Sabbath, indicating that the 'synagogues' mentioned here are available for private prayer probably during the week, and so the meaning 'gathering' is not appropriate. Rather this must be a reference to a place, most likely a building.

Of the three references outside the Gospels and Acts, the use of συναγωγή in the Epistle of James is particularly noteworthy.[179] Here the Christian community is admonished for showing favouritism to certain people:

> For if a person with gold rings and in fine clothes comes into your assembly, (εἰσέλθῃ εἰς συναγωγὴν ὑμῶν) and if a poor person in dirty clothes also comes in, and if you take notice of the one wearing the fine clothes and say, 'Have a seat here, please,' (Σὺ κάθου ὧδε καλῶς) while to the one who is poor you say, 'Stand there,' or, 'Sit at my feet,' (Σὺ στῆθι ἐκεῖ ἢ κάθου ὑπὸ τὸ ὑποπόδιόν μου).[180]

By far the majority of commentators think that this reference to a συναγωγή in a Christian context must refer to an assembly.[181] However, we should note that often the assumption that this reference relates to an

---

175 Acts 16.13-16, see Chapter 5, 4.3.1.
176 Mt. 12.9-10; Mk 1.21; 3.1-2; 6.2.
177 Mk 1.21; 6.2.
178 Mt. 6.5.
179 Συναγωγή is used twice in Revelation (2.9; 3.9), and carries the meaning of both place and congregation, see my discussion of Acts 6.9 in Chapter 5, 4.2.1.1.
180 Jas 2.2-3.
181 P.H. Davids suggest that the terminology is used as the setting was a judicial one, rather than one of worship, *The Epistle of James* (NIGTC; Grand Rapids: Eerdmans, 1982),

assembly rather than a building is just that, an assumption: συναγωγή is used elsewhere in the New Testament to mean a Jewish place of meeting; therefore, because it is being used here of Christian believers, it must be something different. This is a far from convincing point of view. A rare exception to this is Rainer Riesner who concludes that 'not only the Christian assembly but a definite room is in view', pointing out that when the author refers to the Christian community he uses ἐκκλησία.[182] He goes on to suggest:

> There is a fixed seating order. Apparently the leader of the service stands or sits on a raised place. This cannot be merely a stool, but presupposes ascending benches or a raised platform. Next to the leaders' position are sitting places. One part of the room is free for standing.[183]

As has been shown above and will be further evidenced in the following chapters, συναγωγή carried more than one meaning; it can be an assembly, a gathering in a domestic home, through to a purpose-built complex. Further, if, as is possible, this was written by James the brother of Jesus, such terminology may well have been used in the earliest Christian community.

Riesner, while more careful in his assessment, goes too far in what he proposes. The language of 'entering' and 'sitting' might suggest description of physical surroundings, that is, a building or room, but it is also possible to enter a 'gathering' and take a seat there, for example, on wooden furniture. Similarly, the proposed ascending benches and separate standing area pushes what the text actually states. It is clear that there is demarcation in the gathering with some having to stand while others are seated. While this may call to mind the orderly seating described in Philo and the DSS mentioned above, we should stop short of presuming the same kind of arrangement.[184]

4.5. *Conclusion*

As before, it will be worth summarizing the major points from this section.

- *Templum*/ἱερόν
  No specific location: Tacitus records that the Jews have no images set up in their *templa*; equating the Jewish religious meeting places with pagan temples.

---

pp. 108–10. Cf. M. Dibelius, *A Commentary on the Epistle of James* (trans. M.A. Williams; Hermeneia; Philadelphia: Fortress Press, rev. edn, 1976), pp. 132–34; D.J. Moo, *The Letter of James* (TNTC; Grand Rapids: Eerdmans, 1985), p. 89; Kee, 'Transformation', p. 14.

182 Citing Jas 5.14, Riesner, 'Synagogues in Jerusalem', p. 207. Cf. Claußen, *Versammlung*, p. 305; W. Schrage, 'συναγωγή', *TDNT*, vol. 7, pp. 837–38.

183 Riesner, 'Synagogues in Jerusalem', p. 207.

184 Cf. Philo, *Omn. Prob. Lib.*, 81; 1QS 6.8-9.

Jerusalem: Agatharchides, like Tacitus, assumes the Jewish gathering places were temples.

Egypt: Ptolemy IV decrees that the Jews should be banned from their ἱερά.

- *Proseucha/*προσευχή

  Egypt: although a reference to a προσευχή in *3 Maccabees* designates a place, it is unlikely that this should be understood as a building.

  Rome: Juvenal uses *proseucha*, loaned from the Greek, to refer to a place.

  Mizpah: Judas Maccabeus gathers his troops at a προσευχή at Mizpah, but it is not clear that this refers to a building.

- συναγωγή

  Palestine: on one occasion in the Septuagint συναγωγή is used of a building; here the trial of Susannah takes place.

  Palestine: a reference in Jas 2.2 may refer to a place rather than an assembly. References in John and Matthew also relate to places, perhaps buildings.

- Rabbinic sources

  The references to a synagogue of the Alexandrians in Jerusalem and a large building in Alexandria may have some accurate historical detail; however, because of clear exaggeration in these accounts they need to be treated with caution. The inability to differentiate between pagan temples and synagogue buildings discussed in the Babylonian Talmud would make good sense of the confusion between these places in other sources reported above.

5. *Conclusion*

James Burtchaell argues that there is abundant documentary evidence but little archaeological evidence for 'synagogues' in the first century; therefore 'synagogues must often have convened in the open, in the land of Israel, or in private premises in the Diaspora: most typically, in the house of an affluent member'. He goes on to suggest that the whole of a Jewish town in Israel would constitute the 'synagogue' and that small villages would travel to their local town 'synagogue'.[185] These seem fairly sweeping assumptions. First, one must question the assertion that there is abundant documentary evidence when all other scholars note how little evidence of any kind there is. Second, some of the literary evidence describes synagogue buildings which appear to have been significantly larger than domestic dwellings; others multiple 'synagogues' in one town. Third, the restrictions on how far a person could walk on the Sabbath

---

185   J.T. Burtchaell, *From Synagogue to Church: Public Services and Offices in the Earliest Christian Communities* (Cambridge: Cambridge University Press, 1992), p. 227.

make it unlikely that villagers would be able to travel very far to a 'synagogue'.

From the literary evidence it is better to conclude that synagogue buildings existed in many of the towns and villages within Palestine. Similarly, in the Diaspora where there was a Jewish population they would gather, particularly on the Sabbath; occasionally in the open, at times in domestic settings, but also in buildings set aside specifically for the purpose. That various terms are used of these meeting places is interesting and may suggest slightly different functions in different locations. However, the use of ἱερόν, for example, by non-Jews is more likely to indicate that they perceived these places as similar to the pagan temples with which they were familiar. Similarly, authors such as Philo had reason to portray the meeting places as equivalent to Hellenistic philosophical schools. In Chapter 4, the function of 'synagogues' will be examined in more detail and at that stage it will be helpful to identify more clearly these potential differences. More immediately we must examine the archaeological evidence available for the first-century period.

Chapter 3

ARCHAEOLOGICAL EVIDENCE FOR THE 'SYNAGOGUE'

1. *Introduction*

The purpose of this chapter is to gather the available archaeological material relevant to the first-century 'synagogue', including the remains of buildings, inscriptions and papyri. In the first chapter, it was noted that material gathered from archaeological data can often be inappropriately used in discussions of the first-century 'synagogue'. Sites from diverse geographical locations and various chronologies are amalgamated to give a false presentation of the institution of this period. Here sources from as early as the third century BCE and possibly as late as the early second century CE will be analysed. This wide time frame is used for two reasons: i) some of the archaeological remains dealt with are not possible to date completely accurately and so we can only give a range of possibilities; ii) it may allow us to trace a trajectory of development from one period to another. Nevertheless, care will need to be taken when using these diverse sources to illuminate the first-century period. Following the example of the last chapter, here the geographical location of each reference will be highlighted. Starting with the Diaspora, we will begin in Italy and move round in a crescent ending in Berenice, before moving on to examine the material from Palestine.

2. *Diaspora*

2.1. *Italy*
2.1.1. *Rome*

In his *Embassy to Gaius*, Philo notes that there was a large Jewish population in Rome, mainly living in the poor Transtiberinum area of the city. He points out that Augustus had looked on them favourably, allowing them to send back the temple tax to Jerusalem and meet in προσευχαί, 'particularly on the sacred Sabbaths when they receive as a body a training in their ancestral philosophy'.[1] It is difficult to corroborate this claim as no archaeological evidence has been found as yet to substantiate it. However, inscriptions from the Roman catacombs point to the existence of at least 11 'synagogues' in Rome with the term συναγωγή being used.[2] Although these inscriptions date from the second century onwards, it is possible that four of the 'synagogues' mentioned existed in the first century CE:[3] these are the 'synagogues' of the Augustesians,[4] Agrippesians,[5] Volumnesians[6] and Hebrews.[7] Three of these synagogues appear to have been named after leading Roman figures dating from around the turn of the era.[8] Noy notes that it is generally

---

1   Philo, *Leg. Gai.*, 156. Cf. Josephus, *Ant.*, 14.214-15. As indicated in Chapter 2, Philo almost universally uses προσευχή for the Jewish meeting places, his use of the term here probably indicating his Alexandrian perspective being transposed onto Rome. But see *JIWE* 2, 602, where the Latin *proseucha* appears in a non-Jewish inscription from Rome; also Juvenal, *Sat.*, 3.296.

2   H.J. Leon, *The Jews of Ancient Rome* (updated edn, C.A. Osiek [ed.]; Peabody: Hendrickson, 1995), p. 136, p. 159; I. Levinskaya, *The Book of Acts in its Diaspora Setting* (*TBAFCS*, vol. 5), pp. 182–85. See also P. Lampe, *From Paul to Valentinus: Christians at Rome in the First Two Centuries* (Minneapolis: Fortress, 2003), pp. 431–32.

3   Some of the other 'synagogues' may also have existed at this time, although because they are named after places it is difficult to argue for any specific time in which they came into existence other than before the inscriptions in which they are mentioned.

4   *JIWE* 2, 96, 169?, 189, 194, 542, 547.

5   *JIWE* 2, 130?, 170, 549, 562. Although it is thought likely that they took their name from someone, most likely Marcus Vipsanius Agrippa or possibly Kings Agrippa I or II, Noy also notes that it may be that the name could have come from a geographical name for an area of the city of Rome, possibly Horrea Agrippiana, *JIWE* 2, 130.

6   *JIWE* 2, 100, 163, 167, 577. Scholars have argued that the 'synagogue' of the Volumnesians was named after the procurator of Syria in 8 BCE, a friend of Herod's and mentioned often by Josephus, *War*, 1.535-42; *Ant.*; 16.277-83, 344–67, see Levinskaya, *The Book of Acts*, p. 185; W. Horbury, 'Herod's Temple and "Herod Days"', in W. Horbury (ed.), *Templum Amicitiae: Essays on the Second Temple Presented to Ernst Bammel* (JSNTSup, 48; Sheffield: JSOT Press, 1991), pp. 103–49 (142). Leon disagrees, arguing that there is simply insufficient evidence for anything other than speculation over who this may be referring to, *Jews of Ancient Rome*, p. 158.

7   *JIWE* 2, 2, 33, 578, 579. There are also 'synagogues' of the Hebrews at Corinth, dated between the first century BCE and the second century CE (*CIJ* 2, 718, see Levinskaya, *The Book of Acts*, pp. 162–66), and in Lydia dated to the third century CE (*CIJ* 2, 754, see Levinskaya, *The Book of Acts*, p. 60).

8   One further inscription may refer to a first-century patron: the 'synagogue' of the Herodians, *JIWE* 2, 292. See the discussion in Leon, *Jews of Ancient Rome*, pp. 159–63, Noy, *JIWE* 2, 292, and P. Richardson, 'Augustan-Era Synagogues in Rome', in K.P. Donfried and P. Richardson (eds), *Judaism and Christianity in First-Century Rome* (Grand Rapids: Eerdmans, 1998), pp. 17–29 (24).

assumed that the synagogue of the Augustesians was named after Augustus himself, perhaps being founded by some of his slaves.[9]

1 Maccabees 8.17-32 notes the first contact between Jerusalem and Rome when an envoy was sent to Rome in the middle of the second century BCE. Cicero mentions a Jewish presence in Rome in 59 BCE that exerted considerable influence.[10] Horace, writing in the last quarter of the first century BCE,[11] and Ovid, around the turn of the era,[12] both mention the influence of the Jews in Rome. Finally, Seneca writing in the 60s CE, is paraphrased by Augustine as saying, 'by introducing one day of rest in every seven they lose in idleness almost a seventh of their life, and by failing to act in times of urgency they often suffer loss'. Augustine then goes on to quote Seneca: 'Meanwhile the customs of this accursed race have gained such influence that they are now received throughout all the world'.[13]

Where does this evidence leave us? It is clear that at the turn of the era there was a fairly large population of Jews in Rome. They enjoyed certain rights, although these were not protected by a universal decree, but were brought about in particular circumstances and in response to Jewish pleading.[14] In order to gain, and keep, these rights the Jews would have relied on good relations with those who had power within the Roman or local civil government.[15] To find 'synagogues' honouring such figures should be no surprise, particularly within Rome itself.[16] From the evidence of the inscriptions, we know of four 'synagogues' that existed in Rome at the turn of the era, the first being the 'synagogue' of the

9   *JIWE* 2, 96; also L.H. Kant, 'Jewish Inscriptions in Greek and Latin', *ANRW* II.20.2, pp. 671–713 (700). Richardson agrees that it was named after Augustus, but thinks it unlikely that the synagogue was formed by his freed men, pointing out that -ησιοι is a Latinism equivalent to -*enses*, meaning 'belonging to' or 'pertaining to', which could indicate freedmen, but does not of necessity have this meaning, 'Augustan-Era Synagogues', p. 21, n. 14. He thinks it far more likely that this was the Jewish communities' way of honouring the emperor and that this would similarly apply to the synagogue of the Agrippesians and the Volumnesians. In view of Augustus' legislation restricting the number of slaves who could be manumitted, the *Lex Fufia Caninia*, Richardson's argument is more persuasive. For text and translation of the *Lex Fufia Caninia* see F. De Zulueta, *The Institutes of Gaius* (2 vols; Oxford: Clarendon Press, 1946), vol. 1, pp. 42–46.

10   Cicero, *Flaccus*, 66–67.

11   Horace, *Satires* I, 4.139-43.

12   Ovid, *Ars Amatoria* I, 75–80.

13   Seneca, *De Superstitone*, cited in Augustine, *De Civitate*, 6.11.

14   P.R. Trebilco, *Jewish Communities in Asia Minor* (SNTSMS, 69; Cambridge: Cambridge University Press, 1991), p. 10.

15   M. Tellbe, *Paul Between Synagogue and State: Christians, Jews, and Civil Authorities in 1 Thessalonians, Romans and Philippians* (ConBNT, 34; Stockholm: Almqvist & Wiksell, 2001), p. 78.

16   Cf. the Mindius Faustus inscription from Ostia which begins, *pro salute Augusti*, and the various inscriptions from Egypt which honour the ruling families, see below.

Hebrews. It may well be that there were others, but, from the evidence we have, we cannot be decisive on this point. Again, because the inscriptions that we possess are from burial sites rather than from synagogue buildings, it is possible to argue that these refer to gatherings rather than to buildings that existed.[17] However, as we shall see in the next section, in nearby Ostia there are the remains of a synagogue building dating to the first century CE. It would seem highly unlikely that a synagogue building existed in Ostia at this time but none in Rome.

2.1.2. *Ostia*

The bibliography on the synagogue building at Ostia had, until recently, largely been dominated by the work of Maria Floriani Squarciapino, who led the excavation of the site in 1961/62,[18] with other scholars occasionally discussing the site in general terms.[19] Unfortunately, no final report of the excavation has been published and this has led to difficulties in discussing the site in detail. In 1986 Meyers and Kraabel noted that discussion of Ostia had all but ceased in the previous decade,[20] and this would be true for most of the following decade also. However, in the last few years the synagogue building at Ostia has been the centre of a scholarly exchange between L. Michael White and Anders Runesson.[21] White argues that Ostia was not originally constructed as a synagogue building but rather was changed at a later date to meet this purpose. Runesson has challenged White's assertions and maintains that the building was from its earliest

17   C. Claußen argues that there were a few synagogue buildings, but the majority of the Jewish population would have met in homes, *Versammlung, Gemeinde, Synagoge: Das hellenistisch-jüdische Umfeld der frühchristlichen Gemeinde* (SUNT, 27; Göttingen: Vandenhoeck & Ruprecht, 2002), p. 295.

18   M.F. Squarciapino, 'La sinagoga di Ostia', *Bullettino d'arte* 46 (1961), pp. 326–37; *eadem*, 'La sinagoga recentemente scoperta ad Ostia', *Rendiconti: Atti della Pontificia Accademia Romana di Archeologia*, ser. 3, 34 (1961–62), pp. 119–32; *eadem*, 'Die Synagoge von Ostia Antica', *Raggi: Zeitschrift für Kunstgeschichte und Archäologie* 4 (1962), pp. 1–8; *eadem*, 'The Synagogue at Ostia', *Archaeology* 16 (1963), pp. 194–203; *eadem*, 'The Most Ancient Synagogue known from Monumental Remains: The Newly Discovered Ostia Synagogue and its First and Fourth Century A.D. Phases', *The Illustrated London News*, 28th September 1963, pp. 468–71.

19   For lists of the authors who have included discussions of Ostia see L.M. White 'Synagogue and Society in Imperial Ostia: Archaeology and Epigraphic Evidence', *HTR* 90 (1997), pp. 23–58 (27–28, n. 16) and A. Runesson, 'The Oldest Original Synagogue Building in the Diaspora: A Response to L. Michael White', *HTR* 92 (1999), pp. 409–33 (411, n. 4).

20   E.M. Meyers and A.T. Kraabel, 'Archaeology, Iconography, and Nonliterary Written Remains', in R.A. Kraft and G.W.E. Nickelsburg (eds), *Early Judaism and its Modern Interpreters* (SBLCP; Philadelphia: Fortress Press, 1986), pp. 175–210 (187).

21   White, 'Synagogue and Society', pp. 23–58; *idem*, 'Reading the Ostia Synagogue: A Reply to A. Runesson', *HTR* 92 (1999), pp. 435–64; Runesson, 'The Oldest Original Synagogue', pp. 409–33; *idem*, 'A Monumental Synagogue from the First Century: The Case of Ostia', *JSJ* 33 (2002), pp. 171–220.

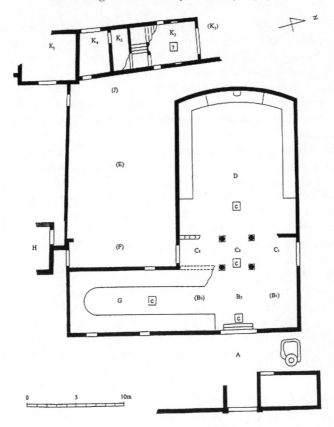

Figure 3.1 Plan of the first phase of the synagogue building.

stage a synagogue complex. The original building could be dated as early as the middle of the first century CE, and, if Runesson is correct, shows a large building existing in the Diaspora at this time. Therefore, because of the potential importance of this building, we will discuss it in some detail, concentrating especially on the debate between White and Runesson.

Ostia sat some 15 km from the city of Rome at the mouth of the Tiber, and operated as its major port. A building, which sat near to the shore and outside the Porta Marina gate, was discovered in 1961 by Squarciapino who identified it as a synagogue building. Although dating to the fourth century in its final stage, the building had clearly been adapted and its initial construction was dated by Squarciapino to the first century CE.[22] The problem, as she noted herself, was knowing whether it had been a

22   Squarciapino, 'La Sinagoga di Ostia', p. 327.

synagogue building in its earliest phase.[23] Arguing that it was, Squarciapino noted the continuity in the building, with the first-century building having a plan very similar to that of the fourth century. Also, there appeared to have been benches running along the side and rear walls of the main building which were similar to the synagogue buildings of Galilee. Finally, she pointed to an inscription, dated to the late second century, but which had been reused in repairs to the floor in the final stage of the building.[24]

In the fourth century the complex included a number of ancillary rooms; the whole structure covering a rectangular area 36.6 m × 23.5 m, with the main hall measuring 24.9 m × 12.5 m.[25] In the first century, the main hall existed (area D) with an additional open room in the southern corner (area G).[26] The wall at the north-western end of the building was curved[27] with a *bema* against it and stone benches around the sides.[28] Finally, outside the building, a well with adjoining cistern was constructed at the same time as the first building.[29]

Michael White disagrees with the chronology set out by Squarciapino. He correctly points out that some of the reasons given for Squarciapino's dating can no longer be relied upon: 'The problem is, of course, that we now know that the Galilean 'type' of synagogue architecture that she presupposed did not exist in this sense in the first century CE'.[30] He examines masonry techniques used to construct the original building, arguing that this style was used from the Flavian period (beginning in 69 CE) through to the middle of the second century CE, but that the expansion of the Porta Marina quarter of Ostia was principally carried out in the Trajanic and Hadrianic periods. He therefore concludes that although the building could be dated as early as the first century, it would only be to the last decade, and prefers a date in the early second century.[31] He points out that too often the first-century date given by Squarciapino has given scholars the false impression that it could date from early in the

---

23   All scholars accept that the fourth-century building was a synagogue, see White, 'Synagogue and Society', p. 28.

24   Squarciapino, 'Synagogue at Ostia', p. 203; *eadem*, 'Most Ancient Synagogue', p. 468.

25   Squarciapino, 'Synagogue at Ostia', p. 196.

26   See Figure 3.1.

27   A.T. Kraabel argues that this points to its use as a synagogue building from the start, 'The Diaspora Synagogue: Archaeological and Epigraphic Evidence since Sukenik', originally published in *ANRW* II.19.1, pp. 477–510, reprinted in *ASHAAD*, vol. 1, pp. 95–126 (116). See also E.M. Meyers and A.T. Kraabel, 'The *bēma*-wall is curved, which suggests that the room was built as a synagogue, not (as at Sardis) converted from some other use' ('Archaeology, Iconography', p. 187).

28   Squarciapino, 'Synagogue at Ostia', p. 203; *eadem*, 'Most Ancient Synagogue', p. 469.

29   Squarciapino, 'Synagogue at Ostia', p. 203.

30   White, 'Reading the Ostia Synagogue', p. 437.

31   White, 'Synagogue and Society', pp. 28–29.

century.[32] Although accepting that in its final phase it was a synagogue building, White compares it with buildings in close proximity and argues that originally it had a second floor and the whole complex was in fact a private *insula*. This housed both domestic accommodation and shops, perhaps with the possibility of a collegial hall also being part of the complex. It was then renovated starting in the mid to later second century for use as a synagogue building. In the late third or early fourth century it went through a major renovation, with the removal of the second floor and the installation of pillars. The fourth and final stage of development saw minor changes to the building made from the middle of the fourth century onwards.

Anders Runesson has examined the work of White, particularly his analysis of the architectural development of the building's history. He argues that White has misunderstood some of the archaeological evidence in his reconstruction of the stages of development.[33] White's theory that a second storey existed in the building in its earlier periods is wrong as: i) the staircase that White hypothesises could not have existed,[34] and ii) White fails to differentiate between two different types of pillars in areas D and C, and consequently argues that all were a later addition to the first-century structure.[35] In conclusion Runesson writes: 'evidence from every detail of the early architecture of the building opposes White's theory... The monumental layout of the edifice from its first phase points to its being a public building.'[36] On the dating of the original building, Runesson points out that the style of masonry used in the building could in fact date as early as 54 CE, and that some brick stamps discovered date to the first century.[37] He concludes: 'It thus seems safe to date the first building to the second half of the first century'.[38]

In a response to Runesson in the same issue of *HTR*, White accepts some of his criticisms; however, he continues to maintain that in its first stage this was not a synagogue building. He posits an interesting chronology for the floors in the building, arguing that rather than the

---

32   *Ibid.*, p. 29 n. 19.

33   E.g., White suggests that the oven, in area G, points in favour of his argument that the building was used as a private *insula*. The problem with this is that these ovens did not appear until the fourth century, Runesson, 'Oldest Original Synagogue', p. 423, n. 55.

34   *Ibid.*, pp. 418–19.

35   Runesson notes: 'despite the fact that they are different in material, height, and diameter', *ibid.*, p. 420.

36   Runesson, 'Oldest Original Synagogue', p. 420.

37   A. Runesson, 'The Synagogue at Ancient Ostia: The Building and its History From the First to the Fifth Century', in B. Olsson, D. Mitternacht and O. Brandt (eds), *The Synagogue of Ancient Ostia and the Jews of Rome: Interdisciplinary Studies* (Stockholm: Paul Åströms Förlag, 2001), pp. 29–99 (81).

38   *Ibid.*, p. 82.

three floors that have been excavated, in fact there may have been as many as five.[39] He points to the style of brick work in area G and suggests that at some stage the original floor of the building was totally removed and a new floor laid at a lower level. He continues to argue for a two-storey building, although he accepts Runesson's argument that the staircase that he had proposed could not have existed.[40] In favour of the second storey, he points to openings in the wall at a height of about 3.4 m which suggest a window or door, 'its position above a layer of brick in three courses gives the appearance of a second level'.[41]

Figure 3.2. Detail of the inside wall of area D showing an opening which has been filled at a later stage.

He points out that Runesson's argument – that the walls of area D are too thin to support a second floor – would suggest that they would also have been too thin to support the ceiling in area D without some additional support. He therefore concludes that some parts of area D contained a second floor built on top of internal walls, and that these walls were then removed at the time the floor was lowered. When these internal walls were

39   White, 'Reading the Ostia Synagogue', pp. 444–48.
40   *Ibid.*, p. 439.
41   *Ibid.*, p. 440. See Figure 3.2.

removed, White suggests, the external walls of area D were reinforced and
the two interior columns added.[42] White maintains that buildings K, E and
H which lie to the south and west of the synagogue hall were constructed
after D and that they may have been built at the same time that D and G
were altered, in the middle of the second century CE.[43] He suggests that
area A was not outside the building but was part of the complex and that
the main entrance to the building came into area A from the road at the
side.[44] White also points out that from 1997 he had accepted that the
building could, in its initial stages, have included a collegial hall.[45]

Figure 3.3. View from room G looking out to area A.

In the most recent article on the Ostian building, Runesson again
responds to White. He accepts that White's hypothesised extra floor(s)
could have existed, but correctly notes that this is an argument from
silence, there being no evidence for their existence.[46] The only evidence of

42   *Ibid.*, p. 441.
43   *Ibid.*, pp. 454–55.
44   *Ibid.*, p. 455.
45   *Ibid.*, p. 456.
46   Runesson, 'Monumental Synagogue', p. 189; a point which White himself acknowledged, 'Reading the Ostia Synagogue', p. 445.

such a floor is the rougher building style in the lower area of the walls in area G^{47} and Runesson points out that the stonework on the outside of these walls 'is in reticulate below the brick course, down to ground level',[48] which would count against White. A more reasonable deduction is that the benches which appear around the walls of area G had existed there from the construction of the building, and therefore the walls would not have required careful finishing as the benches would obscure them.[49]

Runesson correctly points out that White has reinterpreted what he means by an *insula* throughout his articles. In 1999, White argued that he did not intend this term to be limited to 'private houses', but rather 'generally to designate a "block" of contiguous and architecturally interconnected buildings, which might incorporate houses, shops, baths, and other distinct building types, including "public buildings" such as collegial halls'.[50] White had previously argued that in the first phase of reconstruction, area D was turned into an assembly hall, which he concludes took the form of a collegial hall and that this transformation is the point at which area D was transformed into a formal synagogue structure. Runesson incisively notes: 'if White is now prepared to understand the original building to include a collegial hall, he must also be prepared to discuss the identification of this collegial hall as a "formal synagogue structure"'.[51]

Finally, we should note the facilities that were available in this building. As well as the main meeting room there was another room which had stone benches, 1.83 m deep, around its walls and it is suggested that this

47   White, 'Reading the Ostia Synagogue', pp. 445–46. See Figure 3.3.

48   Runesson, 'Monumental Synagogue', p. 191.

49   Runesson also points out that the distance between the floor and the thresholds of the doors into area G is about 0.75 m which would allow the benches to have been constructed below this height, 'Synagogue at Ancient Ostia', p. 78.

50   White, 'Reading the Ostia Synagogue', p. 438. However, it should be noted that this seems to disagree with his definition given in 1997: 'The nature of this building would suggest a private *insula* complex containing both private quarters and shops', L.M. White, *The Social Origins of Christian Architecture* (HTS, 42; 2 vols; Valley Forge: Trinity Press, 1990–97), vol. 2, p. 390; see also vol. 1 where he discusses the buildings identified as 'synagogues' in the Diaspora: 'Of these six, five were renovated from private domestic architecture in that locale', p. 62, also p. 69. We should also note that other scholars have clearly understood White to mean a private building, e.g., Runesson, 'Monumental Synagogue', pp. 178–79, n. 29; Sharon Lea Mattila, who accepts White's arguments on Ostia, states that it seems, along with others, to have 'been renovated from private dwellings typical of the domestic architecture of their particular locale', 'Where Women Sat in Ancient Synagogues', in J.S. Kloppenborg and S.G. Wilson (eds), *Voluntary Associations in the Graeco-Roman World* (New York: Routledge, 1996, pp. 266–86 [267]); R. Hachlili notes that White thinks that the 'building was originally a private house, adapted later to the Jewish community purposes', 'The Origin of the Synagogue: A Re-assessment', *JSJ* 28 (1997), pp. 34–47 (43 n. 55).

51   Runesson, 'Monumental Synagogue', p. 181.

was a *triclinium*, used for communal dining.[52] It may also have functioned as a room in which the Jewish community met to discuss more general matters of concern and it is likely it was used for a number of purposes. As noted, outside the main entrance to the building was a well and cistern; apparently water, lifted from the well, was placed into the cistern perhaps allowing those entering to wash or sprinkle themselves as they passed.[53]

2.1.2.1. *The Mindius Faustus Inscription*

Another piece of evidence from Ostia comes in the inscription which was found in the floor of the synagogue building in its final phase; the fact that it had been reused in the floor indicates that it was obsolete by this time. The first line of the inscription is in Latin, the other six in Greek. Lines 6 and 7 have clearly been erased with the new inscription marking the name of Mindius Faustus as the donor. The erasure on the stone indicates that the gift Mindius Faustus is making follows on from another which had been made earlier, with the name of the original donor erased.[54]

pro salute Aug(usti)	For the safety of the Emperor.
οἰκοδόμησεν κὲ αἰπο[ί]	Mindius Faustus with his family
ησεν ἐκ τῶν αὐτοῦ δο-	built and made (it) from his own
μάτων καὶ τὴν κειβωτὸν	gifts, and set up the ark
ἀνεθηκεν νόμῳ ἁγίῳ	for the holy law.
Μίνδις Φαῦστος με	
[τὰ τῶν ἰ]διῶ[ν][55]	

White has a slightly different translation of the inscription noted above: 'Mindus Faustus [...DIO?...] constructed (the edifice or hall) and made it out of his own gifts, and he set up the "ark" for the sacred law [...]'.[56] For White this indicates two stages in the renovation process by which the existing building became a synagogue. First the construction of the edifice, using the verbs οἰκοδόμησεν and ἐποίησεν, and second the building of the 'ark' using the verb ἀνεθηκεν.[57] White also suggests that given the non-standard orthography in the inscription it could be that the omicron in δομάτων could be read as an omega, that is, δωμάτων. From this he draws a connection with the Theodotos inscription which mentions guest rooms (τὰ δώματα), concluding: 'Read in this way, then, the phrase would refer to the house or rooms from which the synagogue was

---

52   For a full discussion of this room and its function see Chapter 4, 5.2.1.

53   On personal purity see the discussion in Chapter 4, 4.3.2.

54   See the discussion by Noy, *JIWE* 1, 13. This against White's argument that the erasure was a correction, *Social Origins*, vol. 2, 1997, p. 392, n. 163.

55   *JIWE* 1, 13.

56   White, 'Synagogue and Society', pp. 39–40.

57   *Ibid.*, p. 41.

renovated'.[58] For White the inscription marks the donation of his own rooms by Mindius Faustus for the construction of the synagogue building sometime in the second century.[59]

Donald Binder critiques White's work on this inscription pointing out that his alteration of δομάτων is unlikely. He accepts White's argument that the word is rare in pagan literature, but notes that the one place that it is used widely is in the Septuagint. He also correctly points out that the erasure and subsequent insertion of the name Mindius Faustus indicates that this was not the point at which the synagogue building was constructed and suggests that because an ark is mentioned in the inscription, it probably refers to a wooden pedestal for the shrine.[60]

2.1.2.2. *Conclusion*

There is no doubt that White's work has been highly influential in scholarship. This can be seen most emphatically in the extent to which Lee Levine incorporates White's arguments into his discussion of Ostia.[61] As indicated above, the ongoing OSMAP project of the University of Texas, under the direction of White, will shed further light on the building at Ostia. However, here it is appropriate to note a word of caution. As part of a presentation at the annual meeting of the Society of Biblical Literature in 2004, White distributed a handout which, among other things, contained a two-page select bibliography on the Ostia synagogue building. Surprisingly, none of the articles written by Runesson appeared. While those specializing in the area of synagogue studies will be aware of Runesson's work, non-specialists are left with the impression that White's is the only way of interpreting the evidence.

Contrary to White's assertions, the evidence at present shows that the Ostian complex was originally constructed as a synagogue building rather than having been altered from a building which initially had another function. This identification is suggested from a number of factors. i) In its final phase it was clearly used as a synagogue building; further, the Mindius Faustus inscription indicates that this is also the case for intermediate stages. This, along with a similar architectural layout from the first phase suggests continuity of use. ii) Architectural features such as the bowed wall, large meeting room, benches and *bema* indicate that this was constructed as a public building. iii) There were water facilities,

---

58   *Ibid.*, pp. 40–41, n. 49.

59   White, *Social Origins*, vol. 1, p. 79.

60   D.D. Binder, *Into the Temple Courts: The Place of the Synagogues in the Second Temple Period* (SBLDS, 169; Atlanta: Society of Biblical Literature, 1999), pp. 326–31.

61   L.I. Levine, *The Ancient Synagogue: The First Thousand Years* (New Haven and London: Yale University Press), pp. 255–58. See also M. Nanos, *The Mystery of Romans: The Jewish Context of Paul's Letter* (Minneapolis: Fortress Press, 1996), pp. 42–49, esp. p. 42 n. 32; H. Bloedhorn and G. Hüttenmeister, 'The Synagogue', in *CHJ*, vol. 3, pp. 288–90.

available from the first phase, for ritual purification before entering the main building. It is a large structure with extravagant architecture, so much so that Kraabel, who accepts that it was a first-century synagogue building, nonetheless expresses some reservations: 'But would a first century synagogue contain something so "Temple-like" as that four-column entrance?'[62] The answer would appear to be yes.

Although urging caution in viewing Ostia as a microcosm of Rome, White correctly suggests some correlation between the areas.[63] However, in contrast to White who proposes that the archaeological evidence points to 'the relatively late date at which a distinctively Jewish synagogal organization and social life at Ostia and Rome (and elsewhere) arose',[64] the evidence, at present, suggests that there would have been synagogue buildings in Rome in the first century CE.

2.2. Greece
2.2.1. Delos

That a Jewish population existed on the small Aegean island of Delos is first recorded in 1 Macc. 15.16-23 where a letter, dated 139–138 BCE, from the senate, written in support of the Jews in a number of cities, mentions the island. Josephus also records two decrees regarding the Delian Jews; in the first, the local officials noted that the Jews were exempt from military service.[65] The second, a few years later in 43 BCE, mentions a Jewish group who had petitioned the Roman authorities seeking protection from local officials who appear to be restricting their right to carry out religious practices.[66]

In 1912–13, archaeological remains were discovered which were subsequently identified by the excavator, André Plassart, as a synagogue building.[67] The building measured 15.5 m × 28.15 m and had a courtyard to the east, next to the sea. A large room (A/B) measuring 16.9 m × 14.4 m was divided into two at some point in the building's history, one of which was apparently used for assembly as it had benches around two of the walls. There were also a series of smaller rooms, one of which gave access to a cistern under the building. One of the main reasons for its

---

62 Kraabel, 'Diaspora Synagogue', p. 499.
63 White, 'Synagogue and Society', pp. 52–53.
64 *Ibid.*, p. 52.
65 Josephus, *Ant.*, 14.231-32, dated 49 BCE.
66 Josephus, *Ant.*, 14.213-16.
67 A. Plassart, 'La Synagogue Juive de Délos', *RB* 11 (1914), pp. 522–34 (531). See also, P. Bruneau and J. Ducat, *Guide de Délos* (Paris: E. de Boccard, 2nd edn, 1966), p. 129. N.B. The designation of the building as GD 80 in this volume will be used from now on. See figure 3.4.

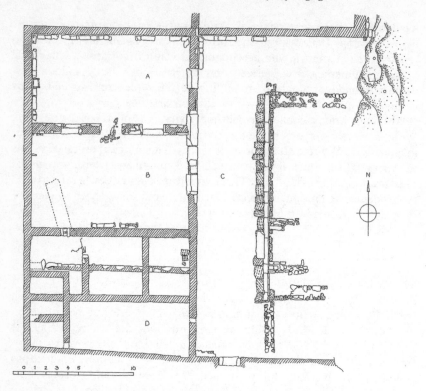

Figure 3.4. The Delos Synagogue, GD 80.

identification as a synagogue building was the discovery of three inscribed bases on the site which bore dedications to θεός ὕψιστος.[68] Further, another inscription found in a house near to the proposed synagogue building notes a donation to a προσευχή.[69] However, Belle Mazur thought that Plassart's identification was unsafe and that the building was in fact a cultic house, noting that there was no definite article before προσευχή and that this should therefore be translated as 'prayer'. She also pointed out that the use of θεός ὕψιστος should be understood as a reference to Zeus, particularly as two of the bases on which these had been found looked as though they had had figures on top of them, which she

68   *CIJ*, 727, 728, 729 = *IJO*, Ach60, Ach62, Ach63, a fourth has ὕψίστῳ alone, *CIJ*, 730 = *IJO*, Ach61; cf. the Egyptian προσευχαί which are dedicated in the same way, *JIGRE*, 9, 27.

69   *CIJ*, 726 = *IJO*, Ach65, Ἀγαθοκλῆς | καὶ Λυσίμα-|χος ἐπὶ | προσευχῆ. One of those mentioned in this inscription is Lysimachos, a name which also appears in one of the ὕψιστος inscriptions.

thought would indicate a pagan background.[70] The debate then continued with scholars on both sides of the argument.[71]

Philippe Bruneau gives four reasons for identifying the building as a synagogue: i) its orientation towards the east or Jerusalem; ii) the three doors giving entry to the building can be found in other synagogues; iii) the presence of benches and iv) the cistern which could have been used for ritual ablutions.[72] The importance of the orientation of the building is questionable, as Bruneau himself acknowledges. Similarly, while the cistern may be a ritual bath, it should be noted that there appears to be no way of entering the room in which it is found, from ground level; although it may be, as Binder suggests, that it would have been accessed from the roof or a second storey.[73] However, the fact that the building is at the edge of the shore might suggest that the sea was used for ritual washing, and the stone basin in area C (the stoa) could also have been used for this purpose.[74]

More importantly, in the same article, Bruneau reported the discovery, in 1979–80, of two further inscriptions on the shore around 90 m north of the building.[75] These inscriptions honour local Delians for benefactions towards a Samaritan group on the island:[76]

[?οἱ ἐν Δήλῳ]
Ἰσραηλῖται οἱ ἀπαρχόμενοι εἰς ἱερὸν ἅγιον Ἀρ-
γαριζεὶν ἐτίμησαν *vac.* Μένιππον Ἀρτεμιδώρου Ἡρα-
κλειον αὐτὸν καὶ τοὺς ἐγγόνους αὐτοῦ κατασκευ-
άσαντα καὶ ἀναθένθα ἐκ τῶν ἰδίων ἐπὶ προσευχῇ τοῦ
θε[οῦ] ΤΟΝ [--]
ΟΛΟΝΚΑΙΤΟ [---- καὶ ἐστεφάνωσαν] χρυσῷ στε[φά-]
νῳ καὶ [---]

---

70   B.D. Mazur, *Studies on Jewry in Greece* (Athens: Printing Office Hestia, 1935), p. 21. Also, some lamps with pagan motifs were found, see Kraabel, 'Diaspora Synagogue', p. 111. Although previous scholarship assumed that all Jews were opposed to any form of figural representation, recently it has been recognized that the assimilation of local practices took place in some Jewish communities and this may explain these lamps.

71   For summaries of the debate see, E.R. Goodenough, *Jewish Symbols in the Greco-Roman Period* (13 vols; New York: Pantheon Books, 1953–68), vol. 2, pp. 71–75; Kraabel, 'Diaspora Synagogue', pp. 109–12; L.M. White, 'The Delos Synagogue Revisited: Recent Fieldwork in the Graeco-Roman Diaspora', *HTR* 80 (1987), pp. 133–60 (136–38); Binder, *Temple Courts*, pp. 303–305.

72   P. Bruneau, "Les Israélites de Délos' et la juiverie délienne', *Bulletin de Correspondance Hellénique* 106 (1982), pp. 465–504 (490–91).

73   Binder, *Temple Courts*, p. 301.

74   *Ibid.*, p. 303.

75   Bruneau, 'Israélites de Délos', pp. 467–75.

76   That this was a Samaritan group can be seen from the reference to *Argarizein*, Mount Gerizim, cf. Jn 4.20.

KA[--]
T[--]

> The Israelites (on Delos) who make offerings to hallowed, consecrated *Argarizein* honour Menippos, son of Artemidoros, of Herakleion, both himself and his descendents, for constructing and dedicating to the *proseuchē* of God, out of his own funds, the _____ (building?) and the walls and the _____, and crown him with a gold crown and _____?[77]

This marks the construction of a Samaritan προσευχή, with the term occurring in the same inarticular manner as was seen in the previous inscription, and would confirm that both should be understood as referring to a building.[78] It is possible that the Samaritan building pre-dated the Jewish one, or even that the Jews and Samaritans shared the same building. However, as the Samaritan inscription was found some 90 m from building GD 80 it seems likely that two buildings existed.[79]

With there now being a general scholarly consensus that this was a προσευχή at some point, there remains a debate about the chronology of its use. The building in Delos has uniformly been identified as being domestic architecture in its original form which was then altered to form a public building.[80] In recent years, a great deal of the material written

---

77   Text from *IJO*, Ach66, translation from White, 'Delos Synagogue', pp. 143–44. This inscription is dated to 250–175 BCE, the other to 150–50 BCE.

78   See White, 'Delos Synagogue', pp. 142–43; Binder, *Temple Courts*, p. 305; Levine, *Ancient Synagogue*, pp. 102–03. But see *IJO*, p. 231 which considers both as referring to a prayer or vow.

79   A.T. Kraabel raises the possibility that GD 80 could have belonged to the Samaritans, 'New Evidence of the Samaritan Diaspora has been Found on Delos', *BA* 47 (March 1984), pp. 44–46 (46). Binder recognizes that this is a real possibility and that it could explain some of the pagan material discovered, *Temple Courts*, pp. 314–15 and pp. 473–74; also R. Pummer, 'Samaritan Synagogues and Jewish Synagogues: Similarities and Differences', in S. Fine (ed.), *Jews, Christians, and Polytheists in the Ancient Synagogue* (New York: Routledge, 1999), pp. 118–60 (120–21). White is sure that there were two buildings, 'Delos Synagogue', p. 154; also P. Richardson, 'An Architectural Case for Synagogues as Associations', in B. Olsson and M. Zetterholm (eds), *The Ancient Synagogue: From its Origins to 200 C.E.: Papers Presented at an International Conference at Lund University, October 14–17, 2001* (ConNT, 39; Stockholm: Almqvist & Wiksell, 2003), pp. 90–117 (106).

80   Goodenough reports that Mazur 'has given good reason to suppose that the building was originally a house', *Jewish Symbols*, vol. 2, p. 71. Subsequently scholars have taken this to mean a domestic house: see H. Shanks, *Judaism in Stone: The Archaeology of Ancient Synagogues* (New York: Harper and Row, 1979), p. 43; Kraabel, 'Diaspora Synagogue', p. 111; Hachlili, 'Origin of the Synagogue', p. 42; *eadem, Ancient Jewish Art and Archaeology in the Diaspora* (Leiden: Brill, 1998), p. 36; R.E. Oster, 'Supposed Anachronism in Luke-Acts' Use of ΣΥΝΑΓΩΓΗ', *NTS* 39 (1993), pp. 178–208 (192); Levine, *Ancient Synagogue*, p. 100; Claußen, *Versammlung*, p. 295; Trebilco, 'Diaspora Judaism', in R.P. Martin and P.H. Davids (eds), *Dictionary of the Later New Testament and its Developments* (Leicester: IVP,

about the site has come from L. Michael White. He argues that the original domestic building was constructed sometime in the second century BCE, and then, around the beginning of the first century BCE, was altered to form a synagogue building. At this stage the portico was embellished which, White argues, included the stairs, a tristoa and the partitioning of room A/B. After the Mithridatic raids of 88 BCE, the προσευχή was again renovated and this included the building of a wall on the east of room A/B. That this renovation took place after 88 BCE is indicated by the use of stone from the gymnasium which was destroyed at this point, and perhaps took place around the time of the decrees of Josephus.[81]

Recently, Donald Binder has questioned the identification of the original building as a domestic structure arguing that it has no parallel in domestic architecture in Delos. He brings a number of arguments against White's analysis of the original building:

1. The dimensions of the assembly room, 16.9 m × 14.4 m, are considerably larger than any of the rooms found in domestic architecture on the island.
2. The stylobate running parallel to the eastern wall of the assembly room was part of the original structure. At 18 m in length, it is also longer than any of those found in the courtyards of private homes.[82]
3. The diameter of the columns which sat on the stylobate would have been no less than 65 cm and indicate a height somewhere around 5 m.[83]
4. The tristoa proposed by White does not take into account the fact that there has been considerable erosion of the site by the sea.[84] Plassart's original plan indicates that the walls of the portico were evident to a length of 28 m and 15 m for the north and south walls respectively. These dimensions are too large for a tristoa; rather, a

---

1997), p. 291; R.A. Horsley, 'Synagogues in Galilee and the Gospels', in H.C. Kee and L.H. Cohick (eds), *Evolution of the Synagogue: Problems and Progress* (Harrisburg: Trinity Press, 1999), pp. 46–69 (49); as does White, see below.

81 White, 'Delos Synagogue', pp. 151–52; *idem*, *Social Origins*, vol. 1, pp. 64–67; vol. 2, p. 332.

82 Binder points out that the southern wall of the portico is bonded to the original structure of the building; the northern wall is not because it was damaged and subsequently repaired, *Temple Courts*, p. 308, n. 160.

83 *Ibid.*, p. 308. White indicates that the columns would have been between 45 cm and 55 cm wide, 'Delos Synagogue', p. 150.

84 White bases his figures on Bruneau's plan. However, in Plassart's original plan of 1913, the beach is shown to be considerably further away (26 m from the north/south stylobate), 'La Synagogue Juive de Délos', the plan appears on the page before the article.

large peristyle is more likely, particularly when compared with other buildings on the island.[85]

5. Mazur compared GD 80 to the guild house of the Poseidoniasts (GD 57) and argued that it was the building of another association.

Binder's arguments for GD 80 having been erected as some form of public building rather than converted from a domestic dwelling are persuasive. However, as he recognizes, this does not allow us to be more positive in our understanding of the building's Jewish heritage. It could have been erected as a προσευχή either by Jews or Samaritans, or as a temple or guild house by a pagan group, and then subsequently damaged in the Mithridatic war of 88 BCE after which it was renovated by the Jews. Further excavations on the site may help to answer some of these questions.

Comparisons of the building with others on Delos indicate that there are similarities between it and collegial halls and local temples in the area.[86] Such similarities were also noted between the synagogue building at Ostia and voluntary-association buildings. When we examine the architectural features, there appear to be further parallels with Ostia: there is a single stone bench around two of the walls in the two main meeting rooms; the building was situated close to the sea, and water was also available from the large cistern or the stone basin in the portico; other rooms were available for use. As mentioned, the main room in the building was split into two by a partition wall which Binder suggests was to segregate the sexes.[87] However, the only other indication we have of such separation is with the Therapeutae of Egypt and thus segregation is unlikely.[88] Another possibility is that the room was used as a dining area for communal meals which are specifically mentioned in the decree quoted by Josephus.[89] One other feature is a marble chair which sat in the middle of the western wall of area A. It has been suggested that this is a Seat of Moses as referred to in Mt. 23.2; however, many similar seats have been found elsewhere on Delos, so this seems unlikely.[90]

The προσευχή on Delos is important to our discussion. Its categorization as renovated domestic space has led to too many scholars misunderstanding the style and layout of the building or the way in

---

85   Binder notes that there is no evidence of a tristoa among any of the buildings of Delos, *Temple Courts*, p. 311.

86   Mazur, *Studies on Jewry*, pp. 18–19; White, *Social Origins*, vol. 2, p. 339. Although clearly this is understandable if the building had originally functioned as a pagan temple which was appropriated by the Jews.

87   Binder, *Temple Courts*, p. 316; also Runesson, *Origins*, p. 187.

88   Cf. B.J. Brooten, *Women Leaders in the Ancient Synagogue: Inscriptional Evidence and Background Issues* (BJS, 36; Atlanta: Scholars Press, 1982), pp. 123–24.

89   Josephus, *Ant.*, 14.214.

90   White, *Social Origins*, vol. 2, p. 337.

which it was used. As a large public building it has similarities to the synagogue building at Ostia, and that some of its functions were also similar seems probable.

2.3. *Bosphorus*

In the Bosphorus region, which lies on the northern shore of the Black Sea, eight inscriptions have been found that make reference to προσευχαί and συναγωγαί. They are dated to the first or second centuries CE and record the manumission of slaves.[91] Such records of manumission were common in the ancient world and these inscriptions follow the pattern found elsewhere.[92] To give one example:

[---]+ A + +[---]κα-
κου ἀφίμι ἐπὶ τῆς προσευ-
χῆς Ἐλπί<δ> α [ἐμ]α[υ]τῆς θρεπτ[ὴν]
ὅπως ἐστὶν ἀπαρενόχλητος
κληρονόμου χωρὶς τοῦ προσ-
καρτερεῖν τῇ προσευχῇ ἐπι-
τροπευούσης τῆς συναγω-
γῆς τῶν Ἰουδαίων καὶ θεὸν
σεβῶν

.... I .... (son/daughter) of ...cacus, release in the prayer-house Elpis?, my home-bred slave-woman(?), so that she(?) is unassailable and unmolested by every heir, except for doing service to the prayer-house. (Done) with the community of the Jews and God-fearers(?) providing joint guardianship.[93]

Here συναγωγή is used of the Jewish community, while the manumitted slave is bound by some ongoing commitment to the προσευχή. Other inscriptions show these manumission ceremonies took place within the προσευχή, indicating some form of building. Recently, there has been a great deal written on whether the slave had a continued responsibility to attend the προσευχή in religious observance, or to serve the prayer-house in some way.[94] The God-fearers and their relationship with the Jewish community have also come under similar scrutiny; however, neither of

---

91   *IJO*, BS5, BS6, BS7, BS9, BS17 (προσευχή here is reconstructed), BS18, BS2O, BS24.

92   See *IJO*, p. 272.

93   Text and translation from *IJO*, BS7, variously dated to the first or second century CE, see *IJO*, p. 280 n. 54.

94   For a summary of the various views see E.L. Gibson, *The Jewish Manumission Inscriptions of the Bosporus Kingdom* (TSAJ, 75; Tübingen: Mohr Siebeck, 1999), pp. 134–50. See also Levinskaya, *Book of Acts*, esp. chs 4, 6 and appendix 3; Binder, *Temple Courts*, pp. 439–45; *IJO*, pp. 273–74.

these debates is of major relevance to our discussion.[95] What is interesting is that the community freed their slaves within these προσευχαί, apparently perceiving them to be similar to the temples that were used by pagan groups for the same purpose.[96]

During the 1990s, a group of scholars began excavation work at Chersonesus in south-western Crimea. Here further evidence of a Jewish presence in this region was uncovered including a possible first-century CE building which lay below or in the immediate vicinity of a Christian basilica, and which might be one of these προσευχαί.[97] Subsequent research continues to indicate that this was a synagogue building; however, it has now become clear that it should be dated to the late fourth or early fifth centuries.[98]

2.4. *Asia*
2.4.1. *Acmonia*

An inscription, which is dated to the end of the first or early second century CE, records the renovation of a building which had originally been given to the Jewish community by Julia Severa, a prominent figure in the city of Acmonia:

τὸν κατασκευασθέ[ν]τα ο[ἶ]κον ὑπὸ
Ἰουλίας Σεουήρας Π. Τυρρώνιος Κλά-
δος ὁ διὰ βίου ἀρχισυνάγωγος καὶ
Λούκιος Λουκίου ἀρχισυνάγωγος
καὶ Ποπίλιος Ζωτικὸς ἄρχων ἐπεσ-
κεύασαν ἔκ τε τῶν ἰδίων καὶ τῶν συν-
καταθεμένων καὶ ἔγραψαν τοὺς τοί-
χους καὶ τὴν ὀροφὴν καὶ ἐποίησαν
τὴν τῶν θυρίδων ἀσφάλειαν καὶ τὸν
[λυ]πὸν πάντα κόσμον οὕστινας κα[ὶ]
ἡ συναγωγὴ ἐτείμησεν ὅπλῳ ἐπιχρύ-
σῳ διά τε τὴν ἐνάρετον αὐτῶν δ[ι]άθ[ε]-
σιν καὶ τὴν πρὸς τὴν συναγωγὴν εὔνοιάν
τε καὶ σ[που]δήν [99]

***

95   E.g., Levinskaya thinks that this group of inscriptions was produced by a group of God-fearers, *Book of Acts*, p. 209.

96   Other notable details in these inscriptions are the mention of local kings and emperors in a similar way to Egyptian inscriptions (see below), as well as the inclusion of a pagan formula, *IJO*, BS20. Again, this indicates the assimilation of accepted local practices by the Jewish community, see D.R. Edwards' discussion, 'Jews and Christians at Ancient Chersonesus: The Transformation of Jewish Public Space', in Kee and Cohick, *Evolution of the Synagogue*, pp. 158–73 (163–65).

97   R.S. MacLennan, 'In Search of the Jewish Diaspora: A First-Century Synagogue in Crimea?', *BARev* 22.2 (1996), pp. 44–51 (69).

98   See Edwards, 'Jews and Christians', pp. 166–70.

99   *MAMA* 6, no. 264.

This building was erected by Julia Severa; P(ublius) Tyrronios Clados, archisynagogos for life, and Lucius, son of Lucius, archisynagogos, and Popilios Zoticos, archon, restored it with their own funds and with money which had been deposited, and they donated the (painted) murals for the walls and the ceiling, and they secured the windows and made all the rest of the ornamentation, and the congregation honoured them with a gilded shield on account of their virtuous disposition, goodwill and zeal for the congregation.[100]

Although it is possible that the donation was of a domestic structure that was then renovated to form a synagogue building, it is more likely that the original gift was the erection of a specific synagogue building.[101] Julia Severa was not a Jew, indeed local coins record that she was a high priestess of the imperial cult in the city at the time of Nero.[102] The donation of the building must therefore have taken place around 55–80 CE, with the renovation recorded here coming sometime afterwards.[103] The level of decoration in this building is worth noting; although it is tempting to compare this with the artwork found in the later Dura Europos synagogue, we do not know exactly what those of Acmonia might have looked like. Two marble capitals have been found at Acmonia decorated with a Torah scroll and a menorah and it is likely they are from a synagogue building, possibly that of Julia Severa.[104] Certainly there appears to be a level of artwork in this building which is not found in the Palestinian synagogue buildings of a similar period. Also, the need for secured windows would suggest that it contained items that would have been worth stealing.[105]

---

100   Translation based on Trebilco, *Jewish Communities in Asia Minor*, pp. 58–59.

101   The term οἶκος here carries the meaning building rather than house, see the discussion in White, *Social Origins*, vol. 2, p. 308, n. 47; Levine, *Ancient Synagogue*, p. 111 n. 193. Binder notes that had an existing building been gifted it is more likely that δίδωμι rather than κατασκευάζω would have been used, *Temple Courts*, p. 287, n. 107.

102   Schürer, *HJP*, vol. 3.1, p. 31. For details of Julia Severa's lineage see, B. Levick, *Roman Colonies in Southern Asia Minor* (Oxford: Oxford University Press, 1967), pp. 106–107; S. Mitchell, *Anatolia: Land, Men, and Gods in Asia Minor* (2 vols.; Oxford: Clarendon Press, 1993), vol. 2, p. 35. For a 'family tree' see, P.A. Harland, *Associations, Synagogues and Congregations: Claiming a Place in Ancient Mediterranean Society* (Minneapolis: Fortress, 2003), p. 141, fig. 23.

103   A.R.R. Sheppard, 'Jews, Christians and Heretics in Acmonia and Eumeneia', *AnSt* 29 (1979), pp. 169–80 (172). White correctly points out that the continued mention of Julia means that she, or her family, were still prominent, and therefore the inscription should be dated no later than the early second century, *Social Origins*, vol. 2, p. 309, n. 48.

104   *MAMA* 6, p. 347; also Trebilco, *Jewish Communities in Asia Minor*, p. 60.

105   Claußen, *Versammlung*, p. 103.

2.5. *Egypt*
2.5.1. *Introduction*

As has been previously mentioned, the first evidence we have of Jewish meeting places comes from Egypt in the third century BCE where they are described as προσευχαί. Although no buildings have been uncovered from Egypt which have been identified as these προσευχαί, there are a number of inscriptions and papyri which help us gain information regarding their architecture and function. Limiting our references to the Second Temple period, nine inscriptions[106] and three papyri[107] mentioning προσευχαί date to this time.

Συναγωγή appears twice: once in an inscription and once in a papyrus. The inscription, dated to the late Ptolemaic or Roman period, appears on the base of a statue[108] and Horbury and Noy conclude that this does not refer to a building, but rather a group or association, and that it is unlikely that a Jewish group would have erected a statue in their meeting places; therefore this reference would have belonged to a non-Jewish group.[109] Levine, in contrast, is sure that this was a synagogue building. He draws attention to another inscription which records a dedication to a Sambathic association (σ]υνόδῳ Σαμβαθικῇ *JIGRE*, 26) which is also inscribed on a statue base. He proposes that these did not come from fully fledged Jewish communities and concludes: 'we may well have here evidence of communities whose conception of Judaism did not preclude such images'.[110] In view of the debate, and because this is the only reference we have where συναγωγή could be used of a building, it would appear we should be cautious. Συναγωγή also appears in a papyrus, dated to the second half of the first century BCE, where a συναγωγή is said to have been held ἐν τῇ προσευχῇ.[111] As Kasher correctly points out, here, the group that is meeting is described as a σύνοδος[112] and therefore the συναγωγή in this case is not to be understood as the body that was

---

106   *JIGRE*, 9, 13, 22, 24, 25, 27, 28, 117, 125. Two other inscriptions may fall within our period: *JIGRE*, 126 clearly refers to a building, 'Papous built the proseuche on behalf of himself and his wife and children. In the 4th year, Pharmouthi 7', but is dated to the first or early second century CE. See also D. Noy, 'A Place of Prayer in Roman Egypt', *JTS* 43 (1992), pp. 118–22. Of *JIGRE*, 105, dated mid-second century BCE to early second century CE, Horbury and Noy note: 'the restoration of proseuche is extremely uncertain...and even if correct might be in the sense of "prayer" rather than "place of prayer"'.

107   *CPJ* 1, 129, 134 (3 occurrences), 138.

108   *JIGRE*, 20, Ἀρτέμων | Νίκωνος πρ(οστάτης) | τὸ ια΄ (ἔτος) τῇ | συναγωγῇ | [...]υτηκηι. (Artemon son of Nikon, *prostates* for the 11th year, to the synagogue).

109   *JIGRE*, 33.

110   Levine, *Ancient Synagogue*, pp. 81–82.

111   *CPJ* 1, 138.

112   Although the papyrus is very badly preserved: the term σύνοδος is reconstructed three times.

convening but as the act of gathering together.[113] In passing, it is interesting to note that this association, which may have been a burial society, met in the προσευχή, suggesting that the prayer-houses could be used for a wide range of community affairs. We will deal with the evidence we have on a geographical basis starting in northern Egypt with the city of Alexandria and then moving south, before dealing with some references which have no geographical identity.

2.5.2. *Alexandria*

First, an inscription from Gabbary near the western harbour in Alexandria. Although from the end of the Ptolemaic era, it is very similar to many others from throughout the period:

[ὑπὲρ] βασ[ιλίσ|ση]ς καὶ β[ασι|λ]έως θεῶι [με]|γάλωι ἐ[πηκό]|ωι (?),
Ἄλυπ[ος τὴν] || προσε[υχὴν] | ἐπόει [?*vacat*] | (ἔτους) ιε΄ Με[χείρ ...]

On behalf of the queen and king, for the great God who listens to prayer, Alypus made the proseuche in the 15th year, Mecheir ...[114]

As in many of the Egyptian προσευχαί inscriptions, the building is dedicated to the royal family. Fraser notes the similarity between the Jewish dedicatory inscriptions and those of pagan temples of the time.[115] Dion concludes that the Jews and other groups needed the authorization of the royal family to meet unhindered and were willing to dedicate their meeting places to them. However, in so doing the Jewish communities stopped short of giving the ruling family any divine title.[116] Here the προσευχή is being given by one person, Alypus, or perhaps by his family. In some inscriptions it is the whole Jewish community that is mentioned, while in others the Jewish community with the help of a named individual appears.

An earlier inscription from Hadra, dated to the second century BCE, gives us further details about the structure of these buildings:

[---] | [--θε]ῶι ὑψίστωι | [--τ]ὸν ἱερὸν | [περίβολον καὶ] τὴν προσ |
[ευχὴν καὶ τὰ συγ]κύροντα.

...to God, the highest...the sacred precinct and the proseuche and its appurtenances.[117]

---

113 A. Kasher, 'Synagogues as "Houses of Prayer" and "Holy Places" in the Jewish Communities of Hellenistic and Roman Egypt', in *ASHAAD*, vol. 1 pp. 205–20 (209–10); also Levine, *Ancient Synagogue*, p. 80.

114 *JIGRE*, 13, dated 37 BCE.

115 P.M. Fraser, *Ptolemaic Alexandria* (2 vols.; Oxford: Clarendon Press, 1972), vol. 1, pp. 282–83.

116 P.E. Dion, 'Synagogues et Temples dans L'Égypte Hellénistique', *ScEs* 29 (1977), p. 45–75 (55–57). See also J.G. Griffiths, 'Egypt and the Rise of the Synagogue', *JTS* 38 (1987), pp. 1–15 (3); Levine, *Ancient Synagogue*, p. 76.

117 *JIGRE*, 9.

As with many inscriptions, large parts of it have had to be reconstructed and we therefore need to be cautious in how we handle these parts. Nonetheless, as well as the προσευχή building, there are additional συγκύροντα, a word which also appears in an inscription from Nitriai in the Nile delta;[118] here it is translated as appurtenances, which Horbury and Noy think could have included a gateway. Also, in the inscription ἱερόν appears with a lacuna after it, which has been supplemented with περίβολον. Dion points to a number of inscriptions from pagan temples that use the same term and suggests that in common with these temples, this would refer to a surrounding wall.[119] Kasher, however, suggests that it may be that the ground in which the προσευχή stood was considered sacred.[120]

2.5.3. *The Nile Delta Area*
2.5.3.1. *Schedia*

There are five inscriptions from the Nile delta dedicating προσευχαί.[121] The first comes from Schedia, which lay on the coast about 22 km to the east of Alexandria. It, along with *JIGRE* 117, is the oldest evidence we have of προσευχαί in Egypt:

ὑπὲρ βασιλέως | Πτολεμαίου καὶ | βασιλίσσης | Βερενίκης ἀδελ|φῆς καὶ γυναικὸς καὶ || τῶν τέκνων τὴν προσευχὴν | οἱ Ἰουδαῖοι.

On behalf of king Ptolemy and queen Berenice his sister and wife and their children, the Jews (dedicated) the proseuche.[122]

Again, the same kind of language is seen with the Jews dedicating their προσευχή on behalf of the royal family.

2.5.3.2. *Athribis*

Athribis lay approximately 150 km inland of Alexandria. We have two inscriptions from the town both from the same period, sometime in the first or second century BCE. The first follows the pattern we have seen above:

---

118 ὑπὲρ βασιλέως Πτολεμαίου | καὶ βασιλίσσης Κλεοπάτρας | τῆς ἀδελφῆς καὶ βασιλίσσης Κλεοπάτρας τῆς γυναικὸς | Εὐεργετῶν, οἱ ἐν Νιτραίς || Ἰουδαῖοι τὴν προσευχὴν | καὶ τὰ συνκύροντα. 'On behalf of king Ptolemy and queen Cleopatra the sister and queen Cleopatra the wife, Benefactors, the Jews in Nitriai (dedicated) the proseuche and its appurtenances'. *JIGRE*, 25.

This inscription is dated between 140 and 116 BCE.

119 Dion, 'Synagogues et Temples', p. 60.

120 Kasher, 'Synagogues as "Houses of Prayer"', pp. 215–16. See also Goodenough, *Jewish Symbols*, vol. 2, p. 87. Cf. Philo, *Flacc.*, 48.

121 One of which is quoted above, see n. 118.

122 *JIGRE*, 22.

ὑπὲρ βασιλέως Πτολεμαίου | καὶ βασιλίσσης Κλεοπάτρας, |
Πτολεμαῖος Ἐπικύδου, | ὁ ἐπιστάτης τῶν φυλακιτῶν, | καὶ οἱ ἐν
Ἀθρίβει Ἰουδαῖοι, | τὴν προσευχὴν | θεῶι ὑψίστωι.

On behalf of king Ptolemy and queen Cleopatra, Ptolemy son of
Epikydes, chief of police, and the Jews in Athribis (dedicated) the
proseuche to the Most High God.[123]

The other inscription from this area, as well as mentioning the προσευχή,
contains details of an additional structure apparently attached to it:

ὑπὲρ βασιλέως Πτολεμαίου | καὶ βασιλίσσης Κλεοπάτρας | καὶ τῶν
τέκνων | Ἑρμίας καὶ Φιλοτέρα ἡ γυνὴ | καὶ τὰ παιδία τήνδε ἐξέδραν ||
τῆι προσευχῆ(ι).

On behalf of king Ptolemy and queen Cleopatra and their children,
Hermias and his wife Philotera and their children (gave) this exedra to
the proseuche.[124]

Horbury and Noy note that *exedra* could describe a variety of structures
at this time, 'ranging from free-standing outdoor sitting-places to sub-
divisions of or annexes to private houses and public buildings, including
gymnasia, temples and churches'. They conclude that here, 'it seems likely
to be a room with one open side, annexed to the main hall, provided with
seating, and used for meeting and discussion, perhaps including judicial
and teaching sessions'.[125] Fraser argues that it could refer to a raised
podium or *bema* at the back of the *proseuche*, and compares it to the one
at Ostia;[126] while Goodenough suggests benches, perhaps even the 'Seat of
Moses'.[127] Donald Binder, in line with his general thesis, points to the
temple as a possible influence arguing that the term is used in the LXX for
Ezekiel's description of the various priestly chambers:

Although it is unlikely that the exedra in the *proseuchē* of Athribis
served only a priestly population, the similarity in terminology may not
be coincidental. Some parallel in function might therefore be inferred,

123   *Ibid.*, 27.
124   *Ibid.*, 28.
125   *Ibid.*, p. 49.
126   Fraser, *Ptolemaic Alexandria*, vol. 2, p. 443 n. 773.
127   Goodenough, *Jewish Symbols*, vol. 2, p. 85. See also L.H. Feldman who translates
this inscription: 'In honour of King Ptolemy and Queen Cleopatra and their children,
Hermias and his wife Philotera and the children [gave] this place for sitting [portice] for the
proseuche', 'Diaspora Synagogues: New Light from Inscriptions and Papyri', in S. Fine (ed.),
Sacred Realm: The Emergence of the Synagogue in the Ancient World (New York: Yeshiva
University Museum, 1996, pp. 48–66 (50)).

with the exedra at Athribis functioning as a dining facility or a place
where a *neōkoros* kept the sacred articles of the *proseuchē*.[128]

Binder concludes by pointing to Philo's emphasis on the educational
function of the προσευχαί and that it may have served as a chamber for
study. In view of the range of meanings that this word can have, it is
difficult to be conclusive about exactly what function the building may
have had. Binder is right to draw back from overemphasizing the influence
of the temple. Similarly, Philo's focus on education may not be without
apologetic purposes. It would appear that the more general conclusions of
Horbury and Noy are more secure: the exedra may well have met a variety
of needs for the Jewish population in Athribis.

2.5.3.3. *Xenephyris*

An inscription from Xenephyris comes from the period of Ptolemy VIII
Euergetes II's reign (145–116 BCE). It details what appears to be another
structure associated with a προσευχή:

ὑπὲρ βασιλέως Πτολεμαίου | καὶ βασιλίσσης Κλεοπάτρας τῆς |
ἀδελφῆς καὶ βασιλίσσης Κλεοπάτρας τῆς γυναικός, οἱ ἀπὸ |
Ξενεφύρεος Ἰουδαῖοι τὸν || πυλῶνα τῆς προσευχῆς, | προστάντων
Θεοδώρου | καὶ Ἀχιλλίνος.

> On behalf of king Ptolemy and queen Cleopatra the sister and queen
> Cleopatra the wife, the Jews of Xenephyris (dedicated) the gateway of
> the proseuche when Theodore and Achillion were presiding.[129]

Griffiths compares the use of πυλών here with other Egyptian sources
concluding that this terminology was used of the 'massive entrance to a
temple with its two flanking towers', in Egyptian temples. However, he
goes on to say that there is no need to assume that the προσευχή in
Xenephyris was monumental: 'Probably the whole building, including the
pylon, was of modest proportions'.[130] Kasher, building on the reference to
a ἱερὸς περίβολος in one of the other inscriptions, argues, 'one can
conclude that the synagogue at Xenephyris stood on a plot of land
surrounded by a wall or a stone fence so that the gate-house allowed
supervision of those who came there'.[131] Binder notes that the word *pylon*
was used by Josephus and the LXX most often to refer to the gates of the
Temple; he also highlights the use of προστάτης, arguing that this
indicates a high degree of institutionalization in the προσευχαί of Egypt.[132]

---

128   Binder, *Temple Courts*, p. 244.
129   *JIGRE*, 24.
130   Griffiths, 'Egypt and the Rise of the Synagogue', p. 10.
131   Kasher, 'Synagogues as "Houses of Prayer"', p. 216.
132   Binder, *Temple Courts*, pp. 242–43.

2.5.4. *The Fayum*
2.5.4.1. *Arsinoe-Crocodilopolis*

We have six inscriptions or papyri from the town of Arsinoe-Crocodilopolis in the Fayum. Although they cover a period beyond that of the first century CE, it is worth noting them all as they give a glimpse of the position of the Jews in this area over a number of centuries. The first reference comes in an inscription dated between 246 and 221 BCE:

ὑπὲρ βασιλέως | Πτολεμαίου τοῦ | Πτολεμαίου καὶ | βασιλίσσης |
Βερενίκης τῆς ‖ γυναικὸς καὶ | ἀδελφῆς καὶ τῶν | τέκνων οἱ ἐν Κροκ[ο] |
δίλων πόλει Ἰου[δαῖ] | οἱ τὴν προ[σευχήν] ‖ [- - - -]

On behalf of king Ptolemy, son of Ptolemy, and queen Berenice his wife and sister and their children, the Jews in Crocodilopolis (dedicated) the proseuche. . .[133]

This inscription follows the formula we have noted above, although it would have had at least one more line of text which is likely to refer to other buildings associated with the *proseuche*.[134]

The next reference to Jews in this area comes in a papyrus dated 4 November 182 BCE and details a loan agreement made between two Jews of the city.[135] We then have a land survey dated to the late second century BCE which covers, in some detail, the various land holdings in the city and what they were used for. It refers to a προσευχή which was situated at the boundary of the town beside a canal, perhaps positioned here for the use of the water. The προσευχή had ownership of some land, which had been leased out to an Egyptian peasant, as well as a ἱερὰ παράδεισος, translated as a consecrated garden.

Col. II

[βο(ρρᾶ) ἐχο(μένης) Ἑρμι]όνηι Ἀπολλωνίδου ἱερᾶς παρα(δείσου)
(ὧν) ὑποδο(χείου) (τέταρτον), περιστε(ρῶνος) ἐρή(μου) λʹ βʹ
χέ(ρσου) εή. γεί(τονες) νό(του) Δημητρίου Θρα(κὸς) χέ(ρσος), βο(ρρᾶ)
προσευ(χή), λι(βὸς) περίστασις πό(λεως), ἀπη(λιώτου) Ἀργα(ίτιδος)
διῶρυ(ξ).

βο(ρρα) [ἐ]χ[ο(μένης)] προσευχῆς Ἰουδαίων διὰ Περτόλλου
διὰ μι(σθωτοῦ) Πετεσούχου τοῦ Μαρρήους
ἱερᾶς παρα(δείσου) γ (ἥμισυ) (τέταρτον) ιʹ ςʹ, [σ]τεφά(νοις) καὶ
λαχά(νοις) α (ἥμισυ)

---

133   *JIGRE*, 117. This inscription, along with *JIGRE*, 22 are the earliest *proseuche* dedications we have.
134   *JIGRE*, p. 202.
135   *CPJ* 1, 23.

γεί(τονες) νό(του) Ἑρμιόνης τῆς Ἀπολλωνίδου, βο(ρρᾶ) καὶ λι(βὸς)
περίστασις τῆς πό(λεως), ἀπη(λιώτου) Ἀργα(ίτιδος) διῶρυ(ξ).
βο(ρρᾶ) ἐχο(μένη) [ε]ἰσβαί(νουσα) λι(βὸς) παρὰ τὴν πό(λιν) σχοι(νίου)
δ (ἥμισυ)

Σαραπίων ὁ παρὰ τῆς βα(σιλίσσης) ἱερὰ α, (ὧν) οἰκιῶν
ἐρή(μων) (ἥμισυ), ἐρή(μου) (ἥμισυ). [[. . . . .]]

Col. III

β. . .[. . .].α.[
γεί(τονες) νό(του) προσευχῆς Ἰουδαίων, βο(ρρᾶ) [καὶ λι(βὸς)
περίστα(σις)] πόλεως,
ἀπη(λιώτου) Ἀργαίτιδος διῶρυ(ξ).
ἕως περιστάσεως πό(λεως) βο(ρρᾶ).

Col. II

Situated to the north, a consecrated garden the property of Hermione
daughter of Apollonides (5 $^{13}/_{32}$ arourai). Of these, a quarter (of an
aroura) occupied by a storehouse, $^{1}/_{32}$ by an empty dovecote, and 5 $^{1}/_{8}$
are waste land. Neighbours: to the south, waste land belonging to
Demetrios the Thracian; to the north, a *proseuche*; to the west the city
boundary; to the east the canal of Argaitis.
Situated to the north, a Jewish *proseuche* represented by Pertollos, and a
consecrated garden cultivated by a tenant, Petesouchos son of Marres,
of 3 $^{13}/_{16}$ arourai and 1 $^{1}/_{2}$ arourai planted with flowers and vegetables.
Neighbours: to the south Hermione daughter of Apollonides; to the
north and west the city boundary; to the east the canal of Argaitis.
Situated to the north, and narrowing to the west outside the city for 4 $^{1}/_{2}$
schoinia, Sarapion, who holds from the queen 1 aroura of sacred land,
of which half is occupied by empty houses, and half is unoccupied.

Col. III

. . . Neighbours: to the south the Jewish *proseuche*; to the north and west
the city boundary; to the east the canal of Argaitis. Northwards as far as
the city boundary. . .[136]

There is some debate in *CPJ* over whether the land belonging to the
προσευχή is likely to have been referred to as sacred. They conclude that
in view of the reference to ἱερὰ παράδεισος leased by Hermione, 'It may
therefore be suggested that the whole place was part of a ἱερὰ γῆ – "sacred

---

136   *CPJ* 1, 134. Translation from *CPJ*; however, where they have translated προσευχή as
'synagogue', we have '*proseuche*'.

land", or "land of gods", divided into plots with various lessees.'[137] Discussing the size of this complex Donald Binder writes:

> The property occupied by the *proseuchē* was quite capacious: its area, given as 3 $^{13}/_{16}$ arourai, is equal to about 10,427 square meters or just over two-and-a-half acres. Similarly, the sacred garden leased by the members of the *proseuchē* recorded as 1 $^{1}/_{2}$ arourai, is about 4,102 square meters or a little over an acre of land. The size of these properties and the monumental nature of the inscription attached to the *proseuchē* (if it is indeed the same as the one mentioned in *JIE* 117) make it difficult to speak of this structure as a renovated house.[138]

In a footnote Binder goes on to write:

> While the *proseuchē* proper may not have taken up the entire two-and-a-half acres, because the surveyor was meticulous about noting ancillary buildings (as with the dovecote in l. 15) and waste land (e.g., ll. 15, 16), we can be fairly certain that only the *proseuchē* was located on this land, and that its complex filled the entire area mentioned in the survey.[139]

The problem with this is that the document does not say what Binder seems to understand by it. The entire area (3 $^{13}/_{16}$ plus 1 $^{1}/_{2}$ arourai) is in fact leased to a tenant by the προσευχή.[140] We do not know whether the area of ground that the προσευχή occupied is included in this measurement, or if it should be treated separately; we certainly need to be cautious in perceiving this to be a large complex. Nonetheless, what we do have is further evidence of a building called a προσευχή and clearly identified as Jewish within the city of Arsinoe-Crocodilopolis. Whether it should be identified with the one in *JIGRE* 117 is impossible to know.

We then have two papyri: the first, dated 16 May 73 CE, lists those due to pay various taxes, including a reference to paying the Jewish tax. The area mentioned covered only one part of the city, called the 'quarter of Apollonios' camp', and fifteen people are mentioned in total: five men, their wives, four children and a woman of 61.[141] The second, dated 105 CE, is a census return which indicates that Jews lived in a certain quarter of the city called 'the quarter of Apollonios Hierax'.[142] The final piece of information we have comes in a papyrus detailing the water system in the city in the year 113 CE. Among those mentioned are two Jewish houses of prayer:

---

137 *CPJ* 1, p. 249. See also Kasher, 'Synagogues as "Houses of Prayer"', p. 216.
138 Binder, *Temple Courts*, p. 238.
139 *Ibid.*, p. 238 n. 25.
140 See *CPJ* 1, p. 248.
141 *CPJ* 2, 421.
142 *CPJ* 2, 430. It is not clear whether this area of the city is the same as that mentioned in *CPJ* 2, 421.

From the archontes of the proseuche of the Theban Jews 128 dr. monthly... From the eucheion likewise 128 dr.[143]

It is interesting to note that they are charged heavily for their water in comparison to other establishments.[144] It could be that this was because large quantities of water were used by the local Jews for ritual cleanliness and sacred meals; there may have been guest accommodation attached which required water, or alternatively they could have been supplying water to the local Jewish community.[145]

2.5.4.2. *Alexandrou-Nesos*

A papyrus dated 11 May 218 BCE contains a petition from a woman who had a cloak stolen by someone who apparently took refuge in a προσευχή. She appeals to the king to intervene and have it returned to her:

> To King Ptolemy, greetings from...who lives in Alexandrou Nesos. I have been wronged by Dorotheos, (a Jew who lives in the) same village. In the 5th year, according to the financial calendar, on Phamenoth...(as I was talking to) my workmate, my cloak (which is worth...drachmai) caught Doretheos' eye, and he made off with it. When I saw him (he fled) to the Jewish *proseuche* (προσευχῆι τῶν’Ιουδαίων) (holding) the cloak, (while I called for help). Lezelmis, a holder of 100 arourai, came to help (and gave) the cloak to Nikomachos the verger to keep till the case was tried. Therefore I beg you, my king, to command Diophanes the strategos (to write to the) epistates telling him to order Dorotheos and Nikomachos to hand over the cloak to him, and, if what I write is true (to make him give me the) cloak or its value; as for the injury... If this happens, I shall have received justice through you, my king. Farewell.[146]

As well as confirming the existence of another προσευχή in the Fayum during the third century BCE, this papyrus also raises the question: why did Dorotheos flee to the προσευχή? Three possible reasons have been proposed: i) he hoped to find friends who would help him conceal his cloak; ii) if both parties were Jews, he might seek to plead his case in the προσευχή; or iii) he sought refuge in a place of asylum, the προσευχή.[147] Pagan temples were used as places of refuge, and, in view of the following inscription, it seems likely that the Jewish meeting places in Egypt were used in a similar way.

---

143   *CPJ* 2, 432.

144   The bath of Severianus is charged 72 dr. 18 ob., and a variety of fountains are charged 36 dr. 9 ob., see *CPJ* 2, p. 221.

145   See *CPJ* 2, p. 221; Levine, *Ancient Synagogue*, p. 80.

146   *CPJ* 1, 129. Translation from *CPJ*, although where they have translated προσευχή as 'synagogue', '*proseuche*' has been used.

147   See *CPJ* 1, p. 240.

2.5.5. *No Geographical Location*

The following inscription was bought in Cairo but is of unknown origin. It dates to 47–31 BC and replaced an earlier inscription from 145–116 BCE.

βασιλίσσης καὶ βασι|λέως προσταξάντων | ἀντὶ τῆς προανακει |
μένης περὶ τῆς ἀναθέσε | ὡς τῆς προσευχῆς πλα||κὸς ἡ ὑπογε-
γραμμένη | ἐπιγραφήτω [*vacat*] |βασιλεὺς Πτολεμαῖος Εὐ|εργέτης τὴν
προσευχὴν ἄσυλον. | *Regina et* || *rex iusser(un)t.*

On the orders of the queen and king, in place of the previous plaque about the dedication of the proseuche let what is written below be written up. King Ptolemy Euergetes (proclaimed) the proseuche inviolate. The queen and king gave the order.[148]

Again, this inscription is similar to those we have seen above, although here the προσευχή is declared inviolate. Griffiths points out that the right of asylum in a sacred place was well known in Israel, Greece and Egypt. Further, he argues: 'In Egyptian belief the god was deemed to be supreme in his own temple, so that refuge to transgressors was warranted in the temple and its surroundings'.[149] That the Jews saw their meeting places as sacred can also be seen in an inscription from Alexandria which cannot be more securely dated than belonging to the Roman period.[150]

2.5.6. *Conclusion on Egypt*

Egypt provides us with a great deal of information relating to the meeting places used by the Jews and it is worth summarizing the main points:

- Some of the meeting places of Egypt exhibit fairly elaborate architecture with the actual προσευχαί buildings having other structures attached.
- In this area συναγωγή is used of the Jewish community.
- The Jews were prepared to dedicate their προσευχαί to the ruling families, but did not ascribe to them divine names.
- The buildings were viewed as sacred places much in the same way as pagan temples.

Recently Heather McKay has cautioned against confusing different terms and different locations in scholarly consideration of the 'synagogue'.[151] It is certainly true that in the past scholars have failed to differentiate between words, and 'synagogue' has been used too often to translate a variety of terms. Although we have tried to identify clearly which word is

---

148   *JIGRE*, 125.
149   Griffiths, 'Egypt and the Rise of the Synagogue', p. 11.
150   *JIGRE*, 17.
151   H.A. McKay, 'Ancient Synagogues: The Continuing Dialectic Between Two Major Views', *Currents in Research: Biblical Studies* 6 (1998), pp. 103–42.

being used in any source, we must ask whether the use of these terms suggests significantly different organizations, or whether they should be seen as local expressions of what was largely the same institution. This is a question that will be explored in more detail in Chapter 4.

2.6. *Cyrenaica*
2.6.1. *Berenice*

Three dedicatory inscriptions from Berenice in North Africa mention a variety of individuals and their gifts to the Jewish population there, a community which was termed a *politeuma* and led by *archons*. The first, dated 8–6 BCE, recorded the contribution of a Roman citizen, probably a Jew,[152] who paid for walls to be painted and a floor plastered, his donation being made to what is described as an ἀμφιθέατρον.[153] The second honoured a Roman official for his administrative excellence and the help he offered to the Jewish community; it was to be erected in the most prominent position in the ἀμφιθέατρον.[154] There is much debate about what this word refers to: some think it is just a regular Roman amphitheatre used for entertainment and assembly,[155] while others argue that it was a Jewish building where the community met, and therefore should be understood as a synagogue building.[156] As such, it is suggested it was given the name because of the seating arrangement around three of the walls as seen in other sites.

The following counts in favour of understanding this as a civic structure: there is evidence of Jews having particular areas set aside for

---

152   That they resolved he should be exempt from liturgies of every kind would suggest that he was a fellow Jew. J.M. Reynolds suggests that he was probably a member of the *politeuma*, 'Inscriptions', in J.A. Lloyd (ed.), *Excavations at Sidi Khrebish Benghazi (Berenice)*, vol. 1, *Buildings, Coins, Inscriptions, Architectural Decoration* (Supplements to Libya Antiqua, 5; Hertford: Stephen Austin and Sons, 1977), pp. 233–54 (247).

153   R. Tracey, 'Jewish Renovation of an Amphitheatre', in G.H.R. Horsley, *New Documents Illustrating Early Christianity: A Review of the Greek Inscriptions and Papyri published in 1979* (Grand Rapids: Eerdmans, 1987), pp. 202–209 (203). See also Reynolds, 'Inscriptions', no. 18.

154   See Reynolds, 'Inscriptions', pp. 244–45, no. 17. This inscription is dated 24 CE, and the resolution took place on the Feast of Sukkoth.

155   E.g., Schürer, *HJP*, vol. 3, p. 104; Goodenough, *Jewish Symbols*, vol. 2, pp. 143–44; Tracey, 'Jewish Renovation', pp. 208–209; Harland, *Associations*, p. 226.

156   E.g., S. Applebaum, *Jews and Greeks in Ancient Cyrene* (SJLA, 28; Leiden: Brill, 1979), pp. 164–65; T. Rajak, 'Jews as Benefactors', in B. Isaac and A. Oppenheimer (eds), *Studies on the Jewish Diaspora in the Hellenistic and Roman Periods* (Te'uda, 12; Tel-Aviv: Ramot, 1996), pp. 17–38 (27–30); Levine, *Ancient Synagogue*, pp. 91–93; S.J.D. Cohen, *From the Maccabees to the Mishnah* (Philadelphia: Westminster Press, 1987), pp. 109–10; J.M.G. Barclay, *Jews in the Mediterranean Diaspora: From Alexander to Trajan (323 BCE – 117 CE)* (Edinburgh: T&T Clark, 1996), p. 237; Binder, *Temple Courts*, pp. 140–45.

them within theatres in other locations;[157] although a plaster floor would not have been found in the main area of an amphitheatre, other floors existed which could have been plastered; the assimilation of Jews into local practices has been shown elsewhere and so it is quite possible that they took part in civic gatherings; the donation is noted as being to all the citizens of the city, which would appear strange if only the Jewish community benefited. However, against this understanding is the fact that at this time the public building that became known as an amphitheatre was not clearly defined as an institution, therefore the term could be used of other buildings.[158] Also, the plaque erected in the amphitheatre marks the contribution to the Jewish *politeuma*; it seems unlikely that this would be how such a gift would be marked if it was being given to the city's amphitheatre.[159] Further, the person is to be honoured at each assembly and at the new moon: would the Jewish population have used the civic amphitheatre for their gatherings perhaps weekly on the Sabbath? Finally, as Reynolds notes, if the city did have an amphitheatre no evidence for it has been found, and, 'if a civic amphitheatre is intended, Berenice was richer and more enterprising in the Augustan period than has been suspected, and equipped with one of the more novel amenities of the time'.[160] On balance it seems likely that this was a specifically Jewish building.

The third inscription from Berenice has become one of the most cited in 'synagogue' studies. It records the names of those who contributed to the renovation of a synagogue building, including the amount they paid. The stone has been broken and although eighteen names appear, the complete number of donors is unknown. Among those mentioned are 10 *archons* and one priest who each contributed 10 drachmae; of the others mentioned the most that anyone gave was 28 drachmae.[161] Before the list of names comes the following:

(ἔτους) β' Νέρωνος Κλαυδίου Καίσαρος Δρούσου | Γερμανικοῦ Αὐτοκράτορος Χοιάχι ν. ϛ' *vac.* | ἐφάνη τῇ συναγωγῇ τῶν ἐν Βερνεικίδι | Ἰουδαίων τοὺς ἐπιδιδόντος εἰς ἐπισκευ|ὴν τῆς συναγωγῆς ἀναγράψαι εἰστή|λην λίθου Παρίου *vac.*

In the second year of the emperor Nero Claudius Caesar Drusus Germanicus, on the 6th of Chorach. It was resolved by the congregation

---

157   E.g., *SEG*, 4.441, see also Reynolds, 'Inscriptions', p. 247.
158   See Levine, *Ancient Synagogue*, p. 92 n. 110.
159   *Ibid.*, p. 92. See also Applebaum, *Jews and Greeks*, p. 161.
160   Reynolds, 'Inscriptions', p. 247.
161   In the first inscription seven *archons* are noted and in the second nine. It has been suggested that this may indicate an increase in the Jewish population in Berenice in the intervening period, see Applebaum, *Jews and Greeks*, p. 163; Binder, *Temple Courts*, p. 263.

of the Jews in Berenice that (the names of) those who donated to the repairs of the synagogue be inscribed on a slate of Parian marble.[162]

This inscription, dated to 55 CE, uses συναγωγή to refer both to the Jewish congregation and, importantly, to the building that is being renovated. It would appear that what the Jewish community in Berenice had previously referred to as an ἀμφιθέατρον was now termed a συναγωγή. We can only speculate over why this change in vocabulary took place; it may be that the former had begun to take on the more fixed meaning of a civic institution, or that the latter was becoming used of the Jewish meeting places.[163]

2.7. *Summary of Diaspora Buildings*

As with the literary material gathered in the previous chapter, various terms are used to describe buildings used by Jewish communities in the Diaspora. In addition, it is worth noting other points of interest:

- In Rome and Berenice prominent local officials are honoured in inscriptions, and in Acmonia an important pagan woman acted as benefactor, providing a building for the Jewish community.
- The archaeological remains of buildings at Ostia and Delos provide us with examples of synagogue buildings in the Diaspora. The monumental architecture, particularly of Ostia, indicates a wealthy Jewish population. Dining facilities were attached to the building in Ostia and one of the rooms in Delos may also have been used for this purpose.
- As well as the προσευχή itself, in Egypt additional buildings were attached.
- The Egyptian buildings were described as sacred and used as places of refuge. In the Bosphorus the manumission of slaves took place within the προσευχαί indicating that they were viewed as similar to pagan temples.
- An inscription from 55 CE gives us the earliest clear use of συναγωγή for a building.

3. *Palestine*

3.1. *Judea*
3.1.1. *Jerusalem*

One of the most important discoveries in connection with 'synagogue' studies generally, and 'synagogues' in Jerusalem specifically, was that of

---

162   Greek text from Reynolds, 'Inscriptions', no. 16, see also, *SEG* 17.823. Translation based on Oster, 'Supposed Anachronism', p. 187.

163   See Levine, *Ancient Synagogue*, p. 96.

the Theodotos inscription. Found in a water cistern, in December 1913 by Raymond Weill during his excavations of 'The City of David', it measures 75 cm × 41 cm × 20 cm and is inscribed on limestone;[164] it reads:

Θεόδοτος Οὐεττηνοῦ ἱερεὺς καὶ | ἀρχισυνάγωγος, υἱὸς ἀρχισυν[αγω]
|γ[ο]υ, υἱωνὸς ἀρχισυν[α]γώγου, ᾠκο|δόμησε τὴν συναγωγ[ὴ]ν εἰς
ἀν[άγν]ω||σ[ιν] νόμου καὶ εἰς [δ]ιδαχὴν ἐντολῶν, καὶ |τὸν ξενῶνα κα[ὶ
τὰ] δώματα καὶ τὰ χρη|σ[τ]ήρια τῶν ὑδάτων εἰς κατάλυμα τοῖ|ς
[χ]ρῄζουσιν ἀπὸ τῆς ξέ[ν]ης, ἣν ἐθεμε|λί[ω]σαν οἱ πατέρες [α]ὐτοῦ καὶ
οἱ πρε||σ[β]ύτεροι καὶ Σιμων[ί]δης.

Theodotos (son) of Vettenus, priest and archisynagogos, son of an archisynagogos, and grandson of an archisynagogos, built the assembly hall for the reading of the Law and for the teaching of the commandments, and the guest room, the chambers, and the water fittings, as an inn for those in need from foreign parts, (the synagogue) which his fathers founded with the elders and Simonides.[165]

For the majority of the last century this inscription was dated to sometime before the destruction of Jerusalem in 70 CE.[166] However, in the past decade or so, that consensus has been challenged, principally by Howard Kee who argues that it comes from a later period. He states, 'metaphorically, it is on this single inscribed stone that there has been erected a highly dubious scholarly construct: the supposed architectural and institutional synagogue of the first century'.[167] Kee has written a number

164   R. Weill, *La Cité De David: Compte rendu des fouilles executes, à Jérusalem, sur le site de la ville primitive. Campagne de 1913–1914* (Paris: Paul Geuthner, 1920), p. 186. Also G.M. Fitzgerald, 'Notes on Recent Discoveries', *PEFQS* 53 (1921), pp. 175–86 (175).

165   Text and translation from J.S. Kloppenborg Verbin, 'Dating Theodotos (CIJ II 1404)', *JJS* 51 (2000), pp. 243–80. Cf. *CIJ* 2, 1404; *SEG* VIII, 170.

166   G.A. Deissmann, *Light from the Ancient East: The New Testament Illustrated by Recently Discovered Texts of the Graeco-Roman World* (London: Hodder and Stoughton, 1910), p. 439; E.L. Sukenik, *Ancient Synagogues in Palestine and Greece* (Oxford: Oxford University Press, 1934), p. 69; Goodenough, *Jewish Symbols*, vol. 1, p. 179; Schürer, *HJP*, vol. 2, p. 425.

167   H.C. Kee, 'Defining the First-Century CE Synagogue: Problems and Progress', *NTS* 41 (1995), pp. 481–500 (483). Heather McKay agrees: 'In short the Theodotos inscription is not certain evidence of the existence of a pre-70 CE synagogue in Jerusalem; it may well belong to a much later building. And any constructions built on the evidence of the stone are not data in themselves', *Sabbath and Synagogue: The Question of Sabbath Worship in Ancient Judaism* (Religion in the Graeco-Roman World, 122; Leiden: Brill, 1994), p. 245; *eadem*, 'Ancient Synagogues', p. 127. See also the more measured comments of M.J. Martin, 'Interpreting the Theodotos Inscription: Some Reflections on a First Century Jerusalem Synagogue Inscription and E.P. Sanders' "Common Judaism"', *ANES* 39 (2002), pp. 160–81.

of articles over the last 10 years putting forward his view,[168] and there have also been several responses to his conclusions.[169] As many scholars have covered the material in such detail I do not intend to rehearse all of the arguments. However, it is important to note that Kee's analysis has at times been muddled or misleading.[170]

In an excellent article, John Kloppenborg Verbin has re-examined the material relating to the Theodotos inscription and the evidence for its date.[171] He judiciously deals with the palaeographic material and compares Theodotos with two balustrade inscriptions from the Herodian Temple[172] and one that records the donation for paving the Temple.[173] These give evidence of the diversity of style and quality in inscriptions at this time, but show similarities that allow Verbin to come to the conclusion that, 'although it is impossible to identify the cutter of the Theodotos inscription with any of the Herodian Temple cutters, the style of lettering falls within the range illustrated by these three public documents.'[174]

Kee marshals two further arguments in defence of his position: first, scholarship has wrongly assumed that subsequent to the events of 70 and 135 CE Jews would not have been able to live in Jerusalem; second, the Theodotos inscription was found in a cistern of a Roman bath, a date for which is likely to have been after the city was rebuilt by Hadrian as Aelia

---

168   H.C. Kee, 'The Transformation of the Synagogue after 70 C.E.: Its Import for Early Christianity', *NTS* 36 (1990), pp. 1–24; *idem*, 'The Changing Meaning of Synagogue: A Response to Richard Oster', *NTS* 40 (1994), pp. 281–283; *idem*, 'Defining', pp. 481–500.

169   K. Atkinson, 'On Further Defining the First-Century CE Synagogue: Fact or Fiction? A Rejoinder to H. C. Kee', *NTS* 43 (1997), pp. 491–502; Oster, 'Supposed Anachronism', pp. 178–208. The two most detailed analyses of his work on the Theodotos inscription are Kloppenborg Verbin, 'Dating Theodotos', pp. 243–80, and R. Riesner, 'Synagogues in Jerusalem', in R. Bauckham (ed.), *The Book of Acts in its Palestinian Setting* (*TBAFCS*, vol. 4), pp. 179–211.

170   E.g., in 1990 Kee argued that immediately after the discovery, 'several responsible archaeologists and epigraphers who saw it prior to publication dated it to the time of Trajan or of Hadrian in the second quarter of the second century', 'Transformation of the Synagogue', p. 7. By 1995, he argued that the 'initial assessment of it by archaeologists knowledgeable about Palestinian finds was that it was from the *later* Roman imperial period', 'Defining', p. 482 (emphasis mine). In contrast to Kee's assertions, when we examine the reports of this find, there appears to be a general consensus that the inscription dates to the first century CE, and probably to before 70 CE. See the initial notice of Weill's discovery in *Revue Biblique* (1914), p. 280; *idem*, *La Cité De David*, p. 190. See also the discussion in L.H. Vincent, 'Découverte de la 'synagogue des affranchis' à Jérusalem', *RB* 30 (1921), pp. 247–77.

171   Kloppenborg Verbin, 'Dating Theodotos', pp. 243–80.

172   *CIJ* 2, 1400 and *SEG* VIII, 169.

173   *SEG* XXXIII, 1277.

174   Kloppenborg Verbin, 'Dating Theodotos', p. 271.

Capitolina.[175] On the first point: while it is likely that Jews were indeed able to live in Jerusalem after the two revolts, it is improbable that they would have been able to construct a large 'synagogue' complex during this time.[176] Regarding the cistern, Weill at no time states that it was part of a Roman bath, and more recent examination of the evidence suggests that it was in fact a *miqweh*.[177] Further, recent excavations of the City of David show that after 70 CE the area remained unoccupied until Byzantine times.[178] This general archaeological evidence again makes Kee's proposals seem unlikely. Finally, given the explicit statement within the inscription that facilities were being provided for those travelling from abroad, we must ask, would pilgrims have continued to visit Aelia Capitolina when the temple no longer existed?

The synagogue buildings of Theodotos not only provide an insight into what might have been incorporated into such structures in the early first century CE, but also give us details of some of the activities that went on in and around such buildings. Although the description of 480 'synagogues' in Jerusalem may indeed be an exaggeration, in the Theodotos, we have evidence of one synagogue building.

3.1.2. *Jericho*

In 1998, Ehud Netzer reported that he had discovered a synagogue building within the Hasmonean winter palace in Jericho. The complex, which measured about 28 m × ca. 20 m, went through three stages of development in the period 75–50 BCE before being destroyed by an earthquake in 31 BCE.[179] Here we will not detail the various changes the

175   Kee goes on to suggest it could have been as late as the fourth century CE, 'Defining', p. 483.

176   Previously it has been recognized that after 70 CE one Roman legion was sent to Jerusalem and that after 135 CE another was then put in place. However, M. Avi-Yonah, having examined the evidence for when this second legion was sent, concludes that the transfer actually took place in 115/116 CE. Considerable road building also took place in strategic places to allow easy movement of Roman soldiers to areas of potential conflict, and all this would suggest that Jerusalem continued to be an unstable place during the period between the two revolts, 'When did Judea become a Consular Province?', *IEJ* 23 (1973), pp. 209–13.

177   See Kloppenborg Verbin, 'Dating Theodotos', p. 254; R. Reich, 'The Synagogue and the *Miqweh* in Eretz-Israel in the Second-Temple, Mishnaic, and Talmudic Periods', in *ASHAAD*, pp. 291–92. Kee may well have been influenced by the report of the find that appeared in the *American Journal of Archaeology*, which lists among the finds 'a cistern with Roman baths', G.L. Robinson, 'Where Archaeological Investigation left off in Palestine and Assyria', *AJA* 21 (1917), p. 84.

178   See, Y. Shiloh, *Excavations at the City of David:* Vol. 1, *Interim Report of the First Five Seasons, 1978–82* (Jerusalem: Hebrew University of Jerusalem, 1984), p. 8; Kloppenborg Verbin, 'Dating Theodotos', p. 259.

179   E. Netzer, 'Synagogue from the Hasmonean Period Recently Exposed in the Western Plain of Jericho', *IEJ* 49 (1999), pp. 203–21 (216). See Figure 3.5.

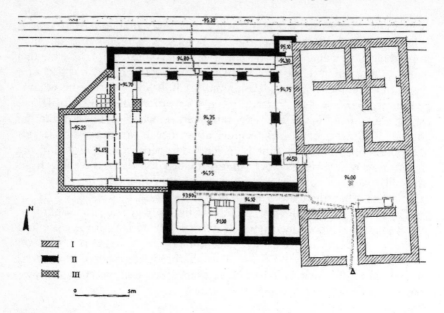

Figure 3.5 Plan of the Jericho synagogue building, showing the various building stages.

building underwent, focusing rather on its layout in the final phase of development.

While the main assembly room would have been the focus of this complex, there are a number of rooms attached to it. To the east of the hall are seven rooms and a small courtyard, and to the south are three rooms, one of which contains a *miqweh*.[180] This ritual bath was fed from a conduit to the north of the building: the water ran through the assembly hall in a small channel, opened up into a basin within the northern benches, and then flowed on to the *miqweh*.[181] Inside, the main assembly hall measured 16.2 m × 11 m and around it were twelve pillars: two rows of five along the north and south with an additional pillar at each end. A single bench, 50 cm high, ran around all four sides of the building sitting between each of the pillars; this higher floor level then continued back to the walls forming an aisle around the building. In addition, on the north wall, were two further tiers of benches which precluded the possibility of

---

180 Netzer suggests that some of these rooms may have been used to accommodate occasional guests, *ibid.*, p. 214.

181 The main immersion pool measured 2.6 m × 2.2 m and was 3.2 m deep. Alongside was a second pool of similar dimensions but without steps which may have been used as an *otzar*.

an aisle along this wall.[182] In the north-eastern corner of the assembly room was a small niche, 1.55 m wide and 1.5 m deep and divided into two compartments: the lower was 60 cm high and was accessed by a very small low entrance; the upper compartment was larger and may have had a platform within it. Netzer suggests that the lower compartment functioned as a *genizah* while the other would have contained Torah scrolls.[183] During the final phase of alterations to the building, a *triclinium* and kitchen were added to the west of the assembly hall. The *triclinium* formed an extension to the hall and was open to it, which meant that as well as the wall being removed at this point, one of the pillars had to be moved so that it did not obstruct the view into the hall. Clearly, if this was the reason for the pillar being moved then there would have been a group reclining in the *triclinium* while others gathered in the hall. Within the *triclinium* a U shaped stone bench, 1.4 m wide, was constructed and covered in plaster. At the same time a small triangular room was also added which functioned as a kitchen.[184]

Netzer's main reason for designating this a synagogue building is its similarities to others of this period, particularly Gamla. Both had benches around the building with a walkway behind; a ritual bath fed by a channel which went through the building; additional rooms attached; pillars or columns; and a (Torah?) niche.[185] David Stacey is more sceptical both of Netzer's general discussion of the Hasmonean site, and the synagogue building in particular. He contends that the complex would have been the home of the chief administrator of the estate, and that the assembly room was used mainly for commercial purposes. Nevertheless, he does acknowledge that it may also have been used by the estate officials on the Sabbath for 'religious requirements'. But he asks: 'If a building served primarily for the secular administration of an estate and any religious activities held in it only served a very small part of the community, was it really a communal institution and could it really be called a synagogue?'[186] While the variety of functions of the 'synagogue' have been stressed throughout this work, if the principal function of the building was

---

182 Along the eastern and southern walls the aisle was 1.75 m wide; the western aisle was 2 m, *ibid.*, pp. 207–10.

183 *Ibid.*, pp. 212–13; E. Netzer, 'Eine Synagoge aus hasmonäischer Zeit', *Antike Welt* 5 (2000), pp. 477–84 (479).

184 Netzer, 'Synagogue from the Hasmonean Period', p. 213.

185 *Ibid.*, pp. 219–20. See also Y. Rapuano who discusses similarities between the building at Jericho and room 4 at Qumran, 'The Hasmonean Period "Synagogue" at Jericho and the "Council Chamber" Building at Qumran', *IEJ* 51 (2001), pp. 48–56.

186 He proposes that labourers would have been hired; celebratory meals held; and produce of the estate displayed to potential buyers in the assembly room, 'Was there a Synagogue in Hasmonean Jericho?' [cited 8 October 2004]. Online: http://www.bibleinterp.com/articles/Hasmonean_Jericho.htm.

as a commercial hall and only very secondarily used for Sabbath gatherings, then Stacey would be right to question its identification. However, his suggestion that the stone benches were used as places to display small quantities of the oil produced on the estate seems unlikely as they were only 50 cm high.

Ma'oz has also examined the site at Jericho and comes to very different conclusions. He argues that this was an ornamental or vegetable garden surrounded by a portico. He points out that the pilasters in the portico are constructed from the cheapest available material employing primitive building techniques, not what would be expected in a synagogue building. The *triclinium* identified by Netzer was a seating area from where the garden could be admired and which he notes was common in Hellenistic and Roman architecture.[187] In reply to Ma'oz, Netzer points out that while the building may lack the finish seen in other synagogue buildings, it is, nevertheless, a solid construction. He argues that if it were to be identified as an ornamental garden then measures to protect the walls and pillars from the effects of irrigation would be expected. Other sites which have been uncovered at Jericho, and clearly identified as ornamental gardens, incorporate measures such as the use of hydraulic plaster to cover foundations.[188] As in other sites we have examined, further assessment of this building will undoubtedly shed more light on its function. At present the arguments favour the conclusions of Netzer, but we should acknowledge that they are far from conclusive.

3.1.3. *Qumran*

The Qumran scrolls indicate that the community had a more complex liturgy than is found elsewhere at the same period: prayer, hymn singing, and Scripture reading were all included and, at times, were carried out communally.[189] This being the case, the community must have met in a particular place, probably a building, to carry this out.[190] However,

---

187   U.T. Ma'oz, 'The Synagogue that wasn't in the Hasmonean Palace in Jericho: A Response to an Article by Ehud Netzer, Ya'akov Kalman and Rachel Loris (Qadmoniot 32, 1998, 17–24)', *Qadmoniot* 32 (1998), pp. 120–21, (Hebrew).

188   E. Netzer, 'A Hasmonean Period Synagogue in Jericho: A Response to a Review by Uri Tzvi Ma'oz (Qadmoniot 118)', *Qadmoniot* 33 (2000), pp. 69–70, (Hebrew).

189   See the discussion in Chapter 4, 2.2 and 3.5.

190   Cf. Philo, *Omn. Prob. Lib.*, 81. A possible allusion to such a place comes in the Damascus Document: 'And everyone who enters a house of prostration should not enter with impurity requiring washing; and when the trumpets of the assembly sound, he may advance or retreat, but they should not stop the whole service, for it is a holy house', CD 11.21–12.1. However, it is not clear to what the 'house of prostration' refers. It could be the Jerusalem temple, or buildings set aside within the Essene communities. L.H. Schiffman, 'The Dead Sea Scrolls and the Early History of Jewish Liturgy', in L.I. Levine (ed.), *The Synagogue in Late Antiquity* (Philadelphia: The American Schools of Oriental Research, 1987), p. 35; A. Steudel, 'The House of Prostration CD xi 21 – xii 1 – Duplicates of the

throughout the site at Qumran there is no building which can be clearly identified as performing the function of a synagogue building. There are rooms which were proposed by the excavator as assembly rooms and these may also have been places where the liturgical elements took place.[191] The largest building at the site, room 77, was used for dining, and it is suggested that it is likely that it performed such a dual purpose.[192] While the documents of Qumran offer us a more detailed insight into the practices of the community, we must recognize that the archaeological remains are considerably more ambiguous in relation to 'synagogue' studies.

3.1.4. *Masada*

Masada was a Herodian palace that became the centre for a group of rebels in the revolt of 66 CE. The first major survey and reconstruction of the site was carried out in 1963–65 by a team of some 200, and the preliminary findings were published in 1965 by Yigael Yadin.[193] Assessing the archaeological evidence of Masada has been difficult as it has taken nearly 30 years for the final reports to be published.[194] In the initial report, attention was drawn to a room, part of which was built into the casement wall of the settlement and, it was suggested, this may have been used as a synagogue building.[195] Originally the building was rectangular, about 12 m × 15 m, with a dividing wall across which created a vestibule area and the main hall. Yadin suggests that the building may have been constructed as a synagogue building as, 'it seems most unlikely that Herod would have denied a place of worship for the Jewish members of his court'.[196] He goes on to propose that it was used as stables after the Herodian period when the Romans occupied the site, as a layer of animal

---

Temple', *RevQ* 61 (1993), pp. 49–68 (59); and Levine, *Ancient Synagogue*, pp. 61–62, argue for a community building. Binder is a little more cautious, *Temple Courts*, p. 455, while D.K. Falk, *Daily, Sabbath, and Festival Prayers in the Dead Sea Scrolls* (STDJ, 27; Leiden: Brill, 1998), pp. 243–45, and Runesson, *Origins*, pp. 334–35, argue for Temple. 1QM 3.4 is suggested as another possible allusion to a 'synagogue,' see Binder, *Temple Courts*, pp. 454–55, and Runesson, *Origins*, p. 335.

191   R. de Vaux, *Archaeology and the Dead Sea Scrolls, The Schweich Lectures of the British Academy* (Oxford: Oxford Universtiy Press, 1959), pp. 10–11.

192   Atkinson, 'Further Defining', p. 501; Binder, *Temple Courts*, p. 463; Levine, *Ancient Synagogue*, p. 62; Runesson, *Origins*, p. 335.

193   Y. Yadin, 'The Excavation of Masada 1963/64, Preliminary Report', *IEJ* 15 (1965), pp. 1–120 + plates.

194   E. Netzer, *Masada – The Yigael Yadin Excavations 1963–1965, Final Reports, III: The Buildings: Stratigraphy and Architecture* (Jerusalem, Israel Exploration Society, 1991).

195   Yadin, 'Excavation of Masada', pp. 78–79.

196   He also argues that the architectural plan and the orientation of the building point to it originally functioning as a synagogue. Y. Yadin, 'The Synagogue at Masada', in L.I. Levine (ed.), *Ancient Synagogues Revealed* (Jerusalem: Israel Exploration Society, 1981), p. 21. See figure 3.6.

dung had been found under the second floor which had been laid by the Zealots.[197] Other changes that were made to the building during the revolt include: the removal of the internal wall; the addition of a small room in the north-west corner, and of benches around the walls – four benches around three of the walls and only one on the northern wall.[198]

The reasons given by Yadin for suggesting that this was a synagogue building are:

1. The addition of the room which would have served as a dwelling for a priest.
2. The existence of a cistern north of the building which could have been used as a *miqweh*.[199]
3. Fragments of scrolls and silver sheqels were found near to the building.[200]
4. The orientation of the building was towards Jerusalem.[201]

To these reasons he later added the fact that other items had also been discovered including an ostracon inscribed 'priestly tithe' and another 'Hezekiah' which Yadin thinks may have been the name of the priest.[202]

By the time of the final report, its author, Ehud Netzer, was much more confident that the building was indeed a synagogue.[203] It is interesting to note that the most important evidence which suggests such a use for this building continues to be the discovery of Scripture. In addition to the

---

197   Because of its 'coarse and rather careless construction', Netzer is confident that it was certainly not originally built as a synagogue, suggesting that the remnants of animal dung below the floor point to it having been built as stables. However, as Netzer himself acknowledges, the problem with this suggestion is that the original floor of the building was made of a delicate plaster, not the kind of flooring one would expect to find in a stable. Whatever the chronology of use for the building, Netzer argues that the use of the building as stables does not preclude it being subsequently used as a synagogue building on the grounds of ritual impurity, Netzer, *Masada III*, pp. 412–13. But see P.V.M. Flesher, who argues that it would seem sacrilegious to build a synagogue on top of a dung heap, 'Palestinian Synagogues Before 70 C.E.: A Review of the Evidence', in *ASHAAD*, vol. 1, p. 36.

198   The benches were 35 cm high and 45 cm wide, Netzer, *Masada III*, p. 406.

199   None of the *miqwaoth* found at Masada lie exactly beside the proposed 'synagogue' and therefore it is difficult to clearly identify if they were associated with the building, leading some to question drawing any conclusions from these.

200   Yadin, 'Excavation of Masada', p. 78 and pp. 103–14, details the finds.

201   However, Paul Flesher correctly points out that had the building been chosen for its orientation towards Jerusalem then it would appear a little strange that the alterations made to it meant that the wall to which the worshippers would have faced became irregular and, he suggests, not conducive to worship, 'Palestinian Synagogues', p. 36. S. Fine suggests that the additional room would have housed the Torah scrolls and was purposely built opposite the entrance serving as a focal point, *This Holy Place: On the Sanctity of the Synagogue During the Greco-Roman Period* (Notre Dame: Notre Dame Press, 1997), p. 30.

202   Yadin, 'Synagogue at Masada', p. 20.

203   Netzer, *Masada III*, p. 402.

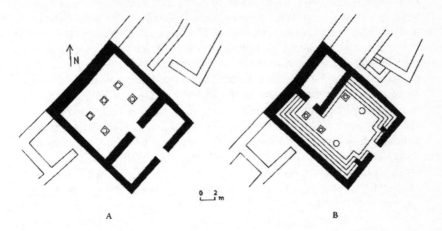

Figure 3.6 The two stages of the Masada synagogue building.

fragments of scrolls found near to the building, parchments were
discovered in a pit in the small room which had been added to the
synagogue building.[204] This contained fragments of the books of
Deuteronomy and Ezekiel.[205] The second reason given by Netzer,
however, is the architectural layout of the building. As indicated above,
a series of benches had been added to the building during the time of the
Sicarii. In contrast to Yadin, Netzer had the evidence of other discoveries
made during the second half of the twentieth century which have a similar
architectural arrangement, and which have also been identified as
synagogue buildings; the benches around the walls of the building were
comparable to those found elsewhere.

It is worth making some general comments on the relative strengths of
the arguments for and against identifying this as a synagogue building.
First, the orientation of the building: the entrance to the building is from
the south-east, and the wall opposite does face towards Jerusalem. Had it
been originally constructed as a synagogue building, then its position may
have been deliberate, but it is not possible to know if this was the case.
Flesher is correct when he notes that the alterations made would appear a
little odd if the orientation towards Jerusalem was important, and it could
just be that this building was one that was suitable for the purposes of the

204   Netzer suggests that this was 'most probably a *genizah* (a repository for worn and
disused sacred scripts),' *ibid.*, p. 410. Flesher argues that the presence of scroll fragments
cannot prove the purpose of the building, pointing out that fragments were found in other
buildings at Masada which were not identified as synagogue buildings, 'Palestinian
Synagogues', p. 37, n. 33.

205   Netzer, *Masada III*, p. 410.

Zealots and that any orientation towards Jerusalem was either of no concern, or was fortuitous. Second, the *miqweh*: again it is difficult to make conclusive arguments from this. The *miqweh* is not immediately next to the proposed synagogue building, although Reich gives good reasons to explain why this is the case. Even so, the presence of a *miqweh* would not of necessity point to the identification of the building as a synagogue. Third, the architectural features: the addition of stone benches around the walls of the building would indicate that it was used as a meeting hall, although clearly this does not necessitate its identification as a synagogue building; however, it is similar to the benches found in other possible 'synagogue' sites. It also seems likely that the additional room at the north-west end of the hall was used to house the Torah when it was not used in the synagogue. Fourth, the fragments of scrolls and the *genizah*: Flesher is correct to point out that scroll fragments were found in other buildings at Masada which were not identified as synagogue buildings. However, the discovery of the *genizah* within the building containing fragments of scripture count in favour of this identification. Although individually the above would make poor arguments for identifying Masada as a synagogue building, the cumulative effect, although not conclusive, is stronger.

3.1.5. *Herodium*

The history of the palace fortress of Herodium is similar to that of Masada. It was constructed by Herod the Great and sits on top of a hill just to the south of Jerusalem.[206] The first excavations, which took place between 1962 and 1967, were led by Virgilio Corbo with subsequent restoration work by Gideon Foerster in 1969. During the revolts of 70 and 135 CE, the palace was taken and used by the Zealots who altered the *triclinium* to form what has been identified as a synagogue building.[207] Internally, the *triclinium* measured 15.15 m × 10.6 m and had a large

---

206   Josephus reports that is was 60 stades from Jerusalem on a hill which had been raised and rounded off in the shape of a breast, *Ant.*, 15.324. For further details see M.J.S. Chiat, *Handbook of Synagogue Architecture* (BJS, 29; Chico: Scholars Press, 1982), pp. 204–207.

207   In his original report, V.C. Corbo indicated only that the transformation of the building took place during the Jewish wars, 'L'Herodion di Giabal Fureidis: Relazione Preliminare della Terza e Quarta Campagna di Scavi Archeologici', *Liber Annuus* 17 (1967), pp. 65–121 (101). However, he later estimates that the changes took place during the second revolt, 'Gébel Fureidis (Hérodium)', *RB* 75 (1968), pp. 424–28 (427); *idem*, *Herodion I: Gli Edifici della Reggia-Fortezza*, (Jerusalem: Studium Biblicum Franciscanum, 1989), p. 107. In his review of the final report, Joseph Patrich notes that it is not clear why Corbo makes this change as he gives no further evidence for such a view, 'Corbo's Excavations at Herodium: A Review Article', *IEJ* 42 (1992), pp. 241–45 (243). Chiat, (*Handbook of Synagogue Architecture*, p. 207), and G. Foerster, ('The Synagogues at Masada and Herodium', in Levine, *Ancient Synagogues Revealed*, p. 24), both date it to the first revolt, while Flesher points out that no good arguments have been made for the earlier date, 'Palestinian

entrance, 3.46 m wide, on the southern wall which was flanked by two windows. On the southern end of the north and south walls were two further doors of about 1.5 m. During the alteration of the *triclinium* the main entrance was reduced to 1.6 m while the windows and other doors were blocked up. At the same time, three rows of stone benches were added around all four sides of the building leaving a gap only at the entrance. The lower and upper benches were 40 cm wide, while the middle level was 90 cm wide making a walkway around the building.[208] At this time a *miqweh* was also added which abutted the eastern wall of the meeting hall.[209] Again, Herodium offers little that allows us to confidently assert that this is a synagogue building.[210] However, the building is large, capable of seating around 200, so it was clearly used for communal purposes and the *miqweh* next to the building suggests that it was used for some ritual purpose. Further, the benches that were introduced are very similar to ones found in other places which have been more confidently identified as synagogue buildings.

3.2. Beyond Judea[211]
3.2.1. Gamla

Gamla is located on the ridge of a hill in the southern Golan; it is described by Josephus in a number of places as it was a town of which he had first-hand experience.[212] Evidence of habitation on the site goes back as far as the early Bronze Age; however, after a long period during which the site was unoccupied, the first Jews settled there about the middle of the

---

Synagogues', p. 37. Although accepting the difficulties in firmly placing a date on the renovation, Binder has recently given reasons to suppose the earlier war is the more likely time for the renovations, *Temple Courts*, p. 184.

208   Corbo, 'L'Herodion', pp. 101–103; D. Chen, 'The Design of the Ancient Synagogues in Judea: Masada and Herodium', *BASOR* 239 (1980), pp. 37–40. Columns were also added during the renovation. However, there has been much debate about these, see, Corbo, 'L'Herodion', p. 101; Foerster, 'Synagogues at Masada', p. 24; Chiat, *Handbook of Synagogue Architecture*, pp. 205–206; Binder, *Temple Courts*, p. 182, n. 54.

209   Foerster, 'Synagogues at Masada', p. 26; *idem*, 'Herodium', in *NEAEHL*, vol. 2, p. 620. Levine is slightly more cautious, *Ancient Synagogue*, p. 60.

210   Flesher points out that groups such as that of the Zealots would have needed a place to assemble for military reasons and identifying it as a synagogue building is dubious, 'Palestinian Synagogues', p. 37.

211   As well as the building described below, two other potential synagogue buildings have been identified in the region of Galilee: Magdala is now recognized by most scholars as not being a synagogue building but rather a springhouse, see the discussion in Binder, *Temple Courts*, pp. 193–96. Excavators at Chorazin identified a building containing two rows of columns and stone benches around its walls. However, full details of the building were never published and subsequent attempts to identify the site have been unsuccessful, see *ibid.*, p. 198.

212   See, *Life*, 61, 114, 177–85; *War*, 1.105, 2.568-74, 4.1-83; *Ant.*, 13.394, 18.4.

second century BCE, and around 80 BCE Alexander Janneus took control of the town. Following the rebellion of 66 CE, Gamla was besieged by the Romans and finally captured in October 67 CE.

After the site of Gamla was identified in the late 1960s, excavation work began in 1976 under Shmaryahu Gutman. During the first season, a structure was uncovered, adjacent to the city's eastern wall, which Gutman identified as a synagogue building. This comprised a main hall of 19.6 m × 15.1 m[213] along with other smaller rooms, the total complex extending to 25.5 m × 17 m.[214] Within the main assembly hall, a series of four tiers of stone benches ran around all four walls, broken only by the main entrance on the southwest wall;[215] two further smaller entrances gave access to the walkway which existed at the top level of benches, one on the southwest wall, the other at the eastern corner from which a staircase led to the street below. A small niche in the western corner of the building was discovered and it has been suggested that this may have been for storing Torah scrolls. Four rows of four columns sat on a stylobate inside the lower level of benches, and a further stylobate ran across the hall from north-west to south-east.[216] Within the central area between the benches there is no evidence of a stone floor indicating that it was not used as a thoroughfare. The north-east boundary of the hall abuts the casement wall of the city, and within this large wall are further rooms, one of which had benches and was identified by the excavators as a study room.[217] To the south-west of the main hall lies an *exedra* beyond which is a *miqweh*;[218] water was also available within the hall in a basin in the northern corner fed through the city wall by a channel from an

---

213   Z. Ma'oz, 'The Synagogue of Gamla and the Typology of Second-Temple Synagogues', in Levine, *Ancient Synagogues Revealed*, pp. 35–41 (37).

214   S. Gutman, 'Gamala', in *NEAEHL*, vol. 2, p. 460.

215   A further bench existed on the northeast wall.

216   S. Gutman, 'The Synagogue at Gamla', in Levine, *Ancient Synagogues Revealed*, pp. 30–34 (32–33). He suggests that the central stylobate was for two further columns, see also D. Syon and Z. Yavor, 'Gamla – Old and New', *Qadmoniot* 34 (2001), pp. 2–33 (9) (Hebrew). Another suggestion is that this formed the foundation of a platform, or *bema*, see Flesher, 'Palestinian Synagogues', p. 39; Binder, *Temple Courts*, p. 164. In contrast, see the comments of E. Netzer who has recently suggested that the floor would have been completely covered in stone slabs which have been looted. The central row of stones should not, therefore, be understood as a stylobate, 'The Synagogues from the Second Temple Period According to Archaeological Finds and in Light of the Literary Sources', in G.C. Bottini, L. Di Segni and D. Chrupcala (ed), *One Land – Many Cultures: Archaeological Studies in Honour of S. Loffreda* (Studium Biblicum Franciscanum Collectio Maior, 41; Jerusalem: Franciscan Printing Press, 2003), pp. 227–85 (285 n. 9).

217   Gutman, 'Gamala', p. 461.

218   Contra Levine, *Ancient Synagogue*, p. 52, this was not a later addition but was constructed at the same time as the synagogue building, see Syon and Yavor, 'Gamla – Old and New', p. 11. However, J.F. Strange cautions that we cannot be sure that it was a *miqweh*, 'Ancient Texts, Archaeology as Text, and the Problem of the First-Century Synagogue', in

aqueduct.[219] The roof of the building appears to have been constructed from wooden beams with branches, straw and plaster.[220] Finally, a lintel was discovered in the building which features a six-petalled rosette flanked by date palms suggesting ritual use.[221] Originally, evidence pointed to the Gamla building having been constructed between 63 and 40 BCE,[222] with Syon suggesting that it may then have been redecorated after Herod took control of the area after 20 BCE.[223] Further discoveries of coins and other artefacts indicate that it should probably be dated to the turn of the era.[224] Of particular significance is the fact that this building was not altered from earlier architecture but was purpose-built in its present form.

Various reasons have been given for identifying the building at Gamla as a synagogue, and scholars afford these reasons different weight in the argument.[225] Those focusing on the orientation of the building towards Jerusalem have rightly been criticized.[226] However, for the following reasons it should be identified as a synagogue building: i) it was clearly intended to be used for some public function; the benches around all walls, similar to other sites, indicate this purpose; ii) the availability of water facilities indicate the desire for ritual purity; iii) the decoration on

---

Kee and Cohick, *Evolution of the Synagogue*, pp. 27–45 (37–38). In total four *miqwaoth* were found in the city which, D. Syon proposes, indicates that observant Jews constituted most of the town's population, 'Gamla: Portrait of a Rebellion', *BARev* 18.1 (1992), p. 20–37 (30).

219   Gutman, 'Gamla', p. 461. It should be noted that this was a later addition, see Syon and Yavor, 'Gamla – Old and New', pp. 10–11.

220   *Ibid.*, p. 9. The exact form the roof would have taken is the focus of speculation, see *ibid.*, pp. 9–10 esp. the reconstruction, p. 10; Z. Ma'oz, 'Gamla – Old and New, Comments on an Article by D. Syon and Z. Yavor', *Quamoniot* 34 (2001), p. 130 (Hebrew); the reconstruction in Netzer, 'Synagogues from the Second Temple Period', p. 282.

221   Ma'oz, 'Synagogue of Gamla', p. 39. See also the picture in Gutman, 'Synagogue at Gamla', p. 34. Another lintel with the same design has been discovered on the western side of Gamla leading Syon to suggest initially that there was a second synagogue building, 'Gamla', p. 35. Subsequent excavation has revealed another large public building in the city, but its exact function is unknown, see Syon and Yavor, 'Gamla – Old and New', pp. 17–19. On the use of palm branches in a ritual context see, Hachlili, *Ancient Jewish Art and Archaeology in the Diaspora*, pp. 347–51.

222   Gutman, 'Synagogue at Gamla', p. 34.

223   Syon, 'Gamla', p. 24.

224   Syon and Yavor, 'Gamla – Old and New', p. 11. Ma'oz, argues for a date between 23 BCE and 41 CE, 'Synagogue of Gamla', p. 35, although towards the end of his article he does presume that the building was in place before the turn of the era, p. 41; also Flesher, 'Palestinian Synagogues', p. 38.

225   E.g., Gutman, 'Synagogue at Gamla', p. 34; Ma'oz, 'Synagogue of Gamla', pp. 37–41; Oster, 'Supposed Anachronism', pp. 194–96; Atkinson, 'Further Defining', pp. 495–98; Flesher, 'Palestinian Synagogues', pp. 38–39; Strange, 'Ancient Texts', pp. 35–39.

226   As at Masada, the orientation of the building is affected by topography and the existence of the city wall. Therefore, it is difficult to conclude that the building was deliberately focused towards Jerusalem.

the lintel; 4) the fine quality of the stonework used in the construction of the building indicates cultic use.

Unhappy with the identification of Gamla as a synagogue building, some scholars have argued that it should be seen as domestic architecture. Horsley argues: 'What are claimed as "synagogue" buildings in the towns of Magdala and Gamla turned out to be private houses'.[227] This is not the case; the building at Gamla was a significant building measuring 25.5 m × 17 m and clearly intended for public use.[228] The finely cut stonework evidenced in the building was also of a higher quality than that used in houses in the city, and the presence of the decoration on the lintel points towards a ritual function.

3.2.2. *Qiryat Sefer*

In 1995, during the construction of a new town in the foothills of the Judaean Mountains approximately 25 km east of Tel Aviv, an ancient settlement was discovered in which a building was identified as a synagogue.[229] The square building measured 9.6 m × 9.6 m and its construction was different to that of other buildings in the town, with carefully dressed stonework being used on its front. Within the building, a single row of stone benches ran around three of the walls; the depth of the bench on the western and eastern walls was 1.5 m, while the southern wall was 2.4 m. In front of the benches four columns sat directly onto the ground and were surrounded by limestone slabs which made up the floor, and provided support to the columns. Along with pilasters in the walls, these columns would have carried arches which supported a roof structure of wooden beams.[230] Within the building a small piece of plasterwork was discovered which had been painted red and the excavators suggest that the walls and columns of the building were all covered in this painted plasterwork. The main entrance into the 'synagogue' is 1.4 m wide, on the northern façade; a groove within the stonework indicates that a wooden frame would have been in place to hold the door. On the stone lintel above

227   R.A. Horsley, *Galilee: History, Politics, People* (Valley Forge: Trinity Press, 1995), p. 224; *idem*, 'Synagogues in Galilee and the Gospels', p. 49; also, Kee, 'Transformation of the Synagogue', p. 8.

228   I estimate that it had the largest seating capacity of the Palestinian synagogue buildings and could have accommodated 360.

229   See Figure 3.7. As yet, little has been published on this building. Binder (*Temple Courts*, p. 197), Levine (*Ancient Synagogue*, pp. 65–66) and Claußen (*Versammlung*, pp. 184–85) briefly mention it. The only article to be published on the site is, Y. Magen, Y. Zionit and O. Sirkis, 'Qiryat-Sefer, a Jewish Village and Synagogue dating to the Second Temple Period', *Qadmoniot* 33 (1999), pp. 25–32, esp. pp. 27–30 (Hebrew). All the following details come from this article.

230   For a reconstruction of the building see, Magen, Zionit and Sirkis, 'Qiryat-Sefer', p. 29, but see the critique of this in Netzer, 'Synagogues from the Second Temple Period', p. 279.

the doorway is a relief of a rosette placed within a triangle. A further narrow doorway from the building leads to a small room, 3 m × 1.2 m, which was also plastered and the excavators suggest that this would have been used to store items used within the synagogue building.

A large number of coins as well as clay, stone, metal and glass vessels were found on the site. These, along with an analysis of the building styles, allow the excavators to estimate the stages of occupation of the site.[231] Initially, the site was used for seasonal agricultural work, although it became a permanent settlement in the middle of the first century CE. After the first Jewish revolt, the settlement was deserted and was resettled for a short period before the Bar Kochba War, after which it remained unoccupied until the third century CE. Therefore, the building should be dated to somewhere between the middle of the first century and 135 CE. Further, the position of the building in a prominent place in the carefully planned layout of the village points toward the period of the first permanent settlement, that is, the middle of the first century CE.

This is clearly the prominent public building at the site and as such is likely to have functioned as the settlement's synagogue building. The benches and interior columns are comparable to those in other synagogue buildings and the rosette on the door lintel is similar to the ones found at

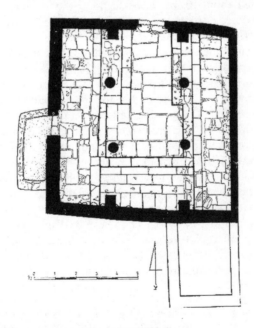

Figure 3.7 Proposed synagogue building at Qiryat Sefer.

231 Magen, Zionit and Sirkis, 'Qiryat-Sefer', pp. 31–32.

Gamla. This building is considerably smaller than any of the others that we have examined and would indicate that within some small villages a synagogue building could be available.

3.2.3. *Modi'in*

Another possible synagogue building was identified, close to Qiryat Sefer, during excavations carried out between 2000 and 2002.[232] On the site at Modi'in, during the Hasmonean period, an earlier Hellenic hall was built over, giving a new hall measuring approximately 10.5–11 m × 7 m. The entrance to the building was in the middle of the longer eastern wall. Within the hall a single row of wide stone benches was uncovered around three of the walls. These were about 20 cm high and, on the eastern and western walls, were 1.5–1.7 m wide while the bench on the northern wall was about 3.5 m wide. The excavators note that they cannot be certain whether this was the original extent of the benches or if there might have been additional layers of benches. A number of coloured plaster fragments (yellow, red and white) were discovered on the site, and it is thought that the hall was decorated in colourful frescoes. The central floor of the hall was made of smoothed field stones and incorporated into this were two raised sections: the first was a square platform (1.1 m × 1.1 m) which protruded about 10 cm above the floor; the second was circular (1m in diameter) and constructed of small field stones and it appears that an object, which continued to be used in the next phase of the building, stood on this base. The function of these installations is not clear; however, it may be that they were used in the reading of the Torah.

During the first part of the first century BCE, a *miqweh* was added in a building to the west of the hall, and in the second half of that century the hall was again altered. The eastern wall was removed and rebuilt to give a new, slightly wider, building which measured 10.5–11.5 m × 8.6 m. Also at this time, two rows of four columns were added to support the roof and two or three rows of stone benches (30 cm high and with a total width of around 1.7 m) surrounded all four walls of the hall.[233] At the centre of the northern benches the excavators have identified a 'special seat'. They are not certain what this was for, and suggest it could have been used by an elder of the community, or as a place to keep or display the Torah. As well as the entrance on the eastern wall, a new entrance was added in the north-eastern corner of the hall. The floor of the hall was made of crushed chalk onto which a new plaster floor was added, probably at the beginning

---

232   A. Onn and S. Weksler-Bdolach, 'Umm-Al-Umdan Ruins: A Jewish Village and a Synagogue Dating back to the Second Temple in Modi'in', *Qadmoniot* 38 (2005), pp. 107–16 (Hebrew). All the following details come from this article.

233   It is not clear whether the columns supported the roof or an additional floor built above the hall, Onn and Shlomit, 'Umm-Al-Umdan Ruins', p. 112.

of the first century CE. The synagogue building, along with the rest of the village of Modi'in, was destroyed in 67 CE. However, shortly afterwards, there is evidence of rebuilding in the village. Inside the hall, on top of the layer of debris left by the destruction, a new plaster floor was laid and a new entrance placed in the northern part of the eastern wall.

The presence of a *miqweh*, Jewish coins, a Hebrew seal in Aramaic and various earthenware vessels similar to those found in other Jewish sites from this period, indicate that Modi'in was a Jewish village. The hall was well appointed with its stone/plaster floor and frescoed walls and would have functioned as a public building. The stone benches and stone pillars are similar to those found in other sites but the raised bases in the centre of the hall are intriguing.

3.2.4. *Capernaum*

Excavations at Capernaum took place during the nineteenth and early twentieth centuries during which time a synagogue building was identified. Investigations of the synagogue building, along with other parts of Capernaum, were continued between 1968 and 1986 by Franciscan archaeologists Virgilio Corbo and Stanislao Loffreda. The impressive synagogue building that had been uncovered was constructed of white limestone and comprised a main meeting hall, a large courtyard attached to the east side of the meeting hall, a narrow porch running the length of the southern wall and a small room attached the north-west corner.[234] Within the meeting hall there were two rows of stone benches along both the east and west walls, and three rows of columns, which rested on a stylobate, creating aisles on the east, north, and west walls.[235]

The dating of this synagogue building has been the subject of great debate, with various scholars suggesting either the second/third century or the fourth/fifth century. However, of greater importance for first-century synagogue architecture was the discovery of, first, a basalt stone pavement around 1.2 m below the central nave of the building, which dated to the first century CE,[236] and second, some walls below the limestone walls of the synagogue building.[237] These were made from black basalt blocks similar to those used in first-century domestic architecture exposed at the site. Originally, it was assumed that these formed a foundation for the synagogue as they were found under all four corners of the building as well as along one of its walls. Further

---

234 S. Loffreda, *Recovering Capharnaum* (Jerusalem: Franciscan Printing Press, 2nd edn, 1993), pp. 33–35.

235 S. Loffreda, 'Capernaum', in *NEAEHL*, vol. 1, p. 294. See Figure 3.8.

236 Various items of pottery were found in and under this floor which date to the first century CE or earlier, J. F. Strange and H. Shanks, 'Synagogue Where Jesus Preached Found at Capernaum', *BARev* 9.6 (1983), pp. 25–31 (29).

237 Loffreda, *Recovering Capharnaum*, pp. 45–49. See Figure 3.9.

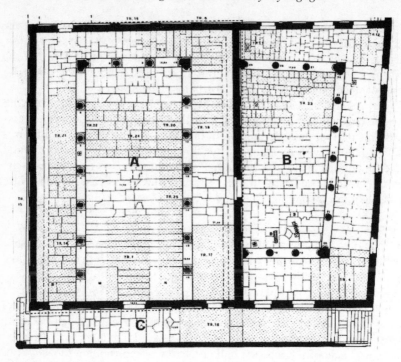

Figure 3.8 Plan of the third to fourth century synagogue building in Capernaum.

excavation found that not only did the basalt walls exist below other walls, but they did not follow exactly the line of the synagogue building above.[238] More evidence that this wall had not been laid as a foundation came with the discovery that it existed only under the main building of the synagogue and not under the courtyard attached to it, which had a foundation of well dressed stone blocks which abutted the basalt walls.[239] As one of the excavators, Loffreda, writes:

> Why this striking difference of foundations? Why did the courtyard which was a secondary unit rest upon excellent foundations, while much poorer foundations were found for the prayer hall which was the most important part of the fourth century synagogue? The only answer we can provide is this: the prayer hall simply reused as foundations the walls of a pre-existing building, while the foundation of the E court was built anew much later.[240]

---

238   It also existed under the stylobate, Loffreda, *Recovering Capharnaum*, p. 47.
239   Strange and Shanks, 'Synagogue where Jesus Preached', p. 30.
240   Loffreda, *Recovering Capharnaum*, pp. 48–49.

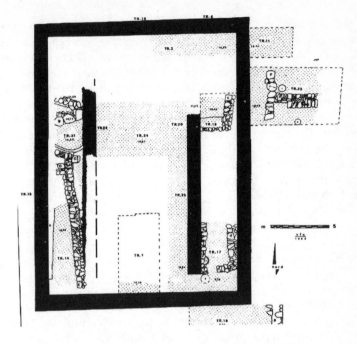

Figure 3.9 Plan of the earlier walls at the Capernaum synagogue building.

The 1.2 m thick walls were also much thicker than those of first-century houses in the area, and the dimensions of the stone pavement, and its composition, which contrasted with the beaten earth floors of houses, also suggested a public building.[241] It would appear clear that the excavators had discovered a public building which dated to the first century.[242]

What is slightly less clear are the exact dimensions of the first-century building. Although there was no indication of any previous building under the central nave of the synagogue, there are the remains of some private houses in the side aisles, which date to the Hellenistic and Roman periods.[243] Corbo concludes that these structures were cleared to make

241   *Ibid.*, p. 45.

242   Binder, *Temple Courts*, pp. 186–93 and Runesson, *Origins*, pp. 182–85, both accept that the earlier building is a synagogue. Claußen acknowledges that the earlier building is not a house and thinks that dating it to the time of Jesus is entirely likely. However, he makes little mention of the details of the building and, perhaps understandably, fails to mention its large size, *Versammlung*, pp. 180–81. Levine is more cautious noting that if this is a first-century synagogue, 'given the meager remains, there is little to be learned about the overall plan of this building', *Ancient Synagogue*, p. 67.

243   There are also remains of a late Bronze Age building dating to the thirteenth century BCE, Loffreda, *Recovering Capharnaum*, p. 45.

way for the first-century building,[244] while Loffreda argues that the original synagogue only occupied the area enclosed between the two inner basalt walls that became the foundation of the later stylobate. He proposes that there was another building between the first-century structure and that of the fourth century which utilised the outer basalt walls.[245] Binder appropriately points out that there are no remains of walls in the north and south which would have connected the inner east and west walls. Further, there is no indication of an additional stratum between the first and fourth century levels.[246] This points towards the first-century building following closely the outline of the later synagogue, although the greater thickness of the earlier building means that the internal dimensions are slightly smaller. It is probable that this earlier public building should also be identified as a synagogue.

3.2.5. *Khirbet Qana*

A possible synagogue building, dating to the first century CE, has recently been discovered at Khirbet Qana in Lower Galilee.[247] Exploratory work on this site has not yet been completed; however, the excavators have found a large room about 20 m × 15 m. At this early stage in the investigation of the site, the presence of architectural characteristics similar to those found in other synagogue buildings has led to it being so identified. Within the building there is evidence of plastered stone benches; foundations for columns; a fragment of a column and an Ionic capital;[248] and fine roof tiles.[249] These items, along with the dimensions of the building, indicate a public rather than a domestic building. Some of the architectural features are certainly similar to those in others which we have identified as synagogue buildings. Further excavation at the site will

244 V.C. Corbo, 'Resti Della Sinagoga del Primo Secolo a Cafarnao', *Studia Hierosolymitana III*, (1982), pp. 314–57 (339). Surprisingly L.J. Hoppe notes that 'the excavators have found no public buildings from the first century at the site', *The Synagogues and Churches of Ancient Palestine* (Collegeville, Minnesota: The Liturgical Press, 1994), p. 35.

245 S. Loffreda, 'Ceramica Ellenisticco-Romana nel Sottosuolo della Sinagoga di Cafarnao', *Studia Hierosolymitana III*, pp. 273–313 (312); *idem*, 'Capernaum', p. 295.

246 Binder, *Temple Courts*, p. 188 n. 60.

247 As yet, little has been published about this site. The following information is drawn from D.R. Edwards, 'Khirbet Qana: from Jewish Village to Christian Pilgrim Site', in J.H. Humphrey, (ed.), *The Roman and Byzantine Near East*, vol. 3 (Journal of Roman Archaeology Supplementary Series, 49; Portsmouth, Rhode Island: JRA, 2002), pp. 101–32, esp. pp. 111–15. In email correspondence, Dr Edwards has confirmed: 'We clearly have an impressive colonnaded building, perhaps built as early as the first (but more probably the second) century', dated 10 July 2006. See also, P. Richardson, *Building Jewish in the Roman East* (Waco: Baylor University Press, 2004), pp. 66–68.

248 The columns were 5 m apart and 2.5 m in from the east and west walls.

249 Elsewhere on the site at Cana a *miqweh* has been found; however, it is some distance from the potential synagogue building so is unlikely to be directly related to its use.

no doubt shed further light on its purpose, but this seems to be another likely candidate.

3.3. *Summary of Palestinian Synagogues*

Within the Palestinian buildings we have examined, certain features are worth noting:

- All except Qumran have stone benches around three or four of their walls; this layout meant that the focus was on the space at the centre of the room.[250] As will be noted in Chapter 4, as the most important liturgical activity that took place within the 'synagogue' was the reading and teaching of the Torah, it seems likely that this took place from this central area, perhaps even from some kind of raised platform. Further, our sources will indicate that discussion of the teaching also took place, and, that the benches would again facilitate this process.
- The importance of Scripture is also emphasised in the *genizah* found at Masada and possibly Jericho. Possible Torah niches exist at Gamla and Jericho and it may be that wooden cupboards were used elsewhere.
- As well as the main assembly room, many of the buildings had additional rooms attached. In many cases it is not clear what their function was, although the Theodotos inscription does indicate some possibilities. In Chapter 4, we will note that a variety of activities could be carried out in the 'synagogue' and that communal dining was important; evidence of such a function is seen in the *triclinium* at Jericho.
- In most cases, these are clearly public buildings. Scholars who have tried to identify them as domestic architecture have either misunderstood the available data, or have relied on others' incorrect identification. Some have correctly noted that these could have been used purely for public assembly and should not be assumed to have had a religious function. However, the *genizah* at Masada, the decoration at Gamla and Qiryat Sefer, and the presence of *miqwaoth* at Masada, Gamla, Modi'in, Jericho and Herodium all point towards these buildings having some ritual function.
- Previous scholarship pointed out the dangers of relying on evidence from buildings that were associated with the Zealot movement, for example, Masada, Gamla and Herodium: they could not be

---

250   It is possible that the centre of some of the buildings was further highlighted by the light coming in through the clestory roof arrangement, see J.F. Strange, 'Archaeology and Ancient Synagogues up to about 200 C. E.', in Olsson and Zetterholm, *The Ancient Synagogue*, pp. 37–62 (43, 53).

assumed to represent wider Jewish practice.[251] This valid caution must now be tempered by the fact that new buildings have been discovered in a variety of locations.

4. *Conclusion*

In this chapter, we have examined the material available to inform our understanding of synagogue buildings; however, the possibility that within some Jewish communities Sabbath gatherings would have taken place within domestic architecture has been highlighted throughout this and the previous chapter. Some communities were too small, did not have sufficient financial capacity, or lacked the political leverage to construct purpose-built places of assembly. In these places it is likely that domestic space of some description would have been used. In some instances these may have been set aside to be used solely by the community, that is, as synagogue buildings, while in others they would have been used for both domestic purposes and Sabbath gatherings. Clearly, identifying these buildings is virtually impossible; however, one inscription from a later period plainly notes such a change within a building:

[..........] + + + | [Κλ.] Τιβέριας Πολύ|χαρμος ὁ καὶ Ἀχύρι|ος ὁ πατὴρ τῆς ἐν | Στόβοις συναγωγῆς, | ὅς πολειτευσάμε|νος πᾶσαν πολε-ιτεί|αν κατὰ τὸν Ἰουδαϊ|σμὸν, εὐχῆς ἕνεκεν | τοὺς μὲν οἴκους τῷ | τετραστόῳ ἐκ τῶν | οἰκείων χρημάτων | μηδὲν ὅλως παραψά|μενος τῶν ἁγίων. τὴν | δὲ ἐξουσίαν τῶν ὑπε|ρῴων πάντων πᾶσαν | καὶ τὴν <δ> εσποτείαν | ἔχειν ἐμὲ τὸν Κλ. Τιβέρι|ον Πολύχαρμον [καὶ τοὺς] | καὶ τοὺς κληρονόμους | τοὺς ἐμοὺς διὰ παντὸς | βίου. ὅς ἂν δὲ βουληθῆ | τι καινοτομῆσαι παρὰ τὰ ὑ- | π᾽ ἐμοῦ δοχθέντα, δώσει τῷ | πατριάρχῃ δηναρίων <μ> υριά- | δας εἴκοσι πέντε · οὕτω γάρ | μοι συνέδοξεν. τὴν δὲ ἐπισκευὴν τῆς κεράμου τῶν | ὑπερῴων ποιεῖσθαι ἐμὲ | καὶ κληρονόμους | ἐμούς.

...... [Claudius] Tiberius Polycharmus, also (called) Achyrius, the father of the synagogue at Stobi, having lived my whole life according to the (prescriptions of) Judaism, in fulfilment of a vow (have donated) the rooms(?) to the holy place, and the *triclinium*, with the *tetrastoa*, out of my personal accounts without touching the sacred (funds) at all. All the right of all the upper (rooms of the building) and the ownership is to be held by me, Claudius Tiberius Polycharmus, and my heirs for all (our?) life. If someone wishes to make changes beyond my decisions, he shall give the Patriarch 250,000 denarii. For thus I have agreed. As for the

---

251   Flesher, 'Palestinian Synagogues', p. 38; Horsley, *Galilee: History, Politics, People*, p. 224; Hoppe, *Synagogues and Churches*, p. 13.

upkeep of the roof tiles of the upper (rooms of the building), it will be done by me and my heirs.[252]

Certain scholars have been overly interested in countering the arguments of Kee·and others and have failed adequately to take into account the possibility of such domestic gatherings. So Richard Oster writes:

> There is no Diaspora evidence from either papyri or epigraphy contemporary with the Second Temple that points to domestic characteristics of synagogues. The places where the Jews met were clearly architectural structures orientated toward their community...Theories comparing primitive Christian house churches with Jewish 'house churches' which were precursors of later synagogues run aground on the dearth of supportive data from the pre-70 period.[253]

While we have established that even within small Palestinian communities like Qiryat Sefer it was possible to have a community assembly hall, or that Capernaum could fund a fairly large synagogue building, we should draw back from assuming that such facilities existed in every village and town throughout the country. Similarly, Diaspora Jewish communities often came under pressure as can be seen in the decrees quoted by Josephus or the pogroms reported by Philo. While certain communities had the financial backing, the political connections and the social stability to provide meeting places for themselves, others lacked some of these conditions and consequently are likely to have met in a domestic setting. As was mentioned in Chapter 1, while establishing clear criteria for the identification of a building as a synagogue might appear to make our task easier, in fact, as greater research is done, deciding on what such criteria might be becomes ever more difficult.

When we examine the patterns of architecture used, again there appears to be division between Palestine and the Diaspora. Certain recurring features are seen within the Palestinian buildings, while those of the Diaspora do not appear to share this pattern.[254] Rather, they resemble the local temples or voluntary organisations. If the architecture follows these patterns, it will be worth considering how this might affect any pattern of worship carried out within them, and whether such practices might vary from one location to another.

---

252 *IJO*, Mac1. This dates to the second or third century CE. See also, C. Claußen, 'Meeting, Community, Synagogue – Different Frameworks of Ancient Jewish Congregations in the Diaspora', in Olsson and Zetterholm (eds), *The Ancient Synagogue*, pp 144–67 (157–58).

253 Oster, 'Supposed Anachronism', p. 193.

254 Although we should remain cautious as there are fewer remains on which to base our observations.

Chapter 4

WORSHIP PRACTICES

1. *Introduction*

In his discussion of Luke's account of the 'synagogue' service in Nazareth, John Nolland writes:

> The major elements of the synagogue service were the recitation of the *Shema* (Deut 6.4-9; 11.13-21; Num 15.37-41), the praying of the *Tephillah* by one of the congregation, a reading from the Torah (probably shared by several people), a reading from the Prophets (both readings accompanied by Aramaic paraphrase), a sermon based on the readings and a final priestly blessing (if a priest was present).[1]

In the last decade or so, virtually every element that Nolland has as part of this first-century service has been questioned.

There would appear to be two major difficulties in addressing the area of worship practices in the first-century 'synagogue'. The first is the lack of detail that we have on the subject, which should make us wary of overly confident assertions on practice. The second is defining what should or should not be considered worship. It is difficult to separate the spiritual from the secular in the first century, with any public act often having a religious element to it. As was seen in the previous chapters, the first-century 'synagogue' would have carried out many different functions, and while it is unlikely that these were all regarded as worship, something such as the manumission of a slave would, nevertheless, have had a religious element to it. In the discussion below we will identify enough material with which to reconstruct some elements of 'synagogue' worship in this period, although we should be aware that the actual practices of communities may well have differed from one another.

---

1 J. Nolland, *Luke* (WBC, 35; 3 vols; Dallas: Word Books, 1989–93), vol. 1, p. 194. Cf. J.A. Fitzmyer, *The Gospel According to Luke* (AB, 28; 2 vols; New York: Doubleday, 1970–85), vol. 1, p. 531; H. Schürmann, *Das Lukasevangelium* (HTKNT, 3; 2 vols; Freiburg: Herder, 1969), vol. 1, pp. 228–29. I.H. Marshall also suggests that there would have been a fixed lectionary cycle for the Torah reading, *The Gospel of Luke* (NIGTC; Grand Rapids: Eerdmans, 1978), pp. 181–82.

In her monograph on 'synagogue' practice Heather McKay defines worship as follows:

> Rites and rituals which pay homage, with adoration and awe, to a particular god or gods. Worship could include sacrificing plants and animals, dancing, playing music, singing hymns or psalms, reading or reciting sacred texts, prayers and blessings. Instruction for, or descriptions of, these types of activity in the texts are regarded by me as evidences of worship either expected of, or carried out by, the religious community.
>
> Prayer to the deity and singing of psalms to or about the deity, exhortations to follow the commands of the deity as understood by the believing community – all these count for me as worship. Community business, discipline sessions and political arguments do not. Reading, studying and explaining sacred texts I do not necessarily regard as worship, *unless* given a place in a planned session of worship. Otherwise I regard these activities as educational, or as serving the purpose of preserving and strengthening group identity, and not necessarily implying worship; the group's understanding of the god as *addressee* of the worship is vital in my definition.[2]

This definition has been criticized by a number of scholars, some more judiciously than others.[3] It is worth pointing out that it has, however, forced scholars to be more explicit in what they mean by 'worship'. In her criticism of McKay's definition, Leonhardt points out that Philo 'would have been surprised by McKay's conclusion that there was no worship on the Sabbath'. She argues that McKay has used modern concepts of what constitutes worship and applied them to a first-century setting.[4]

In this chapter we will survey the available material that might relate to first-century liturgical practices that may have taken place within 'synagogues'. Clearly it is not possible to enter fully into the worldview of a first-century Jew; whether they perceived the various activities that took place within the 'synagogue' as worship is not always clear. Nonetheless, certain elements that would be recognized as worship in both

2   H.A. McKay, *Sabbath and Synagogue: The Question of Sabbath Worship in Ancient Judaism* (Religion in the Graeco-Roman World, 122; Leiden: Brill, 1994), pp. 3–4, (italics hers).

3   See, S.C. Reif, 'Sabbath and Synagogue' (review), *JTS* 46 (1995), pp. 610–12; P.J. Tomson, 'Sabbath and Synagogue' (review), *JSJ* 28 (1997), pp. 342–43; P.W. van der Horst, 'Was the Synagogue a Place of Sabbath Worship Before 70 CE?', in S. Fine (ed.), *Jews, Christians, and Polytheists in the Ancient Synagogue* (New York: Routledge, 1999), pp. 23–37; L.I. Levine, *The Ancient Synagogue: The First Thousand Years* (New Haven and London: Yale University Press, 2000), p. 134 n. 55; J. Leonhardt, *Jewish Worship in Philo of Alexandria* (TSAJ, 84; Tübingen: Mohr Siebeck, 2001), pp. 7–8; A. Runesson, *The Origins of the Synagogue: A Socio-Historical Study* (ConNT, 37; Stockholm: Almqvist & Wiksell, 2001), pp. 194–96.

4   Leonhardt, *Jewish Worship*, p. 8. And it should probably be added, 'western concepts'.

the first and twenty-first centuries are present, and other practices may also have been perceived in such a way, at least in the first century. Finding the correct terminology to deal with the ritual elements that may have taken place within the first-century 'synagogue' is problematic; 'worship' largely reflects later patterns of practice, while 'liturgy' is understood in a different way in the twenty-first century to how it would have been in a first-century setting. Nevertheless, some form of terminology is required in this study, and both liturgy and worship will be used: here they are understood to refer to ritual functions that indicate communication between people and God.

2. Sanctity

2.1. *Introduction*

Before going on to look at some of the practices that went on in first-century 'synagogues', we will explore whether a level of sanctity was attributed to at least some of these buildings. Certainly by the tannaitic period there is evidence that this was the case: what could or could not be done on the site of a derelict 'synagogue' building is discussed, these buildings being compared to the sanctuaries of Lev. 26.31: 'I will lay your cities waste, will make your sanctuaries desolate, and I will not smell your pleasing odors'.[5] This undoubtedly reflects a general movement of sanctity from the temple to the 'synagogue' as it took on some of the roles that the temple had fulfilled.[6] However, did such a movement have its origins in a time when the temple was still standing?

2.2. *The Sanctity of the Building*
2.2.1. *Philo and Josephus*

The terms used by Josephus and Philo would suggest that 'synagogues' were viewed as sacred: both use ἱερόν to refer to them.[7] Philo describes the συναγωγαί of the Essenes as 'sacred spots' (ἱεροὶ τόποι),[8] and the Egyptian προσευχή as a ἱερὸς περίβολος.[9] In a number of decrees

---

5   See S.J.D. Cohen, 'The Temple and the Synagogue,' in *CHJ*, pp. 298–325 (320). S. Fine, 'From Meeting House to Sacred Realm: Holiness and the Ancient Synagogue', in S. Fine (ed.), *Sacred Realm: The Emergence of the Synagogue in the Ancient World* (New York: Yeshiva University Museum, 1996), pp. 21–47 (26).

6   E.g., this can be seen in the Tosefta where the doors of a 'synagogue' are to face east as in the temple, *t. Meg.* 3.22. For a discussion on the increasing sanctity of the 'synagogue' in rabbinic writing see Cohen, 'The Temple and the Synagogue', pp. 319–23.

7   Josephus, *War*, 7.45; *Ant.*, 13.66; Philo, *Deus Imm.*, 7–9.

8   Philo, *Omn. Prob. Lib.*, 81.

9   Philo, *Flacc.*, 48. Philo also suggests that those Alexandrians who wish to take the προσευχαί from the Jews do so in order to turn them into additional sacred precincts (τέμενοί) dedicated to Gaius, *Leg. Gai.*, 137.

recorded by Josephus, the meeting places of the Jews are afforded protection where they were allowed to collect the temple tax and send it to Jerusalem. While this money was collected locally, it was kept in the 'synagogue' along with the Scriptures, so that 'if anyone is caught stealing their sacred books or their sacred monies from a synagogue or an ark (of the law), he shall be regarded as sacrilegious (ἱερὰς βίβλους αὐτῶν ἢ τὰ ἱερὰ χρήματα ἔκ τε σαββατείου ἔκ τε ἀαρῶνος εἶναι αὐτὸν ἱερόσυλον)'.[10] Although here it is the money and Scriptures that are termed sacred, nonetheless this might also have applied to the building. Certainly on one occasion a building was rendered unfit for use by the Jewish community because of the introduction of an image of Caesar. Indeed, Josephus makes the point explicitly that the young men who put up such an image 'set a higher value on audacity than on holiness (ὁσιότης)'.[11] Finally, in relation to Egypt, Anders Runesson has recently pointed out that the place where the Alexandrian Jews went to rejoice after the arrest of Flaccus is described as καθαρωτάτῳ, which is translated by Colson in the Loeb as 'the most open space'.[12] Runesson notes that καθαρός more often carries the meaning of pure or clean and it might well be that Philo is indicating that the Jews went to this place beside the water because there was an element of purity about it.[13]

2.2.2. *Inscriptions and Papyri*

In Egypt the inscriptions and papyri which mention προσευχαί also indicate that at least some of these buildings were treated as sacred. One, dated to the middle of the first century BCE, notes the inviolability of the building granted by the king: 'King Ptolemy Euergetes (proclaimed) the proseuche inviolate ([*vacat*] Βασιλεὺς Πτολεμαῖος Εὐεργέτης τὴν προσευχὴν ἄσυλον)'.[14] This status as a place of asylum may have been the reason that refuge was sought in another προσευχή in Alexandrou-Nesos.[15] Similarly, the ground on which a προσευχή stood could be

---

10 Josephus, *Ant.*, 16.164.

11 Josephus, *Ant.*, 19.300.

12 Philo, *Flacc.*, 122.

13 A. Runesson, 'Water and Worship: Ostia and the Ritual Bath in the Diaspora Synagogue', in B. Olsson, D. Mitternacht and O. Brandt (eds), *The Synagogue of Ancient Ostia and the Jews of Rome: Interdisciplinary Studies* (Stockholm: Paul Åströms Förlag, 2001), pp. 115–29 (121–22).

14 *JIGRE*, 125. This same kind of protection was granted to Egyptian temples, see P.M. Fraser, *Ptolemaic Alexandria* (2 vols.; Oxford: Clarendon Press, 1972), vol. 1, p. 283; P.E. Dion, 'Synagogues et Temples dans L'Égypte Hellénistique', *ScEs* 29 (1977), pp. 45–75 (59); J.G. Griffiths, 'Egypt and the Rise of the Synagogue', *JTS* 38 (1987), pp. 1–15 (10–11); *idem*, 'The Legacy of Egypt in Judaism', in *CHJ*, pp. 1025–51 (1033).

15 *CPJ* 1, 129, see the editor's comments, p. 240 n. 5. See also A. Kasher, 'Synagogues as "Houses of Prayer" and "Holy Places" in the Jewish Communities of Hellenistic and Roman Egypt', in *ASHAAD*, vol. 1, pp. 205–20 (215).

described as holy,[16] and the building may have been surrounded by a ἱερὸς περίβολος.[17] Further evidence of the sacred nature of the buildings can be seen in the way in which they were perceived by pagans as similar to their temples,[18] with practices carried out in pagan temples also taking place within 'synagogues'. Inscriptions from the Bosphorus provide evidence of slaves being manumitted within προσευχαί in the region, a practice which is equivalent to that in pagan temples.[19]

2.3. *The Sanctity of the Person*

Having discussed the sanctity of the building, the question then arises: did those who came to worship in the building need to carry out any act of purification before entering or worshipping? That ritual purity was an issue that concerned Jews of the first century is without doubt:[20] this might relate to the removal of impurity caused by sexual intercourse, bodily emissions, or coming into contact with a corpse.[21] As well as these concerns, ritual washing was also used to bring about a state of purity before worship. So, for example, in the case of the translators of the Septuagint:

> Following the custom of all the Jews, they washed their hands in the sea
> in the course of their prayers to God, and then proceeded to the reading
> and explication of each point. I asked this question: 'What is their
> purpose in washing their hands while saying their prayers?' They
> explained that it is evidence that they have done no evil, for all activity
> takes place by means of the hands.[22]

16   *CPJ* 1, 134.

17   *JIGRE*, 9. However, it should be noted that here περίβολος is assumed to fill a lacuna. One other dedicatory inscription refers to a 'holy place', *JIGRE*, 17; in this fragmentary inscription the term προσευχή does not appear, but it would seem likely that such a building is intended.

18   Agatharchies calls them ἱεροί, Josephus, *Apion*, 1.209; Tacitus *templa*, *Hist.*, 5.5; Addressing the problem in Dora, Petronius wrote that the emperor's 'image was better placed in his own shrine (ναός) than that of another', Josephus, *Ant.*, 19.305.

19   See E.L. Gibson, *The Jewish Manumission Inscriptions of the Bosporus Kingdom* (TSAJ, 75; Tübingen: Mohr Siebeck, 1999), p. 130. Also, van der Horst, 'Was the Synagogue', p. 34.

20   The view that issues of purity were concerned only with the temple cult is criticized by John C. Poirier, who notes the sources that evidence extra-temple purity and argues that some level of purification is associated with Second Temple 'synagogues', 'Purity beyond the Temple in the Second Temple Era', *JBL* 122 (2003), pp. 247–65.

21   See E.P. Sanders, *Jewish Law From Jesus to the Mishnah: Five Studies* (London: SCM, 1990), p. 29.

22   *Ep. Arist.*, 305–306. Cf. Josephus, 'after washing their hands in the sea and purifying themselves (καὶ τῇ θαλάσσῃ τὰς χεῖρας ἀπονιπτόμενοι καὶ καθαίροντες αὑτούς)' *Ant.*, 12.106. Also, Judith bathed before praying: 'She went out each night to the valley of Bethulia, and bathed at the spring in the camp. After bathing, she prayed the Lord God of

As Sanders points out, it is not clear what 'following the custom of all the Jews' might mean; it certainly cannot mean that all Jews washed their hands in the sea. Possibly some form of hand washing was regularly carried out in connection with prayer.[23]

2.3.1. *Palestine*

As has been indicated above, water was regularly associated with Second Temple synagogue buildings. They were either located near to a river or sea, or had facilities for washing close to the building. However, there does appear to be some degree of difference between the facilities used in differing localities. Rutgers writes: '*Mikvaot*, or ritual baths, do not seem to belong to the standard repertoire of structures associated with the Diaspora synagogue'.[24] Reich points out that ritual baths were found in some abundance during the Second Temple period but that after the destruction of the temple, they gradually faded from the scene.[25] He notes that in Palestine immersion pools were used, a fact which appears to indicate a different practice from the Diaspora where no such pools have been found.[26] Sanders argues that all Palestinian Jews viewed immersion in such pools as the correct way of removing ritual impurity. However, Wright correctly criticizes Sanders: although sharing many of Sanders' views, he points out that immersion in rivers, seas or streams would, in all likelihood, have been equally acceptable to Palestinian Jews and would also have been available to Jews in the Diaspora where immersion in special pools was unusual.[27]

Israel to direct her way for the triumph of his people. Then she returned purified and stayed in the tent until she ate her food toward evening', 12.7-9; Judas gathered his army and, 'they purified themselves according to the custom, and kept the sabbath there (κατὰ τὸν ἐθισμὸν ἀγνισθέντες αὐτόθι τὸ σάββατον διήγαγον)', which would probably have been carried out using water, 2 Macc. 12.38; *Sib. Or.*, 3.591-93, pious Jews 'at dawn they lift up holy arms toward heaven, from their beds, always sanctifying their flesh (hands) with water', J.J. Collins, 'Sibylline Oracles', in J.H. Charlesworth (ed.), *The Old Testament Pseudepigrapha* (2 vols; New York: Doubleday, 1983–85), vol. 1, pp. 317–472 (375).

23 Sanders, *Jewish Law*, p. 260.

24 L.V. Rutgers, 'Diaspora Synagogues: Synagogue Archaeology in the Greco-Roman World', in Fine (ed.), *Sacred Realm*, pp. 67–95 (75).

25 R. Reich, 'The Synagogue and the *Miqweh* in Eretz-Israel in the Second-Temple, Mishnaic, and Talmudic Periods', in *ASHAAD*, pp. 289–97 (296).

26 Note, however, the critique of Reich by B.G. Wright, who points out that he appears to presume smaller pools would not have been *miqwaoth* because they could not have been used for immersion, 'Jewish Ritual Baths – Interpreting the Digs and the Texts: Some Issues in the Social History of Second Temple Judaism', in N.A. Silberman and D. Small (eds), *The Archaeology of Israel: Constructing the Past, Interpreting the Present* (JSOTSup, 237; Sheffield: Sheffield Academic Press, 1997), pp. 190–214 (204).

27 Wright, 'Jewish Ritual Baths', p. 208. It should be noted that there is no immersion pool beside the synagogue building at Capernaum; however, its proximity to the Sea of

Rabbinic Judaism saw water that had been drawn as inappropriate for a *miqweh*.[28] Water feeding into a ritual bath either from a spring, or from rain water collected from the roofs of buildings was deemed suitable. However, at times such a supply of water was not possible and a second cistern, an *otsar*, was attached to the main immersion pool. If the water in the immersion pool evaporated or needed to be changed and refilled, the drawn water which had been used could then be made pure by the addition of some water from the additional cistern.[29] While there are examples of this style of installation in the first-century period this may reflect the practices of Pharisaic Judaism as there are also examples of single immersion pools with no additional cistern and to which drawn water must have been added.[30] Therefore, it would appear that the archaeological evidence suggests possible differences within Palestine, even within Jerusalem, where different types of *miqwaoth* have been found from the Second Temple period.[31]

Further evidence of the use of immersion as a means of purity comes from Qumran:

> Concerning the purification with water: No one should bathe in water which is dirty or which is less than the amount which covers a man. No one should purify a vessel in it. And every cavity in the rock in which there is not the amount which covers, if an impure person has touched it, he has defiled its water like the water of a vessel.[32]

Miqwaoth have been found at the site and there is clear indication in the community's literature that bathing was seen as a way of removing impurity as well as a method of initiation into the community.[33]

Galilee might have made it unnecessary. Cf. *m. Miqw.* 5.4: 'All seas are valid as an Immersion-pool', see also, *t. Miqw.* 4.5, 6.3; *t. Mak.* 2.12. The only possible immersion pool in close proximity to a Diaspora synagogue building comes at Delos.

28   *M. Miqw.* 4.5.

29   *M. Miqw.* 6.8. See Sanders, *Jewish Law*, pp. 218–22.

30   E.g., two *miqwaoth* on the Temple Mount are identified by Reich as dating to the pre-Herodian or Hasmonaean period, 'Two Possible *Miqwa'ot* on the Temple Mount', *IEJ* 39 (1989), pp. 63–65. See also the discussion in Sanders, *Jewish Law*, pp. 220–21.

31   R. Reich, 'The Hot Bath-House (*balneum*), the Miqweh and the Jewish Community in the Second Temple Period', *JJS* 39 (1988), pp. 102–107. For a detailed discussion of immersion pools both in rabbinic literature and in a first-century setting, see H.K. Harrington, *The Impurity Systems of Qumran and the Rabbis: Biblical Foundations* (SBLDS, 143; Atlanta: Scholars Press, 1993), pp. 113–39.

32   CD 10.11-13. These details are immediately followed by instruction on how to keep the Sabbath.

33   Wright, 'Jewish Ritual Baths', p. 210.

2.3.2. *Diaspora*
2.3.2.1. *Philo*

In his discussion of the Decalogue, Philo makes the following observation regarding the fourth commandment:

> The fourth, which treats of the seventh day, must be regarded as nothing less than a gathering under one head of the feasts and the purifications ordained for each feast, the proper lustrations and the acceptable prayers and flawless sacrifices with which the ritual was carried out.[34]

Here the worship of the temple is clearly expanded through the reference to the Sabbath. It might be that Philo has in mind Sabbath worship within Jerusalem, although it seems more likely that Sabbath worship elsewhere is also included. Therefore the 'proper lustrations' (περιρραντηρίων τε αἰσίων) here extend to forms of worship beyond that of the temple.[35]

Further evidence for the actual practice of washing comes in a passage which describes the necessary actions for entry into the temple if someone has had contact with a corpse.[36] Philo highlights the activities of pagans and the superiority of Jewish practice:

> The following regulations also shews a farsighted wisdom which should be noted. In almost all other cases men used unmixed water for the sprinkling. By most people it is taken from the sea, by others from the rivers, and by others it is drawn in ewers from the wells. But Moses first provided ashes, the remnants of the sacred fire, obtained in a manner which will be explained shortly. Some of these, he says, are to be taken and thrown into a vessel and afterwards have water poured upon them. Then the priests are to dip branches of hyssop in the mixture and sprinkle with it those who are being purged.[37]

Although the ritual washing of non-Jews is described in the opening sentences above, there is no indication that Philo disassociates Jewish means of purification from this practice. Therefore, it seems likely that this reflects the variety of means used by both Jew and Gentile to purge themselves from impurity, with the superior distinctives of the Jewish practice also highlighted.[38]

Sanders examines the terms Philo uses for the actions to bring about ritual purity after some form of contamination: λουτρόν and περιρραν-

---

34 Philo, *Dec.*, 158.
35 See Leonhardt, *Jewish Worship*, p. 14; p. 261.
36 Philo, *Spec. Leg.*, 1.257-66.
37 Philo, *Spec. Leg.*, 1.262.
38 See Runesson, 'Water and Worship', p. 126. Leonhardt proposes: 'The list, together with the fact that the *proseuchai* were built near water supports the hypothesis that there were purification rites in the *proseuchai*', *Jewish Worship*, p. 266, n. 27.

τήριον. Having compared their use elsewhere in Philo, Sanders argues that the action that is described does not involve bathing, but washing (probably of the hands) and sprinkling from basins.[39] He argues that Philo is reporting an Alexandrian practice and not the action required at the temple.[40] Such practices were probably influenced by pagan customs where *perirranteria* stood at the entrance to temples in which those entering would have dipped their hands and sprinkled themselves.[41]

However, dipping the hands or sprinkling themselves may not have been the only means of purification. In his exposition of Num. 28.2 Philo writes:

> For to whom should we make thank-offering save to God? And wherewithal save by what He has given us? For there is nothing else whereof we can have sufficiency. God needs nothing, yet in the exceeding greatness of His benefices to our race He bids us bring what is His own. For if we cultivate the spirit of rendering thanks and honour to Him, we shall be pure from wrongdoing and wash away the filthiness which defiles our lives in thought and word and deed. For it is absurd that a man should be forbidden to enter the synagogues (ἱερά) save after bathing and cleansing his body (ὃς ἂν μὴ πρότερον λουσάμενος φαιδρύνται τὸ σῶμα), and yet should attempt to pray and sacrifice with a heart still soiled and spotted. The synagogues are made of stones and timber, that is of soulless matter, and soulless too is the body itself. And can it be that while it is forbidden to this soulless body to touch the soulless stones, except it have first been subjected to lustral and purificatory consecration, a man will not shrink from approaching with his soul impure the absolute purity of God and that too when there is no thought of repentance in his heart? He who is resolved not only to commit no further sin, but also to wash away the past, may approach with gladness: let him who lacks this resolve keep far away, since hardly shall he be purified. For he shall never escape the eye of Him who sees into the recesses of the mind and treads its inmost shrine.[42]

Donald Binder has argued convincingly that Philo is not referring to pagan activity, but rather to the Jews entering the 'synagogues'.[43] This is clear from the facts that: i) he identifies the gifts of God to 'our own race' (τὸ γένος ἡμῶν); ii) the reference to ἱερόν is in the plural and therefore does not refer to the temple; and iii) Philo encourages them to cleanse their hearts before entering the ἱερά which, Binder points out, can hardly

39   Sanders, *Jewish Law*, p. 267. Biblical precedent may have been found in passages such as Ps. 73.13.

40   See Sanders, *Jewish Law*, pp. 263–71.

41   See W. Buckert, *Greek Religion: Archaic and Classical* (trans. J. Raffan; Oxford: Blackwell, 1985), p. 77.

42   Philo, *Deus Imm.*, 7–9. Here 'temples' in LCL has been changed to 'synagogues'.

43   Contra Sanders, *Jewish Law*, p. 268, and Leonhardt, *Jewish Worship*, pp. 266–67.

be referring to pagan temples.[44] To this we could add that Philo's description of 'the absolute purity of God' would not be how a Jew perceived the gods/goddesses of the Graeco-Roman world: rather their humanness would have been mocked. Philo here uses the verb λούω to describe the act of purification, which he uses elsewhere for 'bathe'.[45] Therefore, this may suggest differences in practice either among the Alexandrian Jews, or perhaps elsewhere.

The evidence presented would suggest that purity was a matter of concern for Philo, that this concern extended beyond that associated with attendance at the temple in Jerusalem, and that a link can be seen between purity and worship on the Sabbath and in the 'synagogue'. As previously noted, many of the Diaspora 'synagogues' we know of were either close to a natural water source, or had a basin or cistern nearby and some had both. It would seem likely that water was used by those attending the 'synagogue', most likely to wash their hands or sprinkle themselves, although the possibility that they may have immersed themselves cannot be ruled out.

2.4. *Conclusion*

Whether the influence was that of Pharisaic Judaism or Graeco-Roman religion, it appears clear that the Jews saw ritual purity and 'synagogue' practice as connected. It is highly probable that both Jew and Gentile associated sanctity with the building as was the case with pagan temples.[46] As has been shown above, in the works of Philo, Josephus, various pagan sources and inscriptions, the building is seen as sacred.

We can make a clear connection between ritual washing and the extant archaeological sites of synagogue buildings that we have available. Further, that ritual washing was in some ways connected to the worship practices of the Jews seems clear. From the sources available to us it is impossible to make clear claims about different practices in differing localities; however, it does appear that in parts of Palestine among the particularly pious, full immersion in a *miqweh* was the means by which purity was retained. Nevertheless, it is likely that natural bodies of water were also used and in the Diaspora such bodies of water were used frequently for purification. However, Graeco-Roman culture also influenced the Diaspora, and some kind of water source near to the door of the 'synagogue' was used for the washing of hands or sprinkling before entering.

---

44   Binder, *Temple Courts*, pp. 395–97.

45   So Sanders, *Jewish Law*, p. 267.

46   So a Jew who inadvertently bows down before a pagan temple thinking it a synagogue building does not commit a sin according to *b. Shabb.* 72b. This clearly indicates that showing due deference for a synagogue building was taken for granted at this time.

So we have buildings described as ἱερά in Antioch and Egypt, as ἱεροί τόποι in Palestine, and as places of sanctuary in Egypt. Manumission took place in the προσευχαί of the Bosphorus and non-Jews saw the Jewish 'synagogue' as functioning in a way that resembled their temples. There is also evidence of a connection between ritual acts to bring about purity and worship which extends beyond the worship of the temple, and archaeological evidence that would appear to suggest that such ritual acts may well have taken place at a 'synagogue'. Although it is tempting to try and draw a line of demarcation between the practices of Palestinian and Diaspora communities, the evidence is hazier and care needs to be taken in this regard. What we do not know is how this may have been put into practice in communities where 'synagogue' gatherings took place in smaller community buildings or in domestic homes, perhaps in a room in the home of a wealthy member. It may be that in these gatherings the focus of sanctity was more on the activity of the community and more specifically the Torah scrolls, which may have been kept in small wooden Torah shrines. Again, either a natural water supply or a domestic cistern could have been used to maintain ritual purity; however, these final points are speculation.

3. *Scripture Reading and Teaching*

3.1. *Introduction*

Virtually all scholarship on the 'synagogue' of the Second Temple period agrees that Torah reading was a central function in the 'synagogue'.[47] The Torah was perceived as sacred during this period: in the Letter of Aristeas the Scriptures are described as holy or divine for the first time;[48] in a letter to the Jews of Asia Minor in the year 12 BCE we are informed that anyone caught stealing the 'sacred books' from a 'synagogue' (σαββατεῖον) would have his property confiscated;[49] Josephus reports that a Roman soldier was beheaded because he tore up the Torah scroll;[50] and in his account of an incident at Caesarea he states that the Roman governor,

---

47   L.I. Levine, 'The Nature and Origin of the Palestinian Synagogue', *JBL* 115 (1996), pp. 425–48 (438); L.H. Schiffman, 'The Early History of Public Reading of the Torah', in Fine, *Jews, Christians, and Polytheists*, pp. 44–56 (54); Z. Safrai, 'The Communal Functions of the Synagogue in the Land of Israel in the Rabbinic Period', in *ASHAAD*, vol. 1 pp. 181–204 (182); C. Claußen, *Versammlung, Gemeinde, Synagoge: Das hellenistisch-jüdische Umfeld der frühchristlichen Gemeinde* (SUNT, 27; Göttingen: Vandenhoeck & Ruprecht, 2002), p. 213;

48   *Ep. Arist.*, 3; 5; 31; 45, see van der Horst, 'Was the Synagogue', pp. 34–35.

49   Josephus, *Ant.*, 16.163-64.

50   Josephus, *Ant.*, 20.115-16, see also the parallel report in *War*, 2.229-31.

Florus, arrested the Jews because they had removed the Torah scroll from the city.[51]

Various suggestions have been made for the origin(s) of Torah reading in the 'synagogue'. Many scholars have pointed to the *Hakhel* ceremony where the Torah was to be read every seventh year during the festival of Sukkot.[52] Further, the reading and expounding of the law by Ezra at the rededication of the temple is the first instance of a public ceremony and may well have provided the background for the procedures of Torah reading in the 'synagogue'.[53]

3.2. Qumran

At Qumran the daily reading of Scripture is commanded in *The Community Rule*,[54] and Sabbath reading is commented on in 4Q251 1.5. While acknowledging that the public reading of Scripture was part of the life of the community, Schiffman argues that it is wrong to perceive it as 'a ritual reading of the Torah of the kind found in the Pharisaic-rabbinic tradition', but that it may have formed part of their daily study of scripture.[55] One passage from Qumran is worth quoting here:

> And anyone who is not quick to understand, and anyone who speaks weakly or staccato, without separating his words to make his voice heard, such men should not read in the book of the Torah, so that he will not lead to error in a capital matter.[56]

This must relate to the public reading of Scripture; why else would the quality of the reader's voice be important? Also, this indicates that the congregation did not have their own texts to follow, hence the concern for

---

51   Josephus, *War*, 2.292.

52   Deut. 31.10-13. See also the descriptions of this ceremony in *Ant.*, 4.209-10, and *m. Sotah* 7.8.

53   Neh. 8.1-9. I. Elbogen sees Torah reading in the 'synagogues' as an imitation of Ezra's reading (*Jewish Liturgy: A Comprehensive History* [trans. R.P. Scheindlin; Philadelphia: The Jewish Publication Society, 1993], pp. 130–31) as does Binder, who connects the reading of Ezra with the septennial readings, *Temple Courts*, p. 404. Claußen, however, points out that it is not possible to draw a direct line from Ezra's reading to that of the 'synagogue' (*Versammlung*, p. 213), and Schiffman notes that the *Hakhel* reading and that of Ezra are different types; the one being 'a sort of national reading in which a leader, representing the entire people, reads', while the other is an instruction based system, 'Early History', pp. 44–45.

54   1QS 6.7-8.

55   Schiffman, 'Early History', p. 45. Runesson points out that this definition is not valid because it limits the investigation to the practices of only one group, the Pharisees/rabbis, and that the practices of this group are only described in later sources, thus leading to the possibility of anachronism, *Origins*, p. 332.

56   4Q266 5 2.1-3 = 4Q267 5 3.2-5.

accurate reading in order to avoid violation of the law.[57] Schiffman thinks that the reading would have been carried out by a priest,[58] but there is nothing in the text to indicate that this should be the case. Nonetheless, at Qumran it may well be that the focus on the role of the priesthood meant that they would have been the ones to read the Scripture and to teach the community.

3.3. *Josephus and Philo*

The suggestion by McKay, that the Torah-reading ceremonies carried out by the Jews were for educational purposes, appears to receive clear corroboration in the works of Josephus and Philo.[59] Josephus, referring to Moses, reports that on every Sabbath the Jews would assemble in order to hear the Torah being read:

> For ignorance he left no pretext. He appointed the Law to be the most excellent and necessary form of instruction, ordaining, not that it should be heard once for all or twice or on several occasions, but that every week men should desert their other occupations and assemble to listen to the Law and to obtain a thorough and accurate knowledge of it, a practice which all other legislators seem to have neglected.[60]

The picture presented by Philo is very similar. He describes the Sabbath practices of the Jews as taking place in διδασκαλεῖα which 'stand wide open in every city'.[61] The teaching the Jews receive is described as 'the philosophy of their fathers'.[62] However, the διδασκαλεῖα are clearly identified with places of prayer (προσευκτήρια)[63] and the description of the study that went on in the διδασκαλεῖα as philosophy also appears in the συναγωγή,[64] συναγωγίον[65] and προσευχή.[66] This does not negate the arguments of McKay, nor should we flatten out the contours of difference that the use of these different terms may suggest. Nevertheless, to describe the meeting places of the Jews as διδασκαλεῖα, and the practices that went on within them as philosophical study should, at least to some extent, be

---

57   Schiffman, 'Early History', p. 46.
58   *Ibid.*, p. 46
59   See McKay's discussion of Philo and Josephus, *Sabbath and Synagogue*, chapter 3.
60   Josephus, *Apion*, 2.175, cf. *Ant.*, 16.43.
61   Philo, *Spec. Leg.*, 2.62, cf. *Vit. Mos.*, 2.214-16. Cf., also *Dec.*, 40; *Praem. Poen.*, 66.
62   Philo, *Vit. Mos.*, 2.216.
63   *Ibid.*
64   Philo, *Omn. Prob. Lib.*, 81
65   Philo, *Somn.*, 2.127.
66   Philo, *Leg. Gai.*, 156.

attributed to Philo's desire to present Jewish practice in a way that would both be understood and appreciated by a Hellenistic audience.[67]

Two passages from Philo are worth quoting in full. The first is his description of the Sabbath practices of the Palestinian Essenes:

> For that day has been set apart to be kept holy and on it they abstain from all other work and proceed to sacred spots which they call synagogues. There, arranged in rows according to their ages, the younger below the elder, they sit decorously as befits the occasion with attentive ears. Then one takes the books and reads aloud and another of especial proficiency comes forward and expounds what is not understood (εἶθ᾽ εἶς μέν τις τὰς βίβλους ἀναγινώσκει λαβὼν ἕτερος δὲ τῶν ἐμπειροτάτων ὅσα μὴ γνώριμα παρελθὼν ἀναδιδάσκει). For most of their philosophical study takes the form of allegory, and in this they emulate the tradition of the past.[68]

Here we have a picture of a very orderly gathering. The seating in rows according to their age is similar to Philo's description of the Therapeutae[69] and to Qumran.[70] There does not appear to be any particular requirement placed on the ability of the person reading the Scripture; in comparison, the one who then goes on to explain it must be suitably proficient. Again, this is similar to the Therapeutae where the 'senior among them who also had the fullest knowledge of the doctrines' teaches the community;[71] in both these sources this person 'comes forward' in order to carry out his teaching.[72] The architectural remains of Palestinian synagogue buildings examined in the previous chapter indicate that the teacher would move out of his seat on the stone benches, and use the central space to carry this out. Finally, in *Special Laws*, Philo describes the teacher as one with 'special experience' who 'rises' to teach.[73]

The second reference is extant only in the writing of Eusebius. In a discussion on laws, Philo describes the practices at a Sabbath gathering probably in Alexandria:

> What then did he do? He required them to assemble in the same place on these seventh days, and sitting together in a respectful and orderly

---

67   See Schiffman, 'Early History', p. 47. Leonhardt, *Jewish Worship*, pp. 82–83, also p. 293. It could also be that Philo is describing two different things, the 'synagogue' and the 'house of study' (*bet midrash*). However, in the first century CE there is simply no evidence to support such a distinction, see the discussion in Claußen, *Versammlung*, pp. 217–18.

68   Philo, *Omn. Prob. Lib.*, 81–82.

69   Philo, *Vit. Cont.*, 30.

70   1QS 6.8-9.

71   Philo, *Vit. Cont.*, 31.

72   For other references where παρέρχομαι is used to indicate 'coming out to speak' see LSJ, 'παρέρχομαι', VI.

73   Philo, *Spec. Leg.*, 2.62; cf. Acts 13.

manner hear the laws read so that none should be ignorant of them. And indeed they do always assemble and sit together, most of them in silence except when it is the practice to add something to signify approval of what is read. But some priest who is present or one of the elders reads the holy laws to them and expounds them point by point till about the late afternoon, when they depart having gained both expert knowledge of the holy laws and considerable advance in piety.[74]

In common with some of our other references, the responsibility for teaching the community falls on a leader of the community, either a priest or an elder. Here this person also reads the passage of Scripture. The congregation apparently sit passively only interjecting to show approval of particular parts of the reading and perhaps the homily as well.

One way in which the practice of the Egyptian 'synagogues' would have been different from that of Palestine is that the readings would probably have been done in Greek. Philo could not read Hebrew,[75] and appears to have viewed the Septuagint as equal in value: 'The clearest proof of this is that, if Chaldeans have learned Greek, or Greeks Chaldean, and read both versions, the Chaldean and the translation, they regard them with awe and reverence as sisters, or rather one and the same, both in matter and words'.[76] It may also be that in some Greek-speaking Jewish communities within Palestine the preferred language would also have been Greek.

3.4. *Archaeological Evidence*

Some observations can also be made from the archaeological evidence available to us. Most obvious is the 'synagogue' complex described in the Theodotos inscription. Part of the function of this 'synagogue' was 'the reading of the law and the teaching of the commandments (εἰς ἀνάγνωσιν νόμου καὶ εἰς διδαχὴν ἐντολῶν)'.[77] It would appear that two separate components are described, the reading and then the exposition of the commandments. In view of our other sources, this most likely refers to a connected reading and exposition, although it could refer to separate teaching that took place in one of the other rooms of the complex.

Perrot argues that there is a contrast in function between the Diaspora and Palestine: 'May it not be said that unlike the *proseuchae* perhaps of the Diaspora, which appeared primarily as "houses of prayer", the

---

74   Philo, *Hypoth.*, 7.12-13.

75   C. Perrot, 'The Reading of the Bible in the Ancient Synagogue', in M.J. Mulder (ed.), *Mikra: Text, Translation, Reading & Interpretation of the Hebrew Bible in Ancient Judaism & Early Christianity*, (CRINT; Assen: van Gorcum, 1988), pp. 137–59 (155).

76   Philo, *Vit. Mos.*, 2.40. Cf., *m. Meg.* 1.8; 2.1; *m. Yad.* 4.5.

77   Further evidence that Scripture reading was an integral part of a 'synagogue' gathering is seen from the remains of scrolls found at Masada, Y. Yadin, 'The Excavation of Masada 1963/64, Preliminary Report', *IEJ* 15 (1965), pp. 1–120 (103–14), details the finds.

Palestinian synagogues aimed originally at responding to a need for instruction?' Comparing the architectural layout of Gamla, Masada and Herodium, he points out that these 'ancient synagogues were not oriented towards Jerusalem but towards the reader and lecturer in the middle of the building'.[78] While Perrot is right to highlight the differences between 'synagogues' in different geographical locations, it is not possible to go as far as he suggests. The focus of the Palestinian buildings does seem to be the centre of the room, but it could just as easily be argued that the purpose was to allow easy discourse between members of the assembly who could easily face one another. Also, if the raised podium in the building at Ostia was used to read and teach from, the building then became much more like a modern lecture hall.[79]

3.5. *Targumim*

As indicated above, it is likely that in many Diaspora 'synagogues' the reading of Scripture would have been carried out in Greek. However, certain groups may well have contained a large number of people who understood Hebrew (e.g., the 'synagogue' of the Hebrews in Rome?) and here the reading was possibly done in Hebrew. Within Palestine, the opposite is likely: most reading in Hebrew, while a few Greek-speaking 'synagogues' would also have existed within the country. Assessing the usage of languages within Palestine is difficult. Certainly in the first century CE Hellenized cities had been established in which Greek would have been spoken. Jerusalem also would have been a cosmopolitan city where Greek was used regularly, as can be seen from the fact that one third of the inscriptions from the city are in this language.[80] When we move to the area of Galilee a more complex picture emerges. While the populations of cities such as Sepphoris and Tiberias would have had some knowledge of Greek, whether other towns and villages also used the language is less clear.[81] Epigraphic evidence, although helpful, is also liable to give us a distorted view of the situation if used incorrectly: for example, burial inscriptions may be more formal and not reflect the

---

78   Perrot, 'Reading of the Bible', p. 150.

79   See below, 5.2.

80   For a discussion of the relative uses of Latin, Hebrew, Aramaic and Greek see, L.I. Levine, *Judaism and Hellenism in Antiquity* (Seattle: University of Washington Press, 1998), pp. 72–84.

81   While noting some evidence of Greek in first-century Sepphoris and Tiberias, E. Meyers and M. Chancey argue that this should not be understood to reflect widespread use throughout Galilee, 'How Jewish was Sepphoris in Jesus' Time?', *BARev* 26.4 (2000), pp. 19–33 (33).

everyday use of language.[82] It appears that Aramaic would have been the most prevalent language in the area of Galilee, and that Hebrew was also quite widely used, although perhaps for more formal occasions. Upper Galilee was more rural and less involved in trade; therefore, in this area Greek seems to have made fewer inroads.[83]

Whether the reading was then translated into the vernacular is a point of dispute. The older consensus, that such readings existed, was again built on rabbinic foundations.[84] The extant targumim manuscripts we have are dated between the seventh and sixteenth centuries CE and contain material that clearly dates to a late period, for example, a reference to the wife of Muhammad. Within other rabbinic sources, however, we have a reference to Rabbi Gamaliel, who dates to the first century CE, reading the targum in Tiberias. This reference also cites an earlier tradition that a Job targum had existed on the Temple Mount in the time of Gamaliel's grandfather.[85] Whether this reflects the practice of this time is difficult to judge, and even if it did, the scene does not take place within a 'synagogue' setting.

Anthony York, in an article critiquing the view that the Palestinian Targum was contemporaneous with the New Testament, nevertheless points out that there are good reasons to think that some targumim are indeed from the same period or before.[86] Levine gives four reasons for believing that the targumim date from a much earlier period. i) Fragments of Aramaic targumim of Leviticus and Job have been found at Qumran (4Q tgLev; 11Q tgJob; 4Q tgJob).[87] ii) Many studies have found similarities between targumic traditions with those found in other literature dating to around the first century CE. iii) Linguistic similarities have been found between the targumim and Qumran Aramaic, suggesting a common historical setting. iv) A great deal of discussion takes place within rabbinic material, some apparently among second-century sages; later tannaitic sages were not initiating a new practice, but rather were commenting upon,

---

82   See the criticisms of Meyers by S. Freyne, *Galilee from Alexander the Great to Hadrian 323 B.C.E. to 135 C.E.: A Study of Second Temple Judaism* (Notre Dame: University of Notre Dame Press, 1980), p. 141, and the well-advised caution of R.A. Horsley, *Galilee: History, Politics, People* (Valley Forge: Trinity, 1995), pp. 247–50.

83   See, M.A. Chancey, *Greco-Roman Culture and the Galilee of Jesus* (SNTSMS, 134; Cambridge: Cambridge University Press, 2005), pp. 122–65; Horsley, *Galilee: History, Politics, People*, p. 249.

84   E.g., Schürer, *HJP*, vol. 2, pp. 452–53.

85   *T. Shabb.* 13.2; *b. Shabb.* 115a; *y. Shabb.* 16,1,15c. Cf. the discussion of what will defile the hands in *m. Yad.* 4.5.

86   A.D. York, 'The Dating of Targumic Literature', *JSJ* 5 (1974), pp. 49–62 (60–61).

87   M. Sokoloff dates it to the late second century BCE, *The Targum to Job from Qumran Cave XI* (Ramat-Gan: Bar-Ilan University, 1974), p. 9. It should be noted that it is unlikely that a targum of Job would have been used in a 'synagogue' setting, and probably existed for private study.

critiquing, and shaping an already existing institution.[88] Certainly the fragments from Qumran show that targumim did exist in the first century CE, although again the difficulty is knowing whether they were used as a translation of the 'synagogue' reading prior to 70 CE.[89]

From the information we have, it is likely that in most Diaspora 'synagogues' the reading would have been made in Greek and therefore there was no need for a translation. In parts of Palestine the reading would have been in Hebrew, and again no translation would have been required.[90] However, in areas of Palestine where the population more naturally spoke Aramaic or Greek, the Scripture reading that took place within the 'synagogue' may have needed a translation. Whether these targumim were literal translations or were more fluid, acting as a form of commentary, is uncertain.

3.6. *Conclusion on Reading*

The reading of Scripture was clearly a central component, probably *the* central component of the Sabbath gathering in the 'synagogue'. Although there may be apologetic reasons for portraying the Torah-reading ceremonies in didactic terms similar to the Hellenistic schools of philosophy, nonetheless the emphasis on teaching throughout our sources is clear. The purpose of the Torah reading was to impart knowledge, gain an understanding of how God had acted in the past towards his people and to 'advance in piety'.[91] The question then becomes, should such an act be described as worship? Runesson points out that even if we accept McKay's premise, that Torah reading is the only communal activity carried out by Jews on the Sabbath, the fact that Roman decrees identified these as 'sacred rites' must mean that they were at least perceived as fulfilling more than just an educational role.[92] Similarly, Philo describes the activities taking place on a 'holy day' in a 'holy place' indicating that this was not a secular activity.[93] Further, we have pointed out above that the Torah scrolls were recognized by both Jews and Gentiles as sacred, and that the presence of the Torah had a direct bearing on a building being seen as sacred. Therefore, it would seem likely that the study of the Torah was perceived as an act of worship.[94]

---

88   Levine, *Ancient Synagogue*, pp. 148–49; *idem*, 'Nature and Origin', p. 444, n. 78.

89   Perrot, 'Reading of the Bible', p. 155. See also Binder, *Temple Courts*, p. 401, n. 40.

90   In this regard it is interesting to note that all the scrolls of biblical texts found at Masada are in Hebrew.

91   Philo, *Hypoth.*, 7.13.

92   Runesson, *Origins*, p. 195.

93   Philo, *Omn. Prob. Lib.*, 81–82.

94   The importance of the study of Scripture is highlighted in *m. Abot.* 3.6: 'R. Halafta b. Dosa of Kefar Hanania said: If ten men sit together and occupy themselves in the Law, the

Whether some form of fixed lectionary cycle(s) existed during the Second Temple period is much debated; on the current evidence we cannot build a picture of which Scripture was read on specific occasions.[95] However, the suggestion of Reif that festivals and the Sabbaths around them would have been the first to have specific readings seems likely.[96] We have no indication that the person who read the Scripture should be of a particular position in the community or have any special training: the only requirement apparently being that they could be clearly heard. The position of the teacher was more clearly defined; some of our references indicate that a priest or elder should teach the community, others specify that it should be someone competent, or the senior member. It would appear that the role of teacher within the community was important. The correct interpretation of Scripture or of passing on the 'philosophy of their fathers' was a central element of the practices of the 'synagogue'.

What form the sermon took and to what extent there would have been similarities or differences between various communities is again difficult to substantiate. As will be argued below, there is evidence of a broad stream of biblically based material upon which different communities may well have built their construction of worship practices. How the sermon was received and whether there was a debate or discussion is clearer. Binder's suggestion that Paul is presented as always arguing in the 'synagogues' is wrong; διαλέγομαι means simply 'to address'.[97] But there was disputation within the 'synagogue':[98] Jesus' teaching in his home town is greeted with disapproval by those who heard him, followed by a discussion among themselves;[99] and there is a discussion between Jesus and the Jews in the 'synagogue' in Capernaum.[100] Philo also indicates that discussion took place, but generally presents the 'synagogue' gatherings as more orderly.[101] While we have noted that Philo may have reason to present

---

Divine Presence (the Shekinah) rests among them'. This has parallels in Mt. 18.20, and it seems unlikely that rabbinic authors would have copied the Gospel writers; therefore, it is likely that this idea has a first-century provenance.

95   See Perrot, 'Reading of the Bible', pp. 149–54; R.M Campbell, '*Parashiyyot* and their Implications for Dating the Fragment-Targums', in P.V.M. Flesher (ed.), *Targum and Scripture: Studies in Aramaic Translation and Interpretation* (SAIS, 2; Leiden: Brill, 2002), pp. 105–14; S.C. Reif, *Judaism and Hebrew Prayer: New Perspectives on Jewish Liturgical History* (Cambridge: Cambridge University Press, 1993), pp. 63–64. For a more positive view on the existence of lectionary cycles, see, M.D. Goulder, *The Evangelists' Calendar: A Lectionary Explanation of the Development of Scripture* (London: SPCK, 1978), pp. 19–51; Levine, *Ancient Synagogue*, p. 140.

96   S.C. Reif, 'The Early Liturgy of the Synagogue,' in *CHJ*, pp. 852–76 (352).

97   Binder, *Temple Courts*, p. 403. See the discussion in *TDNT*, vol. 2, p. 94.

98   Acts 18.6.

99   Mk 6.2-3.

100   Jn 6.25-59.

101   Philo, *Somn.*, 2.127.

the Jewish gatherings as very sober and orderly affairs, here, nonetheless, the architecture may be suggestive. The Palestinian buildings we examined clearly have their focus in the centre of the building which facilitates an easy exchange between those assembled. In contrast, the buildings at Ostia and Delos are modelled on voluntary associations and are less conducive to such lively debate.

4. *Prayer*

4.1. *Introduction*

Generally scholarly discussion of Jewish prayer around the turn of the era has focused on the formation of the *Amidah*.[102] Scholars have debated whether this was in existence before 70 CE, in some form, or whether it was a creation of the rabbis of Javneh. However, in recent scholarship a question has arisen over whether public communal prayer of any kind existed before 70 CE. Sometimes the debate has revolved around Sabbath worship,[103] at other times communal prayer more generally.[104] One of the potential difficulties of this discussion has been defining the terms or focus of the debate.[105] The focus of this chapter is to establish whether there was any pattern of worship in the first-century 'synagogue'; as a result I will include any evidence of prayer in the 'synagogue' whether that be on the Sabbath or any other day of the week, and will include references to prayer by individuals as well as groups.

As has been seen above, one of the most common terms for the 'synagogue' in the Diaspora is προσευχή and many scholars have pointed out that such a term suggests that these buildings would have been used for prayer of some description. Although this might appear a sensible

---

102   This prayer is also referred to as the *Tefillah*, and the *Shemoneh 'Esreh*, see Levine, *Ancient Synagogue*, p. 510 n. 32.

103   E.g., McKay, *Sabbath and Synagogue, passim.*

104   E. Fleischer argues that although there is clear evidence that piety through personal prayer was held in high esteem, communal prayer is not described nor is it ever linked with the 'synagogue,' either in Palestine or the Diaspora, 'On the Beginnings of Obligatory Jewish Prayer', *Tarbiz* 59 (1990), 397–425, [Hebrew]. However, he defines such prayer as being communal, an absolute obligation and formulaic, (e.g., see pp. 401, 413, 424). L.I. Levine agues that communal prayer was not part of the worship of the Palestinian 'synagogue' until after 70 CE, 'The Second Temple Synagogue: The Formative Years', in L.I. Levine (ed.), *The Synagogue in Late Antiquity* (Philadelphia: The American Schools of Oriental Research, 1987), pp. 7–31 (19–20); *idem*, 'Nature and Origin', pp. 444–45; *idem*, *Judaism and Hellenism*, p. 165. Recently, Levine has a slightly more nuanced account of Palestinian 'synagogue' prayer: 'While there is no evidence for communal prayers in the *typical* synagogues of Judea throughout our period, such prayers did, in fact, exist in certain specific settings', *Ancient Synagogue*, p. 155 (italics mine).

105   See the discussion in the introduction to this chapter, and comments on Levine in the section on Tiberias below.

assumption, when we go to our sources we find very little evidence for prayer around the turn of the era.[106] This lack of evidence has, justifiably, caused some to reassess whether communal liturgical prayer existed at this time. Nevertheless, Donald Binder, citing many sources, makes the point that prayer and sacrifice were prevalent in the ANE at this time: 'Against such a backdrop, even if our sources made no explicit mention of prayer and worship within the synagogues, we would have reason to suspect that prayers were being offered there'.[107] Burtchaell, however, argues that prayer was not as important as sacrifice to Jews: we should not think back from a Christian perspective.[108] This caution is a fair one, but how much access did a Jew, perhaps living in the Diaspora, have to sacrifice? There is certainly evidence of prayer taking place at the time the sacrifice was going on in Jerusalem, with Ezra, Daniel and Judith all choosing the time of sacrifice to pray.[109]

4.2. *Josephus*
4.2.1. *Asia Minor*
4.2.1.1. *Sardis*

One of the decrees recorded by Josephus which we have examined previously gives additional information in respect to prayer. The people of Sardis are to have a place in which 'they may gather together with their wives and children and offer their ancestral prayers and sacrifices to God (εὐχὰς καὶ θυσίας τῷ θεῷ)'.[110] These activities are also to take place when the Jews, apparently all members of the family, come together on 'stated days', presumably the Sabbaths.[111] This decree obviously relates to public worship as any private devotion would not need to be regulated in such a manner. Here prayer as part of the worship of the community is clearly evidenced, and probably took place on the Sabbath. This goes against McKay's general thesis and it should be noted that she fails to discuss this passage.[112] The more puzzling part of this decree is the

---

106   One reason for the lack of evidence may be that the writing of prayers was discouraged: 'those who write down benedictions are as though they burnt the Law-book', *b. Shabb.* 115.

107   Binder, *Temple Courts*, p. 406; cf. E.J. Bickerman, 'The Civic Prayer for Jerusalem', *HTR* 55 (1962), pp. 163–85 (174–76).

108   J.T. Burtchaell, *From Synagogue to Church: Public Services and Offices in the Earliest Christian Communities* (Cambridge: Cambridge University Press, 1992), p. 203.

109   Dan. 9.21; Ezra 9.5; Jdt. 9.1. *Sifre Deuteronomy* also compares prayer to sacrifice, see Levine, *Ancient Synagogue*, p. 516, as does Ps. 141.2. Sir. 50.15-21, Lk. 1.10 and Josephus, *Apion*, 2.193-98, note prayer taking place in the temple at the time of offerings, cf. *m. Tamid* 5.1.

110   Josephus, *Ant.*, 14.260-61, See above chapter 2, 3.2.1.2.

111   Claußen, *Versammlung*, p. 210. Although it is possible that this may refer to new moon celebrations; see Binder, *Temple Courts*, p. 418.

112   The only reference comes in a footnote, McKay, *Sabbath and Synagogue*, p. 78 n. 61.

reference to sacrifices.[113] In the Loeb translation, Marcus suggests that sacrifices should be understood 'in the larger sense of "offerings," '[114] and this is the way most scholars have understood it.[115] Some, however, have suggested that it could be possible that actual sacrifices are meant.[116]

4.2.1.2. *Halicarnassus*

As was noted in Chapter 2, I have argued elsewhere that the decree issued in favour of the Jews in Halicarnassus allowed them to gather and perform their sacred rites on the Sabbaths and to offer prayers beside the sea.[117] As can be seen from the references in Josephus above and from other evidence cited, such an understanding of this decree falls broadly in line with these other sources. What it further does is tie the saying of prayers directly with Sabbath activities, contra McKay. As in Sardis, both men and women are mentioned as having these rights.

---

113 One possible explanation is the similarities between synagogue buildings and pagan temples in which sacrifices would have taken place. We see in Roman authors the inability to differentiate between synagogue buildings and pagan temples and it may be that because the Jews tied some of their prayers, particularly the public prayers of the 'synagogue', with the times of sacrifice in the temple that to an outsider, who did not understand their references, it appears that they are talking about prayers *and* sacrifices, when in fact they are talking about the prayers that accompanied the sacrifice. In the 'synagogue' the sacrifice could not take place but the prayers continued. Cf. Dolabella's letter to the Ephesians granting that they could 'come together for sacred and holy rites in accordance with their law' and to 'make offerings for their sacrifices', recorded by Josephus in *Ant.*, 14.225-27. M. Pucci Ben Zeev argues that this points to the authenticity of the decree from Sardis: 'Had Josephus written the decree by himself, he would have mentioned prayers but with all probability would not have added Θυσίας', *Jewish Rights in the Roman World: The Greek and Roman Documents Quoted by Josephus Flavius* (TSAJ, 74; Tübingen: Mohr Siebeck, 1998), p. 223.

114 R. Marcus, *Josephus*, LCL, vol. 7, p. 589 n. d.

115 Binder, *Temple Courts*, p. 407; Claußen, *Versammlung*, pp. 210–12; Levine suggests that it could refer to the collection sent to Jerusalem by the Jews of Sardis, *Ancient Synagogue*, p. 130 n. 31; See also S.J.D. Cohen, 'Pagan and Christian Evidence on the Ancient Synagogue', in Levine, *The Synagogue in Late Antiquity*, pp. 159–81 (166).

116 E.P. Sanders, 'Common Judaism and the Synagogue in the First Century', in S. Fine (ed.), *Jews, Christians and Polytheists*, pp. 1–17 (p. 7). I. von Görtz-Wrisberg thinks that this may point in the direction of activities normally done in the temple being performed in the Diaspora, 'A Sabbath Service in Ostia: What Do We Know about the Ancient Synagogal Service?', in Olsson, Mitternacht and Brandt, *Synagogue of Ancient Ostia*, pp. 167–202 (172), and M. Goodman comments: 'it is possible that this reference to sacrificial cult reflected a misunderstanding of Jewish religious practice by the city authorities, but, if so, it is worth noting that Josephus was not sufficiently taken aback to comment', 'Sacred Space in Diaspora Judaism', in B. Isaac and A. Oppenheimer (eds), *Studies on the Jewish Diaspora in the Hellenistic and Roman Periods* (Te'uda, 12; Tel-Aviv: Ramot, 1996), pp. 1–16 (5). See also Runesson who goes further, suggesting that the building that the Jews were permitted to erect was a temple and that sacrifices took place there, *Origins*, pp. 465–66. Prayer and sacrifice are also linked by Philo, *Spec. Leg.*, 3.171; *Deus Imm*, 7–9.

117 S.K. Catto, 'Does προσευχὰς ποιεῖσθαι, in Josephus' *Antiquities of the Jews* 14.257-8, Mean "Build Places of Prayer"?', *JSJ* 35 (2004), pp. 159–68.

4.2.2. *Palestine*
4.2.2.1. *Tiberias*

Another reference, which was previously discussed in the chapter on literary sources, takes place in Tiberias. Recounting an event in his life, Josephus makes clear reference to prayer in a προσευχή. He describes how some men had been sent to the city from Jerusalem in order to capture him and bring him back, or, if he resisted, to kill him.[118] The events in the προσευχή take place over three days from the Sabbath to Monday morning, recounting a series of meetings during which those from Jerusalem try to convince the local population that Josephus is an unsuitable commander to have. On the Sunday, one of their number, Ananias, proposed that a public fast should be announced and that they should reassemble on the Monday morning 'in order to attest before God their conviction that without his aid no armour could avail them'.[119] After the group had convened, Josephus recounts, 'We were proceeding with the ordinary service and engaged in prayer (ἤδη ἡμῶν τὰ νόμιμα ποιούντων καὶ πρὸς εὐχὰς τραπομένων), when Jesus rose and began to question me'.[120] Certainly here we have prayer taking place within a προσευχή, but is this communal prayer, or were those gathered just making their morning devotions?[121] Interestingly, McKay seems to accept that this was some form of corporate prayer, but notes that these prayers could be interrupted without comment from Josephus.[122] However, Binder has argued that the Greek construction of this sentence should be translated, 'When we had performed the customary service and had engaged in prayer, Jesus rose and began to question me',[123] indicating an act that had finished. This also seems to make good sense of the situation in which Jesus was trying to delay Josephus until the arrival of John of Gischala and his troops. Only after the prayer session had finished would this have been necessary. However, Binder's further suggestion that 'Josephus means to suggest that some well-established order of worship was followed',[124] may be overstating the case. Nevertheless, νόμιμα does seem to carry the meaning of customary which would suggest that this was a

---

118   Josephus, *Life*, 197–202.

119   *Ibid.*, 290.

120   *Ibid.*, 295.

121   So E.P. Sanders, 'Common Judaism', p. 10; *idem*, *Judaism: Practice and Belief 63 BCE – 66CE* (London: SCM Press, 1992), p. 207.

122   Because it takes place on a Monday and not a Sabbath, McKay excludes it from her consideration of Sabbath worship, considering it 'daily prayer', *Sabbath and Synagogue*, p. 84.

123   Binder, *Temple Courts*, p. 411.

124   Binder argues that νόμιμηα means customary, traditional or legal, *ibid.*, p. 411. Sanders, however, thinks that it does not refer to the regulation of the meeting, but to the regulations relating to the daily morning prayers, 'Common Judaism', p. 10.

pattern of service that would have been understood by Josephus' readers,[125] and that if such a customary practice is associated with public fasts then it may well be that it would also have taken place within a gathering on the Sabbath.[126] Here it is probably better to remain cautious and state that we certainly have praying in a building called a προσευχή, and that this was *probably* something that was carried out communally.

4.2.2.2. *Jerusalem*

One final reference in Josephus, which we referred to in Chapter 2, comes in a section from Agatharchides:

> The people known as the Jews, who inhabit the most strongly fortified of cities, called by the natives Jerusalem, have a custom of abstaining from work every seventh day; on those occasions they neither bear arms nor take any agricultural operations in hand, nor engage in any other form of public service, but pray with outstretched hands in the temples (ἐν τοῖς ἱεροῖς) until the evening.[127]

Again we have a reference to prayer taking place on the Sabbath, reportedly in Jerusalem, although it has been suggested that this may reflect Agatharchides own surroundings in Alexandria.[128] The place that these prayers took place is recorded as 'the temples', most likely referring to synagogue buildings,[129] and, as Binder points out, Josephus' comments, after quoting Agatharchides, appear to show that he was in agreement with the veracity of this report.[130]

4.3. *Philo*
4.3.1. *Alexandria*

After his description of the pogroms of Alexandria, Philo notes that the Jews were able to celebrate the removal of Flaccus and the consequent renewal of freedoms for themselves. He states that they left their houses:

> And when they learnt of the arrest and that Flaccus was now within the toils, with hands outstretched to heaven they sang hymns and led songs of triumph to God who watches over human affairs (προτείνοντες τὰς

125 Gört-Wrisberg, 'Sabbath Service', pp. 172–73.

126 D.K. Falk, 'Jewish Prayer Literature and the Jerusalem Church', in R. Bauckham (ed.), *The Book of Acts in its Palestinian Setting* (*TBAFCS*, vol. 4), pp. 267–301 (279).

127 Josephus, *Apion*, 1.209.

128 McKay does not discuss this reference in *Sabbath and Synagogue*; however, in a paper given to a 1997 SBL meeting, she points out that the reason she does not comment on it is that it refers to Temple prayer, 'Who or What were Synagogues: the People, the Building or the Function?'.

129 On the meaning of temple here, see the discussion above in Chapter 2, 4.1

130 See *Apion*, 1.212; Binder, *Temple Courts*, p. 412. See also Claußen, *Versammlung*, p. 211.

χεῖρας εἰς οὐρανὸν ὕμνουν καὶ παιᾶνας ἐξῆρχον εἰς τὸν ἔφορον θεὸν τῶν ἀνθρωπίνων πραγμάτων). 'We do not rejoice, O Lord,' they said, 'at the punishment meted to an enemy, for we have been taught by the holy laws to have human sympathy. But we justly give thanks to Thee because Thou has taken pity and compassion on us and relieved our unbroken and ceaseless affliction.' All night long they continued to sing hymns and songs of praise and at dawn pouring out through the gates, they made their way to the parts of the beach near at hand, since their meeting-houses had been taken from them and standing in the purest place cried aloud with one accord (τὰς γὰρ προσευχὰς ἀφῄρηντο κἂν τῷ καθαρωτάτῳ στάντες ἀνεβόησαν ὁμοθυμαδόν).[131]

There then follows a prayer made by the people, again thanking God.

There are a number of issues that arise from this account. First, the Jews act together in an act of praise toward God, thanking him for deliverance. Philo states that they stood together and 'cried aloud with one accord'. The fact that the act of gratitude towards God was a communal activity is significant as some scholars have recently questioned whether the Jews would have carried out worship in any way in unison.[132] While this is not an organized session of worship, but rather a spontaneous reaction to the arrest of Flaccus, nonetheless, the fact that they come together for this spontaneous act would suggest that it was an activity they were used to doing together. Second, it would appear that the way they showed their gratitude was to sing and to pray.[133] Again, the fact that this is how they worshipped God on this occasion might suggest that they were used to worshipping together and the most likely occasion for such an activity would be during festivals[134] or at Sabbath gatherings.[135] Levine, on surveying the evidence of prayer in the Second Temple period,

131 Philo, *Flacc.*, 121–22. Here the translation of καθαρωτάτῳ does not follow the LCL, see section 2.2.1 above.

132 See Sanders, although he does allow that the community at Qumran may have prayed their set prayers together, *Judaism: Practice and Belief*, p. 207.

133 McKay contends that the hymns sung should not be seen as the actual or usual hymns of the Alexandrian Jews, but were placed in their mouths by Philo to further his arguments with Caligula. She does, however, concede that they are very similar to hymns of thanks in Psalms and 2 Maccabees, *Sabbath and Synagogue*, p. 69. Van der Horst makes the important point that we should not perceive prayer too narrowly: it could refer to a prose prayer, but may also include a hymn of praise that was sung, 'Was the Synagogue', p. 31. It may be that this is how we should understand the hymns described by Philo, particularly as we are told that they did so with their arms outstretched, (for the connection of prayer with hands outstretched see *3 Macc.* 5.25; Josephus, *Apion*, 1.209; 1 Tim. 2.8). Cf. Burkert's description of similar Greek practices, *Greek Religion*, p. 75.

134 Philo reports that during the Passover celebrations, 'the guests assembled for the banquet have been cleansed by purificatory lustrations, and are there not as in other festive gatherings, to indulge the belly with wine and viands, but to fulfil with prayers and hymns the custom handed down by their fathers', *Spec. Leg.*, 2.148.

135 Görtz-Wrisberg, 'Sabbath Service', p. 171.

including Philo, concludes: 'None mentions public communal prayer'.[136] However, it would appear that this is exactly what is happening in Alexandria. Third, in the morning they went to the shore to continue to praise 'since their meeting-houses had been taken from them'. It seems that in normal circumstances the place where this act of thanksgiving would have taken place would have been the προσευχαί, but as these had been destroyed they were not available and so the people go to the next best place, the shore.[137]

A final point in connection with this account is that it happened at the time of the festival of Sukkot; however, Philo points out that because of the persecutions being suffered, 'nothing at all of the festal proceedings was being carried out'.[138] Görtz-Wrisberg notes that, 'both the yearly pilgrimage festival, Sukkot, and the saying of prayers were seen as activities intimately connected with the Jerusalem Temple', going on to suggest that, 'this indicates that Temple activities may have been practised in the Diaspora'.[139] Heather McKay is far more cautious, preferring to see the joyful response of the people as a 'one-off'.[140] It seems that both authors are, to some extent, correct. It would indeed appear that while the Sukkot festival was being carried out in Jerusalem, some kind of local celebration also took place in Alexandria; however, the particular prayer and praise that Philo reports probably come directly as a result of the arrest of Flaccus and we should be careful about associating it too closely with Sukkot.[141]

---

136 Levine, *Ancient Synagogue*, p. 152.
137 Leonhardt, *Jewish Worship*, p. 79.
138 Philo, *Flacc.*, 117.
139 Görtz-Wrisberg, 'Sabbath Service', p. 171. Binder, whose major hypothesis is that the 'synagogue' was to a great extent modelled on the Jerusalem temple, fails to make this connection, (see below).
140 McKay, *Sabbath and Synagogue*, p. 69.
141 As well as the reference above, an inscription from Berenice mentions a meeting taking place in a 'synagogue' on the feast of Sukkot (see J.M. Reynolds, 'Inscriptions', in J.A. Lloyd (ed.), *Excavations at Sidi Khrebish Benghazi (Berenice)*, vol. 1, *Buildings, Coins, Inscriptions, Architectural Decoration* [Supplements to Libya Antiqua, 5; Hertford: Stephen Austin and Sons, 1977], pp. 233–54 [no. 17]) and, although not specifically tied to worship in the 'synagogue', Philo's description of Yom Kippur is also worth noting. He writes: 'the holy day is entirely devoted to prayers and supplications (λιταῖς καὶ ἱκεσίαις), and men from morn to eve employ their leisure in nothing else but offering petitions (εὐχάς) of humble entreaty in which they seek earnestly to propitiate God and ask for remission of their sins, voluntarily and involuntarily, and entertain bright hopes looking not to their own merits but to the gracious nature of Him Who sets pardon before chastisement', *Spec. Leg.*, 2.196; cf. *Vit. Mos.*, 2.24. This takes place on the day which is described by Philo, following the LXX, as a Sabbath of Sabbaths, leading Binder to ask: 'If diaspora Jews customarily met in the synagogues on the regular Sabbaths, how much more would they have met there on the "Sabbath of Sabbaths"?' *Temple Courts*, p. 420.

4.3.2. *Egypt outside Alexandria*

Philo details some of the corporate activities of the Therapeutic community. As well as Sabbath meetings[142] he describes their feasts held at Pentecost, which, it appears, they repeated every 49 days,[143] and at which food and entertainment were enjoyed. Both men and women were present at this event, although they sat separately.[144] As part of this gathering they prayed before they ate, which was followed by an exposition of a passage of Scripture, perhaps by the president (πρόεδρος).[145] As well as the speaker choosing a passage for discussion, a difficult section could be proposed by a member of the gathering. Then a number of the congregation would rise to sing a hymn to God, either of their own composition or one that was known, before the whole group joined in antiphonal singing.[146] The final part of the gathering came at sunrise when again they raised their hands and prayed before returning to their individual dwellings. Although Philo does not make clear where these activities took place, Binder's suggestion that this would have been in an ancillary room of the synagogue is possible.[147]

4.4. *New Testament*

As in our other primary sources, the New Testament provides little information regarding prayer in the 'synagogue', with the main references to prayer coming either in the context of the temple or the home. The only mention of prayer in relation to a 'synagogue' comes in Jesus' instructions in Mt. 6.5-6 which we noted in Chapter 2:

> And whenever you pray, do not be like the hypocrites; for they love to stand and pray in the synagogues (ἐν ταῖς συναγωγαῖς) and at the street corners, so that they may be seen by others. Truly I tell you, they have received their reward. But whenever you pray, go into your room and shut the door and pray to your Father who is in secret; and your Father who sees in secret will reward you.[148]

Heinemann argues that here Jesus is speaking against the fixed prayer of the 'synagogue',[149] while Fleischer and McKay suggest this shows that a

---

142   See above, Chapter 2, 2.2.1.2.

143   Philo, *Vit. Cont.*, 65. Cf. Binder, *Temple Courts*, p. 469.

144   Philo, *Vit. Cont.*, 69.

145   *Ibid.*, 79.

146   *Ibid.*, 83–85.

147   Binder, *Temple Courts*, p. 418. The description is very similar to the one Josephus gives of the Essenes, *War*, 2.129-31.

148   This account is only in Matthew and therefore we should allow that it may reflect practices of ca. 85 CE.

149   J. Heinemann, *Prayer in the Talmud: Forms and Patterns* (SJ, 9; Berlin: Walter De Gruyter, 1977), p. 192.

'synagogue' was an unsuitable place for prayer.[150] However, the fact that the 'synagogue' is paired with the street corner, combined with the instructions on almsgiving in the previous verses, would indicate that what is being condemned is unnecessary ostentation before others while carrying out private prayer, not communal prayer.[151]

4.5. *The Dead Sea Scrolls*

In discussing the prayer texts of Qumran, Talmon, reflecting an earlier perspective, wrote:

> The propagation of institutionalized prayer among the Qumran Covenanters cannot fully and adequately be explained as arising solely from the historical circumstances of their dissociation from the Temple of Jerusalem and its sacrificial worship. In addition socioreligious factors presumably played a role in this development. One of these, it would appear, was their 'commune ideology' which seriously weakened the position of the individual as a self-contained unit in the group, stressing instead his role and his function as a component of the community's 'corporate personality.'[152]

Despite showing clear connections between the prayers of Qumran and those that developed in the Tannaitic and Amoraic periods,[153] Talmon concludes that 'no definite historical interdependence can be established between the emergence of institutionalized prayer at Qumran and in mainstream Judaism'.[154] While proving any clear historical dependence is difficult, if some of the prayers from Qumran reflect a more widespread practice in Second Temple Judaism then it may be better to conclude that this broader band of communal prayer, often drawing on similar biblical themes, ultimately did go on to form the basis of a more fixed liturgy in later times.

In more recent studies of the DSS, scholars have identified some of the prayer texts as reflecting pre-sectarian material.[155] This clearly has major

---

150   Fleischer, 'On the Beginnings', p. 405; McKay, *Sabbath and Synagogue*, p. 172.

151   R. Beckwith, 'The Daily and Weekly Worship of the Primitive Church', *EvQ* 56 (1984), pp. 65–80 (72); L. Morris, *The Gospel According to Matthew* (Grand Rapids: Eerdmans, 1992), pp. 139–40; R. Gundry, *Matthew: A Commentary on His Handbook for a Mixed Church under Persecution* (Grand Rapids: Eerdmans, 2nd edn, 1994), p. 103. But see Görtz-Wrisberg who suggests that this passage could actually indicate that public prayer was preferred in the 'synagogues', 'Sabbath Service', p. 173.

152   S. Talmon, *The World of Qumran from Within: Collected Studies* (Jerusalem: Magnes Press, 1989), pp. 237–38.

153   *Ibid.*, p. 241.

154   *Ibid.*, p. 243.

155   For a discussion on the methods of identifying the provenance of the documents see D.K. Falk, *Daily, Sabbath, and Festival Prayers in the Dead Sea Scrolls* (STDJ, 27; Leiden: Brill, 1998), pp. 9–16, as well as his introductions to the various liturgical works for the

implications for the way in which they are seen to reflect Judaism more widely than purely the Qumran group which came into existence around the middle of the second century BCE. Recent research into the liturgical function of the texts from the Dead Sea has shown that prayer material is found for daily, festival and Sabbath use.[156] Daniel Falk in his careful assessment of the prayers and hymns argues that many of them point to communal use.[157] Further, he notes that within this communal use there is evidence: i) of a 'liturgical dialogue' where a leader, probably a priest, responds to the prayers of the people with a blessing of peace;[158] ii) of prayer being recited by a leader or leaders with the people responding with 'Amen, Amen';[159] and iii) of a fairly structured form of worship where particular compositions were used for different days of the week, Sabbaths or festivals.[160]

---

provenance of each. Falk notes that in *Words of the Luminaries* and *Festival Prayers* there is no emphasis on boundary markers, no polemic against a corrupt temple structure, nor any emphasis on prayer taking the place of sacrifice. Had these been compositions of the community then these themes would have been expected. He concludes that 'there is no reason to assume that these prayers originated in a group that had withdrawn from the temple,' *ibid.*, pp. 88–89. See also E.G. Chazon, '4QDibham: Liturgy or Literature?', *RevQ* 15 (1992), pp. 447–55; J.R. Davila, *Liturgical Works* (Eerdmans Commentaries on the Dead Sea Scrolls, 6; Grand Rapids: Eerdmans, 2000), pp. 211, 242.

156   For recent works on the liturgical documents from Qumran see, L.H. Schiffman, 'The Dead Sea Scrolls and the Early History of Jewish Liturgy', in Levine, *The Synagogue in Late Antiquity*, pp. 33–48; Talmon, *World of Qumran*, pp. 200–43; B. Nitzan, *Qumran Prayer and Religious Poetry* (STDJ, 12; Leiden: Brill, 1994); Falk, *Daily, Sabbath*; *idem*, 'Prayer in the Qumran Texts', in *CHJ*, pp. 852–76; Davila, *Liturgical Works*.

157   E.g., in *Songs of the Sabbath Sacrifice* human praise is seen as uniting with angelic praise: 'to praise your glory wondrously with the divinities of knowledge, and the praises of your kingship with the m[ost] holy ones', 4Q400, cf. 1QS 6.2-5. See also E.G. Chazon, 'On the Special Character of Sabbath Prayer: New Data from Qumran', *Journal of Jewish Music and Liturgy* 115 (1992/3), pp. 1–21 (10–11); S. Fine, *This Holy Place: On the Sanctity of the Synagogue During the Greco-Roman Period* (Notre Dame: Notre Dame Press, 1997), p. 32.

158   Falk, *Daily, Sabbath*, pp. 53–55. Evidence of priestly blessings in the temple and elsewhere (the 'synagogues'?) may also be found in *m. Tamid* 7.2 (also *m. Sotah* 7.6). But see the discussion of these passages by Levine, who notes that the comparison here may be between the pre-70 practice in the Temple and post-70 'synagogues', *Ancient Synagogue*, pp. 156–57.

159   Falk, *Daily, Sabbath*, pp. 84–85. For other examples of 'Amen' being used at the end of prayers see, 1 Chron. 16.36; Neh. 8.6; Ps. 106.48; Jdt. 13.20 and Tob. 8.8. The report of a large synagogue building in Alexandria states that someone had to stand on a wooden platform and wave a handkerchief so that the congregation would know when to respond, 'Amen', *t. Sukkah* 4.6. See also above Chapter 2, 4.3.

160   The *Words of the Luminaries* has prayers for Sunday to Friday which follow a historical development from creation to the post exilic period, Falk, *Daily, Sabbath*, p. 68. The prayers for the Sabbath, however, contain no historical allusions, but address God with praise, Davila, *Liturgical Works*, p. 241. Chazon points out that the prayers uttered during the week use the historical reminiscences to facilitate petitions to be made to God. However,

Schiffman points out that many of the canonical psalms that were used liturgically at Qumran are the same as those used later in the rabbinic liturgy.[161] It is also worth noting that there is evidence of continuity in the use of particular psalms for certain days of the week: in the Septuagint – Sunday, Psalm 24 (LXX 23); Monday, Psalm 48 (47); Wednesday, Psalm 94 (93); Friday, Psalm 93 (92); Sabbath, Psalm 92 (91) and 38 (37), and in the Mishnah the Levites sing these psalms on the same days with the addition of Psalm 82 on Tuesday and Psalm 81 on Thursday.[162] As well as these clear connections, scholars have suggested that elements that took full form only later can be identified in an early form in the Qumran material. The *Qedushah*, the joining of the earthly and heavenly communities in praising God's holiness and kingship (Isa. 6.3 + Ezek. 3.12 + Ps. 146.10) became part of later Jewish liturgy.[163] Although there is no explicit reference to it in the material from Qumran, Falk argues that in the *Songs of the Sabbath Sacrifice* there is evidence that on Sabbaths, some form of the *Qedushah* was recited.[164] Esther Eshel, who also points to the 'roots' of the *Qedushah* in *Songs of the Sabbath Sacrifice* further notes connections with *Daily Prayers* and argues that in these two texts we have evidence of the differences in later practice, where Palestinian Jews recited the *Qedushah* weekly on the Sabbath, while the Babylonian practice was a recitation four times a day.[165]

---

on the Sabbath no petitions are made, only praise. The contrast is all the clearer by the move from addressing God in the second person to the third. She notes that such a practice can also be seen in rabbinic sources, 'Special Character', pp. 4–5; p. 15 n. 12.

161 Schiffman, 'Dead Sea Scrolls,' p. 36. Also, the *Songs of the Sabbath Sacrifice*, which envisages the Sabbath worship of the angelic priesthood in heaven, has similarities to the book of Revelation, Davila, *Liturgical Works*, pp. 83–84, 91.

162 See the discussion in R. Beckwith, *Calendar and Chronology, Jewish and Christian: Biblical, Intertestamental and Patristic Studies* (Leiden: Brill, 1996), pp. 141–43. See also Leonhardt who has assessed Philo's use of psalms and hymns, both biblical and extra-biblical. She points out that the Psalms is the most frequently referenced biblical book outside of the Pentateuch concluding that Philo's use of these psalms exegetically, points to their being used in a 'synagogue' setting. She acknowledges that this does not mean that this is a universal application, but that it reflects the pattern of worship within perhaps Egyptian or Alexandrian synagogues, *Jewish Worship*, pp. 143–44.

163 Elbogen, *Jewish Liturgy*, pp. 54–62

164 Falk, *Daily, Sabbath*, pp. 138–46; also Nitzan, *Qumran Prayer*, pp. 367–69.

165 E. Eshel, 'Prayer in Qumran and the Synagogue', in B. Ego, A. Lange and P. Pilhofer (eds), *Gemeinde ohne Tempel, Community without Temple: Zur Substituierung und Transformation des Jerusalemer Tempels und seines Kults im Alten Testament, antiken Judentum und frühen Christentum*, (WUNT, 118; Tübingen: Mohr Siebeck, 1999), pp. 323–34 (323–29). It is also worth noting that *Songs of the Sabbath Sacrifice* was found both at Qumran (9 copies) and Masada (1 copy). See also R.S. Sarason, 'The "Intersections" of Qumran and Rabbinic Judaism: The Case of Prayer Texts and Liturgies', *DSD* 8 (2001), pp. 169–81.

4.5.1. *Conclusion on Qumran.*

As has been pointed out by several scholars, the material from Qumran gives us a new perspective on Jewish liturgy. At times it clearly reflects the ideology of one particular group of Jews and is more structured than any of our other Second Temple sources. However, there is also evidence that some of the material may reflect patterns of worship that existed within other groups of Jews in this period. Therefore, to exclude Qumran as reflecting only sectarian practices and therefore virtually ignore it as a possible source of reference, as McKay does, is not sensible.[166]

As indicated above, I conclude that the Jews of Qumran are a particularly pious group who have constructed a complex liturgy to take the place of sacrifice in Jerusalem, from which they are excluded. As such they should not be understood as reflecting the everyday practice of Palestinian Jews in general. However, the fact that similarities can be found to other material from the Second Temple period, and that many of the themes and practices of the Qumran community are then found echoed in the rabbinic sources, would suggest that there were other groups of Jews who shared some of these practices at this time.

4.6. *The* Shema

Having shown above that prayer was an important part of Jewish life, that it at times took place within 'synagogues', and could be carried out communally, can we gain a picture of what these prayers may have been like? The two prayers that are most often associated with a 'synagogue' service are the *Shema* and the *Amidah*, and in a previous generation, scholars argued that these would have been part of the pre-70 liturgy. Recent scholarship points out that there is little evidence for the use of

---

166 McKay, *Sabbath and Synagogue*, p. 59. The comments of van der Horst are appropriate: 'If the Qumran Essenes were so "far removed from mainstream Judaism," it is hard to understand why Judaism in a slightly later period would have totally adopted the Sabbath customs of precisely this sect', 'Was the Synagogue?', p. 31. Equally *inappropriately*, McKay, who accepts that the Qumran community held communal Sabbath worship, creates a false understanding of the worship practices. She argues that i) any prayer that went on in these gatherings would have been modelled on the silent prayer of the priests in the temple, p. 55; and ii) it is not clear whether those who took part in such worship can truly be seen as non-priestly Jews, *Sabbath and Synagogue*, pp. 55–56. In relation to the second point, Binder (*Temple Courts*, p. 466, n. 46) notes that the *Community Rule* details the priestly and non-priestly ranks within the community: 'This is the Rule for an assembly of the Congregation. Each man shall sit in his place: the Priests shall sit first, and the elders second, and all the rest of the people according to their rank', 1QS 6.8-9, cf. 6.2-5; CD 13.2-3. In relation to prayers being said silently, we have already noted that there was a 'liturgical dialogue' between a leader and the congregation. Such an exchange would be difficult to imagine if it were done silently.

these prayers in the 'synagogue' of this period, and it is consequently difficult to prove one way or the other.

Shema means 'hear' and is the first word of Deut. 6.4-9. In Mishnah *Berakot* 1–2 we are told that the Jews would recite this passage along with Deut. 11.13-21 and Num. 15.37-41 in the morning and evening,[167] and, according to Mishnah *Tamid* 5.1, it was recited daily by the priests in the temple.[168] Apart from its use in the temple, the evidence suggests it was said individually at the start and finish of the day, perhaps along with the Decalogue and some benedictions.

Evidence for the use of the *Shema* and Decalogue together comes in the Nash Papyrus: first published in 1903 by Stanley Cook, and coming from Egypt, it contains the first verses of the *Shema* along with the Decalogue,[169] and dates to the second half of the second century BCE.[170] Finding these two scriptural passages on a single piece of papyrus would suggest a catechetical or liturgical use,[171] although it could have been made for use in a *mezuzah* or *tefillin*.[172] As well as in this papyrus, the *Shema* and Decalogue appear together in some liturgical compilations from Qumran, in a number of *tefillin* also found at Qumran,[173] in the Septuagint's addition to Deut. 6.4, and in Mishnah *Tamid* 5.1, which also has the Decalogue preceding the *Shema*. At the end of the first century the Jews stopped using the Decalogue liturgically because of the

---

167　Earlier indications for the use of the *Shema* come in Josephus, *Ant.*, 4.212; *Ep. Arist.*, 158–60; Jesus alludes to the *Shema* in Mk 12.29; for other possible New Testament references see B. Gerhardsson, *The Shema in the New Testament: Deut 6.4-5 in Significant Passages* (Lund: Nova Press, 1996); see also 1QS 10.10, cf. 4Q408 1.6-11. *Sib. Or.*, 3.591-93 talks of Jews praying in their beds in the morning.

168　Clearly this is from a later source and we need to be cautious. We do not know the chronological development of the *Shema*; however, Elbogen suggests that its formation from the three passages of scripture took place over time, with the first passage being the oldest to which the second and then the third were added, *Jewish Liturgy*, pp. 22–23. Reif argues convincingly that, in light of discussion in the tannaitic period, the third section probably did not have the same status even in the second century, 'Early Liturgy', p. 350.

169　W.F. Albright, 'A Biblical Fragment from the Maccabean Age: The Nash Papyrus', *JBL* 56 (1937), pp. 145–76 (145).

170　Albright argues that this is the most likely date, but gives the limits as 165 to 37 BCE, 'Biblical Fragment', p. 172.

171　See L.W. Hurtado, *At the Origins of Christian Worship: The Context and Character of Earliest Christian Devotion* (Grand Rapids: Eerdmans, 1999), p. 32. Sanders suggests it was used for devotional or educational purposes, *Judaism: Practice and Belief*, p. 196.

172　Levine, *Ancient Synagogue*, p. 520 n. 77. However, R. Kimelman, who also argues that this is the best explanation, does allow the possibility that such phylacteries were portable prayerbooks, 'The Šĕmaʿ and its Blessings: The Realization of God's Kingship', in Levine, *The Synagogue in Late Antiquity*, p. 74.

173　Falk, 'Jewish Prayer,' p. 287; Levine, *Ancient Synagogue*, p. 521.

'insinuations of the heretics'.[174] Whether these heretics were Christians or other Jews is a matter of debate; however, this further suggests that it was being used liturgically before this point. Nevertheless, we must recognize that it is difficult to move from this position and go on to posit that the place in which it would have been used was the 'synagogue', or indeed that it would have been used for public rather than private prayer. Evidence in favour of its use communally may be found in Mishnah *Megillah* 4.3 where the use of the *Shema* comes in the context of a discussion of Sabbatical Scripture reading, which it states should not be carried out unless ten men are present.[175] Although this reflects the practice of a later period, the fact that the *Shema* and Decalogue are found together in much earlier sources may suggest this practice was in existence in at least some Jewish communities at an earlier date.

Similar debates have surrounded the *Amidah*, with scholars discussing the extent of the editing work carried out under Gamaliel II at Yavneh.[176] Here they have tried to work back from the final form to see if themes found in the full 18 benedictions arise in inter-testamental literature:[177] such comparisons prompted the conclusion that during the Second Temple period the form of the *Amidah* had reached a fairly advanced stage.[178] Again, more recent scholarly discussion has been considerably more cautious when assessing the sources. Fleischer, pointing to the lack of evidence, takes the most extreme position in the debate, arguing that no formal public prayer took place either in Palestine or the Diaspora.[179] Levine accepts that prayer would have been part of the worship of the Diaspora but would not have taken place within Palestine.[180] However, in connection with the formation of benedictions, Falk correctly notes that Josephus' reference to morning and evening prayers as thanksgiving and an acknowledgement before God of 'the bounties which he has bestowed on them through their deliverance from the land of Egypt' do not seem to make sense unless the *Shema* was accompanied with benediction(s).[181]

---

174   See G. Vermes, *Post-Biblical Jewish Studies* (SJLA, 8; Leiden: Brill, 1975), p. 169. However, the removal of the Decalogue was not complete and it continued to be used in some rabbinic material, see Levine, *Ancient Synagogue*, p. 522, n. 82.

175   Görtz-Wrisberg 'Sabbath Service', pp. 173–74.

176   For the references to its formation see *b. Ber.* 28b and *b. Meg.* 17b.

177   E.g., comparisons with Ben Sira, see Elbogen, *Jewish Liturgy*, p. 394 n. 7; W.O.E. Oesterley, *The Jewish Background of the Christian Liturgy* (Oxford: Oxford University Press, 1925), pp. 55ff; S.J.D. Cohen, *From the Maccabees to the Mishnah* (Philadelphia: Westminster Press, 1987), p. 72. For comparisons with The Prayer of Manasseh, see Bickerman, 'Civic Prayer', p. 170.

178   Elbogen, *Jewish Liturgy*, p. 35; Heinemann, *Prayer in the Talmud*, p. 224.

179   Fleischer, 'On the Beginnings', *passim*.

180   Levine, *Ancient Synagogue*, p. 153.

181   Falk points out that this is the theme of the benediction following the *Shema* in rabbinic liturgy and in *m. Tamid* 5.1, *Daily, Sabbath*, pp. 113–14. This makes more sense than

4.7. *The* Ma'amad

One place in which prayer may have taken place within Palestine is the *ma'amad* gathering. Mishnah *Taanith* 4.2-3 describes the division of the people of Israel into 24 courses or *ma'amadoth*.[182] We do not know when this division came about; however, such a division of the people does appear in 1 Chronicles, and this has been suggested by some scholars as a possible point of origin of the 'synagogue'.[183] We are told that as their representatives met in Jerusalem, the people left at home would gather together to fast and read the creation account in Genesis. Could it be that prayer also accompanied this reading? Reif thinks that it did,[184] and notes that at the time of a sacrifice being made, there was the need for confession of sin, although this may have been made in very few words.[185] The weekday prayers in *Words of the Luminaries* have some similarities to

---

R. Beckwith's understanding that Josephus conceived the *Shema* as a thanksgiving itself, *Daily and Weekly Worship: Jewish to Christian* (Alcuin/GROW Liturgical Study, 1; Bramcote: Grove Books, 1987), p. 16.

182 For other rabbinic references to the courses see, *m. Sukkah.* 5.7-8; *m. Tamid.* 5.1; *y. Taan.* 68a; *t. Taan.* 2.1-2; *b. Arak.* 12b. Neh. 12.1-7 mentions some kind of a division into 22; Josephus also mentions 24 courses, *Ant.*, 7.365-66 and *Life*, 2 where he describes himself as coming from the first course; in *Apion*, 2.108 he mentions only 4 courses but this is extant in Latin only and the suggestion of Schürer that it could be a textual corruption seems persuasive, *HJP*, vol. 2, p. 247. For details of epigraphic evidence for the 24 courses see D.R. Edwards, 'Khirbet Qana: from Jewish Village to Christian Pilgrim Site', in J.H. Humphrey (ed.), *The Roman and Byzantine Near East*, vol. 3 (Journal of Roman Archaeology Supplementary Series, 49; Portsmouth, Rhode Island: JRA, 2002), pp. 101–32 (102–103 n. 7).

183 1 Chron. 24.7-18. Görtz-Wrisberg, 'Sabbath Service', p. 169. M. Hengel suggests that the spread of the 'synagogue' in Palestine could have come through them, 'Proseuche und Synagoge: Jüdische Gemeinde, Gotteshaus und Gottesdienst in der Diaspora und in Palästina', in J. Gutmann (ed.), *The Synagogue: Studies in Origins, Archaeology and Architecture*, (The Library of Biblical Studies, New York: KTAV, 1975), p. 182. But see A. Finkel, 'Jesus' Preaching in the Synagogue on the Sabbath (Luke 4.16-28)', in C.A. Evans and W.R. Stegner (eds), *The Gospels and the Scripture of Israel* (Sheffield, Sheffield Academic Press, 1994), pp. 325–41 (327, n. 1).

184 Although he notes that this was 'not in the formal fashion of later times', Reif, *Judaism and Hebrew Prayer*, p. 58. See also J.J. Petuchowski, 'The Liturgy of the Synagogue', in J.J. Petuchowski and M. Brocke (eds), *The Lord's Prayer and Jewish Liturgy* (London: Burns and Oates, 1978), p. 45; and Cohen, *From the Maccabees*, p. 65; Elbogen, *Jewish Liturgy*, p. 191. L.I. Levine comments: 'The prayer service itself was conceived as a parallel to sacrifices offered at the Temple. When priests of a particular locality travelled to Jerusalem to participate in the Temple ritual, special services were held by their fellow townspeople in the local synagogue', ('Ancient Synagogues A Historical Introduction', in L.I. Levine (ed.), *Ancient Synagogues Revealed* (Jerusalem: Israel Exploration Society, 1981), pp. 1–10 (3). However, later he modifies his position noting that there is no evidence for prayer in these gatherings, only Scripture reading, 'Second Temple Synagogue', p. 17. Fleischer is sure that there was no prayer, 'On the Beginnings', p. 422.

185 He cites Lev. 5.5; 16.21; Num. 5.7, Reif, *Judaism and Hebrew Prayer*, p. 31.

the practices in the regional *ma'amadoth* gatherings, and Falk speculates that this may be the place in which such a practice arose.[186]

4.8. *Other Sources*

There are a number of other sources which may also indicate that prayer played a part in communal Jewish worship. Some of the sources make no reference to the 'synagogue' as the place in which this would have taken place; indeed, some clearly indicate another location. However, they do add to the picture given above that prayer was an important aspect to Jewish life, and it may be that in some of the references the place in which these prayers took place was the 'synagogue'. We will now survey the additional material, chronologically moving from the oldest.

Evidence that Jews gathered together for communal worship comes in the books of Maccabees. Under the direction of Judas Maccabeus, as the Israelites made themselves ready for battle they gathered together to pray and ask for God's mercy.[187] After defeating their enemies, again they offered praise to God in a song of thanksgiving.[188] In a letter to the Lacedemonians Jonathan writes: 'We therefore remember you constantly on every occasion, both at our festivals and on other appropriate days, at the sacrifices that we offer and in our prayers'.[189] Finally, prayer is linked to the Sabbath in 2 Macc. 8.27 when the Israelites stop the pursuit of an enemy army because it is late on the day before the Sabbath:

> When they had collected the arms of the enemy and stripped them of their spoils, they kept the sabbath, giving great praise and thanks to the Lord (περὶ τὸ σάββατον ἐγίνοντο περισσῶς εὐλογοῦντες καὶ ἐξομολογούμενοι τῷ κυρίῳ), who had preserved them for that day and allotted it to them as the beginning of mercy.

Heather McKay argues that this last passage does not reflect regular Sabbath practice but comes in response to the victory gained.[190] In this she is probably correct, but all of the passages from the books of Maccabees do seem to indicate that prayer was carried out communally.[191]

---

186   Falk, *Daily, Sabbath*, p. 91. See also Reif, 'Prayer in the Qumran Texts', p. 859.

187   1 Macc. 3.44. It should be noted that although this does not take place in Jerusalem, but in Mizpeh, this is as a replacement for the Temple, see P. Davies, 'A Note on I Macc. III. 46', *JTS* 23 (1972), pp. 117–21.

188   1 Macc. 4.24; cf. Jdt. 13.17.

189   1 Macc. 12.11.

190   McKay, *Sabbath and Synagogue*, p. 48.

191   L.I. Levine, 'The First-Century Synagogue: New Perspectives', *STK* 77 (2001), pp. 22–30 (25).

Finally, an important reference comes in *Biblical Antiquities*, which probably dates to the first century CE.[192] In a rendering of the Decalogue, God says:

> Keep the sabbath day to sanctify it. For six days do work, but on the seventh day is the Lord's sabbath. You shall not do any work on it, you and all your servants, except to praise the Lord in the congregation of the elders and to glorify the Mighty One in the assembly of the aged (*nisi ut in ea laudes Dominum in ecclesia presbiterorum et glorifices Fortem in cathedra seniorum*).[193]

Here the commandment to abstain from work is combined with an instruction to offer praise to God. The fact that such praise is to be carried out in the 'congregation of the elders' clearly indicates that this is public worship that is being described, although we are not given details of what such worship might involve.[194]

4.9. *Conclusion on Prayer*

As we have covered a good deal of material on prayer, it will be worth summarizing the major points:

- There is a connection in the sources between communal prayer and the Sabbath in Sardis (4.2.1.1); Halicarnassus (4.2.1.2.); Jerusalem (4.2.2.2.); Qumran (4.5.); Palestine (4.8).
- Such communal prayer is identified as taking place at the beach in Alexandria (4.3.1.); within the κοινὸν σεμνεῖον in Egypt (4.3.2.); in a προσευχή in Tiberias? (4.2.2.1.); within ἱερά in Jerusalem (4.2.2.2). It would also have taken place within the προσευχαί of Alexandria had they been available (4.3.1).
- Private prayer could take place within συναγωγαί in Palestine (4.4).

As I have noted above there is a real paucity of evidence when we come to assess the extent to which prayer played a part in the worship of Jews in the first century CE. However, the recognition of this fact has led some scholars to an overly minimalistic interpretation of the data. We must

---

192   Whether it should be dated to the period before or after the destruction of the Temple is debated. D.J. Harrington dates it pre-70, 'Pseudo-Philo', in Charlesworth, *Old Testament Pseudepigrapha*, vol. 2, pp. 297–377 (299–300), as does D. Mendels, 'Pseudo-Philo's *Biblical Antiquities*, the "Fourth Philosophy," and the Political Messianism of the First Century CE', in J.H. Charlesworth, *The Messiah: Developments in Earliest Judaism and Christianity* (Minneapolis, Fortress Press, 1992), pp. 261–75 (266, n. 21). The revisers of Schürer place it some time in the first century, *HJP*, vol. 3.1, p. 329, but see the discussion in H. Jacobson, who dates it to the first half of the second century CE, *A Commentary on Pseudo-Philo's Liber Antiquitatum Biblicarum* (AGJU, 31; Leiden: Brill, 1996), pp. 199–210.

193   *Bib. Ant.*, 11.8. Translation from Jacobson, *Pseudo-Philo's*.

194   See also Binder, *Temple Courts*, p. 413 and Runesson, *Origins*, pp. 345–46.

recognize that silence on the matter does not of necessity mean that it did not exist; it may just be that areas of Jewish worship which differed from the worship found in their pagan counterparts meant that Jewish authors highlighted practices such as Torah reading.[195] Whilst we need to be careful of arguing from silence, in the discussion above it has been shown, nonetheless, that there is evidence that prayer was an important aspect of Jewish life, and that prayer was carried out communally. Further, some of our sources indicate that it took place within the 'synagogue', or would have done had the 'synagogue' been available to them.

Ezra Fleischer has suggested that a distinction needs to be made between prayer as 'personal, spontaneous, occasional and informal devotion and "Prayer" *qua* compulsory religious commandment, imposed upon every man and seen as an institutionalized way for both community and individual to worship God'.[196] Fleischer is correct in noting that universal legislation did not exist in the first century; however, we should not assume, therefore, that no communal prayer took place: this is too much of a dichotomy. As has been noted in regard to architecture, no single blueprint existed in the first century; similarly individual communities developed communal prayer in their own settings. Our search for worship in the 'synagogue' is wider than Heather McKay who focuses purely on the Sabbath. However, van der Horst's critique of McKay seems fair: 'are we to believe that precisely on the Sabbath, in contrast to other days, there was no praying and singing?'[197]

Levine in his discussion of prayer argues that 'Prayer appears to have played little or no role in the *typical* Judean synagogue',[198] but acknowledges that sects such as the Essenes at Qumran may have developed some communal prayer. However, here it has been suggested that similarities in themes found in the liturgies from Qumran and later rabbinic sources suggest a broad stream of biblical motifs which found expression in slightly different ways in diverse communities and at different times. The fluidity in the formation of prayers such as the *Amidah*, where the themes rather than the prescribed wording of the prayer were still being formulated at the end of the first century, suggests that different communities may have developed liturgies in a variety of forms.[199] Gathering together for Sabbath worship is widely attested and

195   Levine, 'Nature and Origin', pp. 431–32.

196   E. Fleischer, 'Rejoinder to Dr Reif's Remarks', *Tarbiz* 60 (1991), pp. viii–ix (English Summaries).

197   Van der Horst, 'Was the Synagogue?', p. 31.

198   Levine, *Ancient Synagogue*, p. 157, (italics mine).

199   Reif, *Judaism and Hebrew Prayer*, p. 70; Beckwith, 'Daily and Weekly Worship of the Primitive Church', p. 69. Heinemann, in the Hebrew translation of Elbogen, adds new material on the *Amidah*. Rather than seeing it as growing in a fairly fixed form with new benedictions being added now and again, he points out that it 'grew and took shape in

the decrees, quoted by Josephus, protecting the Jews' right to pray and to meet and perform their sacred worship indicate that such Sabbath gatherings could well have included prayer.[200]

Finally, a comment on the geographical dimension to this debate. Most references we have to prayer in Jerusalem come in relation to the temple. Again, it is difficult to be decisive, but it may be that the Jews resident in and around Jerusalem who wished to do so used the temple as a place of prayer. Elsewhere in Palestine, the Qumran community gathered to carry out their complex liturgy, probably in room 77. In Tiberias the Jews came together to pray on a fast day in a προσευχή and, while acknowledging the difficulties of dating, the Gospel of Matthew details private prayer within a synagogue building. Therefore, contra Fleischer, it would appear that we have evidence of communal prayer in Palestine. In the Diaspora, προσευχή was the most common term to describe the meeting places of the Jews, strongly suggesting that prayer would have been part of worship carried out there;[201] indeed, prayer is attested in Asia Minor and Egypt.

What is being argued for is not a monochrome picture of Judaism where prayer took place at least weekly on the Sabbath in the local 'synagogue'. Those who have questioned the evidence for prayer, particularly in Palestine, have highlighted an important fact, and what we have sought to do is show that the picture we are left with is a variegated one. Such differences cannot be seen simply by contrasting the Diaspora with Palestine, but rather by recognizing that certain communities appear to have had a more structured liturgy than others.

5. Sacred Meals

5.1. Introduction

Another area of communal life shared by Jews was dining. This is seen most clearly in a decree protecting the rights of the Jews on Delos:

> Now it displeases me that such statutes should be made against our friends and allies and that they should be forbidden to live in accordance with their customs and to contribute money to common

---

many different circles of worship'. Different communities had prayers and benedictions that they used which gradually came together, *Jewish Liturgy*, p. 35. See also Petuchowski who argues that even when Gamaliel II brought the *Amidah* together it was only the order and not the full text that was fixed, 'Liturgy of the Synagogue', p. 54; as does Cohen, *From the Maccabees*, p. 72. Avigdor Shinan argues that such variation continued into late antiquity, 'Synagogues in the Land of Israel: The Literature of the Ancient Synagogue and Synagogue Archaeology', in Fine, *Sacred Realm*, pp. 130–52 (143).

200   E.g., Josephus, *Ant.*, 14.213.

201   Further evidence that prayer took place in these buildings comes in an Egyptian inscription, dated 37 BCE, for, 'the great God who listens to prayer', *JIGRE*, 13.

meals and sacred rites, for this they are not forbidden to do even in
Rome. For example, Gaius Caesar, our consular praetor, by edict
forbade religious societies to assemble in the city, but these people alone
he did not forbid to do so or to collect contributions of money or to
hold common meals.[202]

It is difficult to get a clear picture of what these meals would have
involved. When and how often were they held; where were they held; were
they perceived as sacred and were they attached to some kind of act of
worship, perhaps on the Sabbath or another festival occasion? As Levine
points out, what we can be clear about is that these 'meals were recognized
by Romans and Jews alike as important communal activities which played
an integral part in the corporate life of the Jews'.[203]

Although from a later period, a passage from the Tosefta may be helpful:

> What is the order of a meal [at a communal meal]? As the guests enter,
> they are seated on benches or chairs while all [the guests] assemble [and
> are seated together]. [Once all have assembled] they [the attendants]
> have given them [water] for their hands, each [guest] washes one hand.
> [When] they [the attendants] have mixed for them the cup [of wine], each
> one recites the benediction [over appetizers] for himself. [When] they
> have arisen [from the benches or seats] and reclined [to the second stage
> of the meal], and they [the attendants] have [again] given them [water]
> for their hands, even though each has already washed one hand, he now
> must wash both hands. When they [the attendants] have [again] mixed
> for them the cup, even though each has recited a benediction over the
> first [cup], he recites a benediction over the second [also]. When they [the
> attendants] have brought before them appetizers, even though each has
> recited a benediction over the first [appetizers], he recites a benediction
> over the second, and one person recites the benediction for all of them
> [at this stage of the meal]. One who arrives after three [courses of]
> appetizers [have been served] is not allowed to enter [to join the meal].[204]

With reference to this Smith writes: 'The form of the meal represented
here clearly corresponds to that of the Greco-Roman banquet. Such
features as reclining, three courses, washing the hands, mixing wine with
water, and saying a blessing over the wine are some of the more obvious
elements.'[205]

---

202 Josephus, *Ant.*, 14.214-15. These meals may also be attested elsewhere in *Ant.*,
16.164, see the discussion in chapter 2, 3.2.1.
203 Levine, *Ancient Synagogue*, p. 130.
204 *T. Ber.* 4.8.
205 D.E. Smith, *From Symposium to Eucharist: The Banquet in the Early Christian World*
(Minneapolis: Fortress Press, 2003), p. 146.

5.2. *Diaspora*
5.2.1. *Case Study of Ostia*

The archaeological remains of the synagogue in Ostia provide us with vital data in relation to a Diaspora synagogue building. As discussed above, the building included a *triclinium* as part of the structure in its earliest phase, which is different from the majority of Palestinian buildings for which we have evidence.[206] As in other Roman towns, Ostia had many temples as well as the guild buildings of various voluntary associations, and these buildings often had dining areas associated with them.[207] From Ostia we have evidence of over 40 guilds, although more would have existed,[208] and Meiggs suggests that they would have covered virtually every aspect of the life of the town 'and must have included a considerable proportion of the population'.[209] Trade associations existed, with grain and navigation making up more than half of the known guilds, reflecting Ostia's main commercial activity. There is also evidence of religious and funerary guilds.[210]

At times these associations would have met in a temple of the god/goddess associated with the protection of the cult. However, there is also evidence that some of the wealthier associations had their own guild buildings. One that has been clearly identified in Ostia is that of the builders' guild: this building complex dates to the early Hadrianic period[211] and although larger than the synagogue building,[212] nonetheless shares many of its architectural features. Most notable are: the focus, which when entering the building through the main doorway, is a room with a bowed podium against the far wall; the dining rooms off the main

---

206 See above, Chapter 3, 2.1.2.

207 R. MacMullen, *Paganism in the Roman Empire* (New Haven: Yale University Press, 1981), pp. 34–42; G. Hermansen, *Ostia: Aspects of Roman City Life* (Edmonton: University of Alberta Press, 1982), p. 60; J.N. Bremmer, *Greek Religion* (Oxford: Oxford University Press, 1994).

208 Hermansen, *Ostia*, p. 55. P. Richardson puts the number at 60, 'An Architectural Case for Synagogues as Associations', in B. Olsson and M. Zetterholm (eds), *The Ancient Synagogue: From its Origins to 200 C.E.: Papers Presented at an International Conference at Lund University, October 14–17, 2001* (ConNT, 39; Stockholm: Almqvist & Wiksell, 2003), pp. 90–117 (97).

209 R. Meiggs, *Roman Ostia* (Oxford: Clarendon Press, 2nd edn, 1973), p. 312.

210 Hermansen, *Ostia*, pp. 59–60. Cf. *CPJ* 1, 138 which mentions a meeting of a σύνοδος in a προσευχή in Egypt, perhaps a funerary association, and no. 139, details an association which organised meals that may have taken place within a προσευχή.

211 Meiggs, *Roman Ostia*, p. 324, although the incorporation of the guild occurred around 60 CE, *ibid.*, pp. 330–31.

212 About 41 m × 28 m.

View from the main entrance
showing the bowed podium.

Water basin.

Dining room to the east of the portico.

Figure 4.1 Three views of the Builders' Guild House.

area with stone benches around the walls; and water available in a basin in a corner of the portico.[213]

It seems highly probable that the Ostian Jews were influenced by the architectural design of the guild or temple buildings which they saw around them in Ostia and incorporated some of the features into their synagogue building. If that is the case, then some of the practices of these *collegia* may also have impacted upon the Jewish community.[214] As Hermansen points out, the functions of these voluntary associations were

213   See Figure 4.1. See Meiggs' description of the building, *Roman Ostia*, p. 324; also, Richardson, 'Architectural Case', pp. 103–05.

214   Peter Richardson has argued that Diaspora synagogue buildings functioned and were perceived as *collegia*, and that even in Palestine they retained many of these features, 'Early Synagogues as Collegia in the Diaspora and Palestine', in J.S. Kloppenborg and S.G. Wilson (eds), *Voluntary Associations in the Graeco-Roman World* (New York: Routledge, 1996), pp. 90–109. M. Klinghardt argues that the Jewish gatherings parallel the Hellenistic associations and that it is unthinkable that the deciding aspect of Hellenistic association life,

'worship, banquets, and assemblies'.[215] Philip Harland argues that too many scholars have concentrated on the social element of the associations and downplayed the religious. In connection with meals he writes: 'That banqueting activities could be infused with varying degrees of religious significance for the participants, being viewed as a means of honoring or communing with the gods, further suggests caution in reducing the purposes of associations to the social'.[216] The guilds regularly held meals within their buildings either on a date associated with the god/goddess with which the guild was connected, or perhaps on the anniversary of the birthday of one of their patrons.[217] Given the evidence presented above for meals taking place within Jewish communities, it would seem likely that in Ostia the function of the *triclinium* was to accommodate such meals.

5.2.2. *Elsewhere in the Diaspora*

As well as the *triclinium* at Ostia, it may be that the additional buildings (τὰ συγκύροντα) attached to the προσευχαί in Egypt fulfilled a similar function. A papyrus from Apollinopolis Magna and dating to the first century BCE probably records a Jewish dining club. It contains a list of those who contributed to feasts (πόσεις), and although it gives no indication, it is possible that these took place in the προσευχή.[218] Also in Egypt, every 49 days, the Therapeutae gathered to worship and share a meal. This meal is explicitly described as a sacred banquet (ἱερὸς συμπόσιον),[219] and the most likely place for this meal to happen would have been in a room attached to their 'synagogue' building.

5.3. *Palestine*
5.3.1. *Jericho*

The possible synagogue building recently discovered in Jericho, with its *triclinium* and kitchen attached, is an intriguing addition to our knowledge. The U-shaped stone bench on which those dining would have reclined measured 5.2 m × 4.1 m and was 1.4 m wide, and between it and the wall was a small passageway, 70 cm wide, for those serving. This

---

the Symposium, would have played a lesser role in Jewish 'synagogues', *Gemeinschaftsmahl und Mahlgemeinschaft: Soziologie und Liturgie frühchristlicher Mahlfeiern* (TANZ, 13; Tübingen: Francke Verlag, 1996), pp. 258–59.

215　Hermansen, *Ostia*, p. 60.

216　P.A. Harland, *Associations, Synagogues and Congregations: Claiming a Place in Ancient Mediterranean Society* (Minneapolis: Fortress, 2003), p. 77. See the similar comments of Smith, *From Symposium to Eucharist*, p. 6, and S. Mitchell and M. Waelkens, *Pisidian Antioch: The Site and its Monuments* (London: Duckworth, 1998), p. 83

217　Meiggs, *Roman Ostia*, p. 326.

218　*CPJ* 1, 139.

219　Philo, *Vit. Cont.*, 64–82.

triclinium is much more open to the main assembly room than the one in Ostia and how it would have been used by the community in relation to the function of the assembly room is not clear. What this does provide is another example of a communal dining facility directly associated with a synagogue building.

5.3.2. *Elsewhere in Palestine*

The book of *Jubilees*, written around the middle of the second century BCE,[220] portrays the Sabbath as a day on which to eat and drink:

> And thus he created therein a sign by which they might keep the sabbath with us on the seventh day, to eat and drink and bless the one who created all things just as he blessed and sanctified for himself a people who appeared from all the nations so that they might keep the sabbath together with us. And he caused their desires to go up as pleasing fragrance, which is acceptable before him always.[221]

The picture is of the heavenly and earthly realms uniting, both in worship and in the sharing of a meal.[222] Such a description would suggest a communal activity, and probably reflects the Sabbath practices of the author's community. Further, the eating and drinking that goes on appears to be linked with the worship of the community. It is also worth noting that the desires of the people go up to God which means that prayer was involved in this worship.[223]

Communal dining is a feature of the life of the sectarian communities,[224] but it is not clear that these took place in 'synagogues', or that they were anything other than ordinary daily meals, and as such should not be seen as part of any worship activity.[225] As discussed above, in his report of the disputes in the Tiberias προσευχή, Josephus remarks that the meeting was broken up because of 'the arrival of the sixth hour, at which it is our custom on the Sabbath to take our midday meal'.[226] Again, it is

---

220   See J.C. VanderKam, *The Book of Jubilees* (Sheffield: Sheffield Academic Press, 2001), p. 21.

221   *Jub.* 2.21, cf. 2.31, from O.S. Wintermute, 'Jubilees', in Charlesworth, *Old Testament Pseudepigrapha*, vol. 2, pp. 35–142.

222   *Jub.* 2.18-19.

223   See Wintermute, 'Jubilees', p. 57, n. x.

224   Josephus, *War*, 2.128-33; Philo, *Hypoth.*, 11.11; 1QS 6.4-5; 1QSa 2.17-21.

225   Although the reference to communal dining from Qumran also goes on to state that, 'in the place in which the Ten assemble there should not be missing a man to interpret the law day and night', 1QS 6.6. This may fit well with our suggestion that room 77 at Qumran could have functioned as a dining area and a place of worship. Of the Essenes Josephus writes: 'pure now themselves, they repair to the refectory, as to some sacred shrine' (*War*, 2.129), but Smith points out this is more to persuade his reader that these meals were different to 'run-of-the-mill pagan affairs', *From Symposium to Eucharist*, p. 157.

226   Josephus, *Life*, 279.

not clear whether this meal was shared in the building, in another location, or if each went to their own homes.[227] Finally, the Theodotos inscription mentions the guest rooms and chambers (ξενών καὶ δώματα), part of which may have served as a dining area.

5.4. *Conclusion*

There is clear evidence that in some communities the Jews gathered for communal meals. While these may have been social gatherings, all such gatherings, whether Jewish or pagan, would have involved a ritual element. The evidence would seem to suggest that at least some of these were more directly sacred[228] and may have coincided with the festival gatherings at Jerusalem.[229] It is possible that such meals took place at each new moon and perhaps on each Sabbath, but there is no clear evidence for this.[230] The synagogue at Ostia provides the clearest archaeological data for such practices, to which can now be added the *triclinium* at Jericho; but the additional buildings mentioned in connection with the Egyptian προσευχαί and the Theodotos synagogue may also have been used for such a practice. Although the sources point to communal meals taking place across all geographical locations, it may be that within 'synagogues' which were heavily influenced by Graeco-Roman society, both those in Palestine and the Diaspora, the influence of their banqueting tradition was strong.

6. *Overall Conclusion*

In line with the conclusions in earlier chapters, we are not arguing for a monochrome picture of the worship practices that took place within 'synagogues'. Different communities would have been influenced by the particular social world in which they found themselves, and would have incorporated some of the practices of their environment. However, we should also draw back from a description which leaves us with such a variegated picture of these practices that one almost cannot grasp any item that was held in common. Therefore, it will be useful to summarize the points made above:

- It seems likely that some form of action took place by which a person entering a 'synagogue' purified themselves. The fact that water was so often associated with synagogue buildings suggests that this was an element that was universally practised, although the method

---

227 Cf. Lk. 14.1.
228 E.g., the Therapeutae.
229 See Philo, *Spec. Leg.*, 2.148.
230 For possible connections see Binder, *Temple Courts*, pp. 415–26.

used appears to have varied from one location to another. The fact that purification was required before entry to the 'synagogue' strongly suggests that what occurred there was seen as sacred. This is further bolstered by inscriptions and literary evidence, which describe the meeting places as ἱεροὶ τόποι or as ἱερά.

- As noted, virtually all scholarship accepts that Torah reading was a central component of 'synagogue' practice and was carried out weekly on the Sabbath. Further, it has been shown that this can and should be identified as a form of worship. It seems likely that within virtually any 'synagogue' gathering on a Sabbath, in any geographical location, this would have been a common element.

- As well as Torah reading we also have evidence of prayer and hymn singing. The fact that the meeting places of the Jews were often called προσευχαί must give us some indication of the practices that took place within these buildings. Prayer in the 'synagogue' on the Sabbath is attested by Josephus, and Philo reports that prayer and hymn singing would have been carried out by the Alexandrian Jews in their προσευχαί, had they been available to them. There is also evidence that the 'synagogue' was used for prayer at other times of the week, and that individuals could use the 'synagogue' for their daily prayers. The evidence we have suggests that prayer was a more important element outside of Judaea and this may be because the temple was used for communal prayer within this region.

    It has been shown that the material from the DSS should not be excluded from our consideration on the grounds that it belonged to a sectarian group. The fact that some of the material pre-dates Qumran and that there are links with later more structured 'synagogue' liturgy strongly suggests that this material falls into a broad band of biblically based material which finds a more structured form at Qumran.

- We have argued that communal meals were a part of Jewish community life and that it is likely that these took place within 'synagogues'. Evidence for these is most clearly seen in the archaeological remains that we have at Ostia and Jericho; however, there is evidence that communal dining took place elsewhere. The influence of the symposium may have been strongly felt in the Hellenistic 'synagogues', which incorporated elements of the practice of their communities, perhaps most clearly through the voluntary associations.

In the introduction to this chapter it was noted that it was not possible to understand fully which elements of 'synagogue' practice would have been perceived as worship by a first-century Jew; however, it has been argued above that certain activities were clearly regarded in such a way. Whether other elements, such as the collection and storage of the temple tax, would also have been considered worship is difficult to know.[231]

Harland, using both historical tools and social sciences, argues that the portrayal of both Christian and Jewish groups as sects, completely detached from the cultural settings in which they found themselves, is an inaccurate presentation. Focusing on the communities of Asia Minor, he argues that Jewish groups were involved in the life of the city:

> A complex scenario akin to acculturation, assimilation, and dissimilation (rather than the overly simplistic separationist focus of sectarian typologies) should be imagined for the variety of synagogues and congregations (or individuals) within the polis of the Greek East. While particular groups (or individual members or leaders) might firmly reject certain aspects of the values, symbols, conventions, and institutions of Greco-Roman culture and society, they might also maintain, accept, or adapt others, without necessarily undermining or losing their own distinctive way of life, worldview, or group identity (monotheism being the key).[232]

This understanding of the interaction of Jewish groups with the cultural milieu within which they lived is helpful. It has been argued above that we can perceive areas in which the worship practices of the Graeco-Roman world have been incorporated into Jewish 'synagogue' practices. The level of integration and the particular practices of groups would have varied from place to place. Therefore, we must, on the one hand, hold onto this acculturation to local practice while, on the other, recognize that some elements were particular to Jewish practice and that there is a commonality across geographical and socio-economic boundaries.

---

231 See the comments of Claußen: 'Besides the functions which were religious in the narrower sense, like prayer, the reading, teaching and study of Torah and ritual ablutions in the adjacent *mikwaoth* or waters, synagogue buildings also served as accommodation for guests, the storage of donations and other finance, as asylum-places and as places at which slaves were freed, for conducting legal cases and for all sorts of meetings for local Jewish purposes in the widest sense. Perhaps communal meals also took place there', *Versammlung*, p. 300 (author's translation).

232 Harland, *Associations*, p. 199.

Chapter 5

The 'Synagogue' in Luke-Acts

1. Introduction

In the previous chapters, we have examined the evidence for the first-century 'synagogue' and for the worship practices that took place there. The purpose of this chapter is to study the portrayal of the 'synagogue' in Luke-Acts and compare it to the material gathered. As noted in Chapter 1, in his recent article on the first-century 'synagogue', Kenneth Atkinson remarks: 'When Luke-Acts records Jesus or Paul as entering a synagogue, an edifice similar or identical to the Gamla synagogue is being described'.[1] Other scholars are considerably more sceptical. Luke has been accused of being anachronistic in his portrayal of the 'synagogue' and, along with many other areas of his writing, is thought to have read back the situation that existed towards the end of the first century CE into the period of Jesus' ministry and the formative years of the church. It is argued that his portrayal of events that took place within the 'synagogue' assumes a level of organization that only came into being subsequent to the destruction of the Jerusalem temple with the consequent increase in formalization and structure that took place in the 'synagogue'.

The issues recently raised as to the form and function of first-century 'synagogues' are now making their way into New Testament scholarship. While many commentators continue to assume that a reference to συναγωγή means a building with a set religious function,[2] some modern commentators on Luke-Acts will note the possibility that gatherings rather than buildings may be in mind, and that a variety of activities could

---

1   K. Atkinson, 'On Further Defining the First-Century CE Synagogue: Fact or Fiction? A Rejoinder to H. C. Kee', *NTS* 43 (1997), pp. 491–502 (499).

2   E.g., C.K. Barrett, *Acts* (ICC; 2 vols.; Edinburgh: T&T Clark, 1994–98), vol. 1, p. 323; J.B. Green, *The Gospel of Luke* (NICNT; Grand Rapids: Eerdmans, 1997), p. 209; W. Eckey, *Die Apostelgeschichte: der Weg des Evangeliums von Jerusalem nach Rom* (2 vols; Neukirchener-Vluyn: Neukirchener, 2000), vol. 1, pp. 158–59; J. Jervell, *Die Apostelgeschichte* (KEK, 3; Göttingen: Vandenhoeck & Ruprecht, 1998), p. 225.

have been carried out there.[3] However, although this is noted, it is often inconsistently applied. To give one example: while discussing the 'synagogue(s)' of Acts 6.9, Fitzmyer acknowledges the possibility that συναγωγή does not need to mean a building but may refer to the congregation.[4] However, when he comes to comment on Acts 13.44, Paul's visit to Pisidian Antioch, he writes: 'One wonders how the "whole town" could have fitted into the synagogue',[5] apparently forgetting his earlier comments and the possibility that the author might not be referring to a building. Similarly, although commentators note the archaeological remains of a synagogue building in Capernaum, the details of its architecture are not discussed, and its structure not taken note of in the general discussion of the town or the surrounding area of Galilee.

Therefore, in the following pages we will:

- Outline how recent scholarship has interacted with Luke-Acts and its presentation of 'synagogues'. It will be shown that as the discussion has continued, scholars have often focused on only some of the evidence leading to too great a polarity in the arguments, and that a more nuanced approach should be adopted.
- Use specific passages as case studies where the background material can give a more accurate understanding of how συναγωγή or προσευχή should be perceived, drawing particularly on geographical and archaeological evidence. So, for example, when we are informed that Jesus went to a 'synagogue' in Nazareth and Paul visited a 'synagogue' in Pisidian Antioch, are we to imagine that the experience they had was similar? Does the latest research allow us to present a more accurate picture of what the historical reality might have been like, and does this accord with Luke's description?
- Examine Luke's presentation of 'synagogue' worship and, again incorporating the geographical dimension, compare it to our other sources.
- Assess whether Luke is correct in his presentation, or is justifiably accused of anachronism.
- Using the background material, describe some of the worship practices that may have existed, but that Luke does not provide, for example, purification, prayer and hymn singing as well as communal dining.

---

3 B. Witherington, *The Acts of the Apostles: A Socio-Rhetorical Commentary* (Grand Rapids: Eerdmans, 1998), pp. 255–57; J.A. Fitzmyer, *The Acts of the Apostles* (AB, 31; New York: Doubleday, 1998), pp. 356–58.

4 Fitzmyer, *Acts*, pp. 356–57.

5 Fitzmyer, *Acts*, p. 520.

2. *Terminology*

In line with some of the sources outlined in earlier chapters, the New Testament's use of συναγωγή is limited to certain authors. Michael White writes:

> It must be noted by way of contrast to the prolific mention in Acts (especially in Paul's travels), that Paul, whose genuine letters come from before 70, never once referred to the synagogue, either as institution or edifice, even though he clearly knew Jewish communities or individuals in several localities in Greece and Asia Minor.

From this he concludes: 'All too often the legal status and organization of the sizeable Jewish populations at Antioch and, especially, Alexandria have been wrongly assumed to apply equally to the many small, diverse Jewish communities throughout the Diaspora'.[6]

Of the 56 times that συναγωγή is used in the New Testament, by far the most frequent use comes in Luke-Acts, which has 34 references. In fact, it is striking to note Luke's almost universal use of the term συναγωγή for the meeting places of the Jews,[7] the only exception being the προσευχή in Philippi.[8] As we have seen above, in the early part of the first century there were a variety of nouns used to describe these gathering places, but these are not reflected in the writing of Luke.

3. *Is Luke Anachronistic?*

3.1. *The Minimalists' Perspective*

As noted at the beginning of this chapter, it has been argued that Luke is anachronistic in his description of the first-century 'synagogue', most vociferously by Howard Kee. Subsequently, other scholars have argued in a similar way, or pressed one particular element of the debate. In relation to Luke-Acts, there are four main points put forward by those who hold to a minimalist position:

---

6   L.M. White, *The Social Origins of Christian Architecture*, vol. 1, *Building God's house in the Roman World: Architectural Adaption among Pagans, Jews, and Christians* (HTS, 42; Valley Forge: Trinity Press, 1990), p. 87. D.D. Binder dismisses this disparity too easily: 'The fact that so few references to the synagogues appear in the Pauline writings should not come as a surprise to us: Paul wrote his epistles to congregations he either founded or hoped to visit (Romans) primarily to address internal disputes. Allusions to his involvement with Jewish groups were incidental to this function', *Into the Temple Courts: The Place of the Synagogues in the Second Temple Period* (SBLDS, 169; Atlanta: Society of Biblical Literature, 1999), p. 64.

7   Here I am not equating all Luke's uses of συναγωγή with meeting places, see further below.

8   Acts 16.13-16, see further below.

- First, Luke's use of the term συναγωγή has been inaccurately translated by the English 'synagogue' which is understood as a building with a set pattern of religious activity. Rather, in the first century, this term should be understood to refer to the gathered community and is only occasionally used of a meeting place.[9]
- Second, the use of προσευχή is often assumed to be equivalent to συναγωγή.[10]
- Third, much of the archaeological material available has either been wrongly identified as synagogue buildings, or been incorrectly dated, leading to a misunderstanding of what a συναγωγή might be in Luke-Acts. Particularly in Palestine, the purpose-built synagogue building is a later institution:

> The earliest distinct buildings date from the third century, and vary widely in style and interior arrangements. Thus there is simply no evidence to speak of synagogues in Palestine as architecturally distinguishable edifices prior to 200 C.E. Evidence of meeting places: 'Yes', both in private homes and in public buildings. Evidence of distinctive architectural features of a place of worship or for study of Torah: 'No'.[11]

- Fourth, Luke-Acts projects back the worship practices of the Diaspora 'synagogue' of the late first century CE to the time of Jesus and the early church:

> The clearest evidence from the gospel tradition of the development of formal practices in connection with worship in synagogues comes – not surprisingly – from Luke-Acts. These traces of formalization are what might be expected in a document produced where the development of the synagogue had begun earlier than in Palestine: the diaspora... Thus we have in Luke-Acts the later forms of synagogal worship read back into the time of Jesus.[12]

---

9   So H.C. Kee, 'Defining the First-Century CE Synagogue: Problems and Progress', *NTS* 41 (1995), pp. 481–500 (493).

10   As are many other terms, but here my focus is on the terminology of Luke-Acts.

11   H.C. Kee, 'The Transformation of the Synagogue after 70 C.E.: Its Import for Early Christianity', *NTS* 36 (1990), pp. 1–24 (9). It must be said that others among the 'minimalists' would take a slightly more nuanced approach, well summarized by H.A. McKay: 'They believe that extrapolations from current evidence have to be made in order to reach the traditionalists' position, and they are not willing to make these extrapolations. They do not deny that further evidence could appear that would confirm the traditionalist stance, but they do not accept that stance as being already proved', 'Ancient Synagogues: The Continuing Dialectic Between Two Major Views', *Currents in Research: Biblical Studies* 6 (1998), pp. 103–42 (106–107).

12   Kee, 'Transformation', pp. 17–18. Also, H.A. McKay, *Sabbath and Synagogue: The Question of Sabbath Worship in Ancient Judaism* (Religion in the Graeco-Roman World, 122; Leiden: Brill, 1994), p. 166; J.D. Crossan and J.L. Reed, *Excavating Jesus: Beneath the*

The above summary centres on the work of Howard Kee. As mentioned, Kee's articles have subsequently either been the focus of direct responses or incorporated into the work of scholars. As this discussion progressed the debate has become a little more nuanced, although much of Kee's original argument is maintained by the minimalists. My intention in focusing on Kee is not to create a 'straw-man' to attack, but rather to trace the trajectory of subsequent scholarship.

One of the problems with this exchange is that in certain areas it has simply polarized the debate, and some of the issues concerned have not been thoroughly thought through. Here it will not be possible, or necessary, to identify all that has been written; rather, we will highlight important material which focuses on the presentation of the 'synagogue' in Luke-Acts. In relation to the third point above, the question of the identification of ancient sites, there are archaeologists who should also be considered minimalists. However, most of the discussion over the identification of sites as synagogue buildings has been covered in Chapter 3 and we do not intend to cover it again here, except where it is of direct importance for Luke-Acts.

3.2. *The Debate*

The first major response to Kee came in 1993, in an article by Richard Oster where he states: 'my intention is to respond only to the charge of anachronisms in Luke's picture of the Jewish synagogue during the era of the Second Temple'.[13] Oster highlights the fact that Kee had been selective with the evidence he cited, and correctly points to an inscription from Berenice in which συναγωγή is used both for the gathered community and for a building.[14] He argues that Kee has created a false dichotomy between συναγωγή and προσευχή, failing to acknowledge the breadth of language that would be used of the Sabbath meeting places. However, he also acknowledges that Kee has correctly pointed out that many of the occurrences of συναγωγή in Luke-Acts could be references to 'congregations rather than to synagogues'.[15] One of the problems of this early exchange is confusion over terminology, with both scholars pointing out

---

Stones, Behind the Texts (London: SPCK, 2001), p. 30; R.A. Horsley, *Archaeology, History, and Society in Galilee: The Social Context of Jesus and the Rabbis* (Valley Forge: Trinity, 1996), p. 147.

13   R.E. Oster, 'Supposed Anachronism in Luke-Acts' Use of ΣΥΝΑΓΩΓΗ', *NTS* 39 (1993), pp. 178–208 (179). The first response to Kee had been made earlier by E.P. Sanders in a long footnote, *Jewish Law From Jesus to the Mishnah: Five Studies* (London: SCM, 1990), pp. 341–43, n. 29.

14   Oster, 'Supposed Anachronism', pp. 187–88. Oster also cites other sources that Kee omitted, in which συναγωγή is used of a meeting place.

15   *Ibid.*, p. 190.

the other's shortcomings.[16] Where Kee had focused his discussion on συναγωγή and προσευχή, Oster widened the debate and produced a table listing all the 'Greek words used of Second Temple synagogues'.[17] The problem with this is that 'this table would be inconceivable, because unintelligible, to a "minimalist"'.[18] This is a fair criticism; simply to assume that all the words that Oster lists are equivalent to 'synagogue' in English is inappropriate. Such a variety of terms, for the minimalist, points to variety in the actual meeting-places, if indeed meeting-places are intended.

Following Oster's well-argued article was an essay from Kenneth Atkinson. While accepting that Oster had made many good points against Kee, he is concerned at Oster's 'extreme conservatism concerning the historical reliability of Luke-Acts'.[19] Atkinson focuses his attention on Kee's handling of the archaeological sites at Gamla, Masada and Herodium, arguing that these should be identified as synagogue buildings rather than just meeting halls. In this respect Atkinson's arguments are good, as are his criticisms of Kee's understanding of the evidence:

> Kee's misunderstanding of the archaeological evidence may stem largely from his confused interpretation of the terms used to describe pre-70 CE synagogues. The epigraphic evidence attests to a variety of synagogue structures, ranging from house-synagogues to formal structures designed for Jewish worship and additionally used for various communal functions during the remainder of the week.[20]

This is an excellent summary of the evidence: a variety of buildings were used, from house-synagogues to large purpose-built structures such as the one at Gamla, and these were used in a variety of ways by their communities. The problem with Atkinson is that on the very next page he goes on to say: 'When Luke-Acts records Jesus or Paul as entering a synagogue, an edifice similar or identical to the Gamla synagogue is being described', before apparently returning to his earlier convictions:

---

16 E.g., *ibid.*, p. 185; H.C. Kee, 'The Changing Meaning of Synagogue: A Response to Richard Oster', *NTS* 40 (1994), pp. 281–83 (281).

17 Oster, 'Supposed Anachronism', p. 186. It should be noted that this is a very helpful list which has subsequently been referred to by many. The paradox is that it may be appropriate to translate many of these varied terms with the word 'synagogue' but not do the same with συναγωγή. A. Runesson gives a comparable table of terms, but explicitly notes the ones that were used of buildings and those used of the assembly/community, *The Origins of the Synagogue: A Socio-Historical Study* (*ConNT*, 37; Stockholm: Almqvist & Wiksell, 2001), pp. 171–73.

18 McKay, 'Ancient Synagogues', p. 119.

19 Atkinson, 'Further Defining', p. 492, n. 5.

20 *Ibid.*, p. 498.

The synagogue building itself undoubtedly underwent a long process of development. During the pre-70 CE period a number of synagogue types existed simultaneously, ranging from large magnificent structures, such as the Gamla synagogue, to altered rooms, like Masada and Herodium, to house-synagogues.[21]

There are two major problems with the conclusions of Atkinson. First, he seems to ignore the possibility proposed by Kee, and accepted by others, that συναγωγή can refer to a gathering and not uniformly to a building.[22] Second, he is confused as to the architectural form of a first-century synagogue building. Even if we were to allow that every time Jesus or Paul enters a συναγωγή Luke has a building in mind, why should we think of something similar to the large building at Gamla?

One of the other major contributors to the minimalist position has been Heather McKay. Perhaps the most useful contribution McKay has brought to this debate comes in an article in 1998 in which she gives an overview of the major points of the discussion. Picking up on some of the confusion in earlier material she argues that anyone entering this field must clearly define the terms they are using: specifically, it is wrong to identify both συναγωγαί and προσευχαί as 'synagogues'.[23]

McKay also highlights the particular perspectives of scholars who are active in this field noting that, 'any "ancient synagogues" – whether they were *rooms*, *buildings* or perhaps solely, *groups* of Jews – that we envisage are of necessity constructs, that is, constructs in which both our scholarly judgements and our imaginations play a great, but often unrecorded, part'.[24] This kind of criticism is double-edged; while she is correct to note this issue, what one is left with is a feeling that as a historian all one should record are the bare facts. As Reif has noted, all we are then left with is a

---

21   *Ibid.*, p. 499.

22   'Although Luke-Acts is not in all respects historically accurate, it does remain an important witness to the existence of pre-70 CE synagogues as distinctive architectural edifices. The only anachronisms remaining are those scholars who, in the face of overwhelming evidence, continue to doubt the existence of pre-70 synagogues. *Cadit quaestio*, let us move on to other matters,' *ibid.*, p. 502.

23   McKay: 'evidence relating to buildings known as *proseuchai* cannot be directly applied to 'synagogues', since *proseuchai* are always, clearly, buildings, and 'synagogues' are frequently community groups', 'Ancient Synagogues', p. 115. Presumably here McKay means συναγωγαί when she writes 'synagogues'; bearing in mind her criticisms, it would have been clearer if she had transliterated both terms. Also, προσευχαί are not always buildings, see my discussion of Josephus *Ant.*, 14.257-58, (S.K. Catto, 'Does προσευχὰς ποιεῖσθαι, in Josephus' *Antiquities of the Jews* 14.257-8, Mean "Build Places of Prayer"?', *JSJ* 35 (2004), pp. 159–68), as well as Acts 16.13, 16, in section 4.3.1 below.

24   McKay, 'Ancient Synagogues', p. 104.

series of footnotes.[25] While I accept that the picture we project is a construct, and indeed that this construct will be influenced by the preconceptions we bring, nonetheless it is vital that we do reconstruct as best we can. It is right that our scholarly judgements and historical imagination should inform our understanding of how the 'synagogue' might be understood in a particular geographical location. It is equally important that other scholars point to the weaknesses in our understanding, or that some new piece of evidence or new interpretation, should turn our hypothesis on its head. Surely that is what historical scholarship is all about![26]

In relation to Luke-Acts, McKay notes:

> An important fact that I noted while working with the book of Acts is that although Luke sets out there to describe the work of the apostles at a time later than the work of Jesus, and paints the picture of Paul as a later disciple of Jesus, he assumes the same picture of the synagogue in both volumes of his work, making no allowance for change or development during the time span of thirty years he himself claims to be depicting. This is, for me, an extra piece of evidence that the picture Luke paints of Jesus in the synagogue cannot be historically accurate, even if Luke's picture of the synagogues of Paul's day were to be taken as authentic.[27]

In response to this it should be noted, first, that although the end of Acts portrays a time about 30 years from that covered by the Gospel of Luke, Acts covers large portions of the time between. Second, to use an analogy from today, if many church services have changed little in the past 30 years in a rapidly changing society, why should McKay expect great changes in the 'synagogue' in a society which would have changed at a much slower pace? Arguing for a more dramatic change in the period after the destruction of the temple might be more understandable, but such a change is unlikely between 30 and 60 CE.

Although he has not entered directly into the discussion outlined above, the writing of Michael White has been very influential in 'synagogue'

---

25   S.C. Reif, 'Jewish Liturgy in the Second Temple Period: Some Methodological Considerations', in *Proceedings of the 11th World Congress of Jewish Studies, Jerusalem, June 22–29, 1993* (Jerusalem: Magnes Press, 1994), pp. 1–8 (2).

26   The section on Capernaum below is just such a reconstruction, see section 4.2.2.2.

27   McKay, *Sabbath and Synagogue*, pp. 165–66. Interestingly, in an earlier article she allows that most references to συναγωγή in Acts refer to buildings: 'In the book of Acts, the term "synagogue" often means a building in which Jews met together on the sabbath to read Scripture and listen to teaching. For example, in 15.21, James says "from early generations Moses has had in every city those who preach him, for he is read every sabbath in the synagogues", thus confirming the procedures that we have understood from Philo for προσευχαί and Josephus for synagogues', H.A. McKay, 'From Evidence to Edifice: Four Fallacies about the Sabbath', in R.P. Carroll (ed.), *Text as Pretext: Essays in Honour of Robert Davidson* (JSOTSup, 138; Sheffield: JSOT Press, 1992), pp. 179–99 (195).

studies.[28] He has been involved in an ongoing debate with Anders Runesson on the identity of the earliest phase of the building in Ostia.[29] His conviction that the synagogue buildings at Delos and Ostia were homes in their earliest stages fits well with his general argument that Christianity and Judaism prospered under the expansion of the Roman empire and that these groups moved from meeting in domestic space to purpose-built structures over time and at about the same rate as each other. In his discussion of 'synagogues' in Acts, Witherington, citing White, remarks: 'many, if not most, of the pre-70 synagogues in the Holy Land may have been slightly modified rooms in public buildings or private homes'.[30] I have shown above that White is wrong when he proposes that the buildings at Delos and Ostia were originally domestic houses,[31] and the archaeological evidence gathered from Palestine highlighted the variety of towns and villages that might have a synagogue building. Obviously I do not deny that this is how many 'synagogues' originated, or that in the first century, rural communities or small populations of Jews would have continued to meet in homes. My point is only that too much weight has been given to the arguments of White, and therefore New Testament scholars, such as Witherington, may be overly influenced by his views.

As the scholarly discussion has continued in various articles, four monographs on the subject of the early 'synagogue' have also appeared which interact with the debate to various degrees. First was the massive work of Levine, *The Ancient Synagogue: The First Thousand Years.* Although noting some of the arguments of the minimalists, Levine does not spend much time with this debate. He dismisses much in the conclusions of Kee and McKay, and has a positive view of Luke-Acts as a historical source for 'synagogue' research.[32] Following Levine comes the work of Binder who tends towards a maximalist view of the evidence. Although Binder's work is careful and detailed, he often uses terminology which, for a minimalist, should not be confused; for example, he terms the

---

28   I have already noted White's influence on Levine's discussion of Ostia, see Chapter 3, 2.1.2.2.

29   L.M. White 'Synagogue and Society in Imperial Ostia: Archaeology and Epigraphic Evidence', *HTR* 90 (1997), pp. 23–58; *idem*, 'Reading the Ostia Synagogue: A Reply to A. Runesson', *HTR* 92 (1999), pp. 435–64.

30   Witherington, *Acts*, pp. 255–56 n. 245.

31   Gamla is also incorrectly identified as a house by R.A. Horsley, *Galilee: History, Politics, People* (Valley Forge: Trinity, 1995), p. 224.

32   E.g., *The Ancient Synagogue: The First Thousand Years* (New Haven and London: Yale University Press, 2000), p. 45, n. 11.

προσευχή in Delos a synagogue.[33] Anders Runesson's study focuses on the origin of the 'synagogue'; however, in order to do so he moves backward from the material available from later periods. His definition of terms and his precise treatment of his subject most clearly deal with the issues raised by McKay in her 1999 article.[34] Finally, Carsten Claußen accepts much of the minimalists' perspective in his work. As in all these later studies he is more nuanced in his arguments and accepts that there would occasionally have been synagogue buildings. However, continuing the line pursued by White, he sees the establishment of Jewish and Christian meeting places following a similar trajectory: 'For the first century CE it may be stressed that in the same way that the vast majority of Jewish assemblies gathered in private houses, the early Christians also met like this.'[35] In common with all scholars who have come to this subject from a biblical studies background, Binder, Runesson and Claußen are careful in their use of Luke-Acts as a source. Although all three recognize its importance for the investigation of the subject, they are also careful to point out the potential pitfalls.[36]

3.3. *Conclusion*

The effect of attempts to refute Kee and the minimalist perspective have at times simply heightened the divide between the two groups, with neither side paying adequate attention to the detail of the other's arguments. As has been shown, Kee did not take into account all the sources available in which συναγωγή clearly refers to a building. However, when scholars rightly made this point, highlighting those occasions when it could be used of a building, the impression gained in some New Testament scholarship is that it should continue to be understood in this way. Indeed, in response to Oster's article, Kee himself misunderstands Oster's argument in exactly this way, noting that he 'fails to take into account adequately the range of

---

33 Binder, *Temple Courts*, p. 88. We should note that he does, later in his discussion, make it clear that his position is that προσευχή was the term regularly used of Diaspora synagogue buildings, *ibid.*, pp. 111–18.

34 E.g., 'By the first century several different terms were used to designate the phenomenon referred to in modern literature by the English word "synagogue". The terms could refer to both buildings and assemblies, or only buildings, or, again only assemblies. Furthermore, the assemblies referred to were of different types', *Origins of the Synagogue*, p. 232. See also his table on pp. 171–73.

35 C. Claußen, *Versammlung, Gemeinde, Synagoge: Das hellenistisch-jüdische Umfeld der frühchristlichen Gemeinde* (SUNT, 27; Göttingen: Vandenhoeck & Ruprecht, 2002), p. 307 (author's translation).

36 See especially Binder, *Temple Courts*, pp. 67–75, 78–81.

connotations that συναγωγή has in the pre-70 CE Jewish literature'.[37] So when Witherington, in his commentary on Acts, has an excursus on 'synagogues', he cites the Berenice inscription to show that συναγωγή could be a building but fails to mention that in the same inscription it also refers to the gathering.[38] From this the view of the minimalist is dismissed and the maximalist's perspective continues.[39]

So scholarship has created a dichotomy: where a συναγωγή is mentioned we must decide whether a building or a gathering is in mind. This appears to be too limited a choice. To give a twenty-first-century parallel: if a person says that they are going to *church*, what should we understand them to mean? To some this could mean going to a large building, to others a meeting in a community hall, while a third person may be thinking of a group gathering in a home.[40] Some will think of the architecture; others, of the group of people they are gathered with. When a person talks about *church*, even in their own mind there may be some ambiguity – do they mean the building or the community gathered? Perhaps they have both ideas in mind at the same time. It appears that just such an understanding may also apply to συναγωγή. On occasions it can clearly mean a building, on others clearly a gathering, while some references may have both meanings in mind at the same time.[41]

The other choice that is made is between monumental synagogue buildings and gatherings in domestic space. So, discussing the 'synagogues' mentioned in the New Testament, Hoppe can write: 'it is not clear that these buildings were, in fact, monumental buildings constructed and used primarily for worship. In all likelihood, these "synagogues" were not

37   Kee, 'Changing Meaning', p. 281. Also McKay, 'Oster seems consistently to envisage a "building" as the dominant meaning (though he does not state that this is his position) and the "gathering" as a subsidiary meaning', 'Ancient Synagogues', p. 119.

38   Witherington, *Acts*, p. 255.

39   We should note that the current debate over 'synagogues' is not limited to the Gospels and Acts. The discussion has also made its way into Pauline studies. Two recent monographs on Romans highlight how a particular perspective on the 'synagogue' helps to construct an understanding of the social background to Paul's letter. Mark Nanos incorporates many of the arguments of White and Kee in his picture of Roman Judaism, concluding that homes or small renovated buildings would have been used by the communities, *The Mystery of Romans: The Jewish Context of Paul's Letter* (Minneapolis: Fortress Press, 1996), pp. 42–50, see esp. pp. 42–43, n. 4, p. 377, n. 15. P.F. Esler, in contrast, correctly includes literary evidence of προσευχαί in Rome as well as the archaeological remains from Ostia, concluding that there must have been a number of specially constructed buildings in Rome at the time of Paul's letter, *Conflict and Identity in Romans: The Social Setting of Paul's Letter* (Minneapolis: Fortress Press, 2003), pp. 8–97. Overall the conclusions of Esler are safer, although he may be in danger of assuming too much from the remains at Ostia.

40   I realize that this is a very western perception of what church might mean, but it can easily be applied in a different cultural context.

41   E.g., Acts 6.9; 9.2.

distinguishable from ordinary domestic architecture.'[42] Again this polarization is unhelpful. Different kinds, sizes and styles of architecture were used as 'synagogues' depending on the socio-economic situation of the local Jewish community, and these buildings would have been used for a variety of purposes throughout the week. Such diversity needs to be acknowledged.

Therefore, is there a sign here of anachronism in the New Testament accounts? Does συναγωγή simply refer to the congregations or are buildings in mind? Horsley writes: 'With no archaeological or literary evidence for synagogue buildings in Judean or Galilean towns and villages until the third century or later, it is difficult to justify the standard reading of *synagōgē* in the New Testament as a religious building'.[43] Kee and Horsley both examine the various potential references to 'synagogues' as places in the New Testament, Kee concluding that the account of the Roman centurion building a synagogue for the Jews in Luke 7.5 is the only clear reference to a building,[44] although Acts 18.4-7 does also refer to a place, and it may be that this was a house.[45]

As pointed out in the earlier chapters, there is a real diversity in the terminology used to describe the meeting(place)s of the Jews. They could be called συναγωγή, προσευχή, ἱερόν, διδασκαλεῖον, σαββατεῖον etc., and in certain geographical locations particular terms were more commonly used than others. Similarly, authors often used more than one term for what can broadly be defined as the 'synagogue'. That being the case, we might have expected Luke also to use a greater variety of words for the meeting(place)s: his consistent use of the term συναγωγή does appear odd. Geographically his account of the ministry of Jesus and the early church covers an area from Jerusalem to Rome. It is highly unlikely that in all of these communities the term that would have been applied locally was συναγωγή. From this perspective it appears Luke's use of συναγωγή is anachronistic: not in the way in which he has been seen as anachronistic by Kee and others, but rather in his ubiquitous use of the term. Clearly in some of the places that Luke records a συναγωγή, the local community would have called it something else.[46]

42 L.J. Hoppe, *The Synagogues and Churches of Ancient Palestine* (Collegeville, Minnesota: The Liturgical Press, 1994), p. 14.

43 Horsley, *Galilee: History, Politics, People*, p. 225.

44 Kee, 'Transformation', p. 17; *idem*, 'Defining', p. 490; Horsley, *Galilee: History, Politics, People*, p. 225.

45 Kee, 'Transformation', p. 4; *idem*, 'Defining', p. 491.

46 M. Hengel suggests that this is because the shaping of the Gospels tradition was still influenced by its Palestinian origins, 'Proseuche und Synagoge: Jüdische Gemeinde, Gotteshaus und Gottesdienst in der Diaspora und in Palästina', in J. Gutmann (ed.), *The Synagogue: Studies in Origins, Archaeology and Architecture* (The Library of Biblical Studies, New York: KTAV, 1975), pp. 27–54 (51).

Having acknowledged the strengths and weaknesses in the arguments put forward by those involved in the debate over the presentation of the 'synagogue' in Luke-Acts, and with the evidence which has been gathered in the previous chapters, we will now take a closer look at some of the texts of Luke-Acts as this background information can help us understand the historical reality behind them. Following the pattern of previous chapters we will try to examine these by geographical location.

4. Geographical Locations

4.1. Introduction

Palestine	General ref.		Luke 4.44[47]
	Galilee	General ref.	Luke 4.14-15
		Nazareth	Luke 4.16, 28
		Capernaum	Luke 4.33, 38; 7.5
	Judea	Jerusalem	Acts 6.9; 24.12; 26.11
Diaspora	Syria	Damascus	Acts 9.2, 20
	Cyprus	Salamis	Acts 13.5
	Galatia	Pisidian Antioch	Acts 13.14, 43
		Iconium	Acts 14.1
	Asia	Ephesus	Acts 18.19
	Macedonia	Thessalonica	Acts 17.1
		Beroea	Acts 17.10
		Philippi?	Acts 16.13, 16
	Achaia	Athens	Acts 17.17
		Corinth	Acts 18.7-8

Table 5.1 Geographical spread of 'synagogues' in Luke-Acts.

Where there appears to be some distinction between Luke-Acts and our other sources is in the number and spread of 'synagogues'. The accounts

47   Luke's change of Mark's Γαλιλαία to Ἰουδαία is not to indicate a ministry in the district of Judaea, rather it indicates that Jesus' message is to all Jews, see I.H. Marshall, *The Gospel of Luke*, (NIGTC; Grand Rapids: Eerdmans, 1978) pp. 198–99; J. Nolland, *Luke* (WBC, 35; 3 vols; Dallas: Word Books, 1989–93), vol. 1, p. 216.

of Jesus' movements have him preaching in 'synagogues' throughout Palestine, and Paul throughout the Diaspora. In some of these references the plural συναγωγαί is used suggesting that there were more than one in these cities.[48]

Here the limitations of space will not allow a complete examination of each reference along with a discussion of what the historical situation may have been in that particular setting. Rather, references representative of particular areas will be chosen. Starting in Palestine, the συναγωγαί in Jerusalem will first be discussed; we will then move beyond Judaea to Galilee where the archaeological data gathered in Chapter 3 will be used to inform our understanding of the reference to a συναγωγή in Capernaum. Further, the worship practices in Palestine will be examined, particularly focusing on Jesus' teaching in Nazareth. Moving to the Diaspora, the encounter of Paul and Lydia at a προσευχή in Philippi will be examined; the reasons for Luke's use of this term and whether it should be understood as a building or not will be considered. One further Diaspora site will also be explored in detail: a reference to a συναγωγή in Pisidian Antioch is the only occasion in Luke-Acts where this term clearly does not refer to a building, but should the other reference to a συναγωγή in the city be understood in the same way? The account of Paul's teaching in Pisidian Antioch also gives us details of Diaspora practice and this will be discussed.

4.2. *Palestine*
4.2.1. *Jerusalem*
4.2.1.1. *Acts 6.9*

Acts provides us with three references to 'synagogues' in Jerusalem. The first comes in 6.9 in which Stephen is confronted by Hellenistic Jews:

> Some of those who belonged to the synagogue of the Freedmen (as it was called), Cyrenians, Alexandrians, and others of those from Cilicia and Asia (τινες τῶν ἐκ τῆς συναγωγῆς τῆς λεγομένης Λιβερτίνων καὶ Κυρηναίων καὶ Ἀλεξανδρέων καὶ τῶν ἀπὸ Κιλικίας καὶ Ἀσίας) stood up and argued with Stephen.

There is considerable debate around this passage. First, as to how many 'synagogues' are being referred to here, with suggestions ranging from between one and five.[49] Although also a genitive, Λιβερτίνων, from the

---

48   Jerusalem (Acts 6.9; 24.12; 26.11); Damascus (Acts 9.2, 20); Salamis (Acts 13.5), as well as the general references in Lk. 4.14-15, 44.

49   For one 'synagogue' see, C.J. Hemer, *The Book of Acts in the Setting of Hellenistic History* (ed. C.H. Gempf; WUNT, 49; Tübingen: Mohr Siebeck, 1989), p. 176; Witherington, *Acts*, p. 253; F.F. Bruce, *The Book of the Acts* (NICNT; Grand Rapids: Eerdmans, rev. edn, 1988), p. 124, n. 28; L.T. Johnson, *The Acts of the Apostles* (Minnesota: Liturgical Press,

transliteration of the Latin *libertinus*,[50] is different to the other four references which are all geographical, thus suggesting one synagogue for all the groups mentioned. However, the repetition of the article, τῶν, here indicates that two 'synagogues' may be more likely: 'some of those from the "synagogue" of the Freedmen (as it is called), Cyrenians and Alexandrians, and (some from the "synagogue") of those from Cilicia and Asia'. We then have two 'synagogues' representing specific areas of the Diaspora, one from North Africa and another from Asia Minor. Given the possibility that various geographical locations may have had slightly different 'synagogue' practices it would seem entirely plausible that groups travelling to Jerusalem would be drawn to a practice, and a community, with which they were familiar.[51]

The second point of debate relates to whether this occurrence of συναγωγή should be understood to refer to congregation(s) or building(s).[52] Barrett appears to think of it purely in terms of a building,[53] while Schürer manages to hold both points of view; first he thinks that here (and in Acts 9.2) συναγωγή is being used to denote the 'congregation';[54] however, he then goes on to assumes that Acts 6.9 does refer to a building.[55] Fitzmyer recognizes both possibilities but does not commit to one or the other.[56] Similarly, Witherington is well aware of the debate,

---

1992), p. 108; R. Riesner, 'Synagogues in Jerusalem', in R. Bauckham (ed.), *The Book of Acts in its Palestinian Setting* (*TBAFCS*, vol. 4), pp. 179–211 (204–205); Barrett, *Acts*, vol. 1, p. 323; H. Conzelmann, *Acts of the Apostles* (trans. J. Limburg *et al.*; Philadelphia: Fortress Press, 1987), p. 47. For two, see F.J. Foakes Jackson and K. Lake, *The Beginnings of Christianity* (5 vols; London: Macmillan and Co., 1933), vol. 4, p. 66; E. Haenchen, *The Acts of the Apostles* (Oxford: Blackwell, 1971), p. 271; W. Schrage, 'συναγωγή', *TDNT*, vol. 7, p. 837; Kee, 'Defining', p. 490; Jervell, *Die Apostelgeschichte*, p. 225. Levine, however, argues that because of the large Diaspora presence in Jerusalem and the differences between these groups, five is more likely, *Ancient Synagogue*, p. 53; also Schürer, *HJP*, vol. 2, p. 428, n. 8.

50 Barrett, *Acts*, vol. 1, p. 323. Bruce and others note that because of the following African nations, a reading of Libyans was suggested by Beza and subsequently Dibelius. Bruce remarks that this is tempting in the context, 'but the temptation should be resisted', *The Book of Acts*, p. 124. It is interesting that Nestle-Aland (27th ed.) and UBS (4th ed.) both use a capital Λ in λιβερτῖνος, perhaps indicating that they understand it as a reference to a place or as a title for the 'synagogue'. However, capitalization is often not a recent editorial decision and may have a long background in the history of printed editions. (I am grateful to Dr P.J. Williams for information in this regard).

51 Cf. the discussion of rabbinic evidence for 'synagogues' in Jerusalem, particularly the 'synagogue' of the Alexandrians, in Chapter 2, 4.3.

52 It is interesting to note that two recent German commentators do not discuss this issue at all, Eckey, *Die Apostelgeschichte*, vol. 1, pp. 158–59; Jervell, *Die Apostelgeschichte*, p. 225.

53 Barrett, *Acts*, vol. 1, pp. 323–24.

54 Schürer, *HJP*, vol. 2, p. 428.

55 *Ibid.*, 2.445.

56 Fitzmyer, *Acts*, pp. 356–57.

including a section on current scholarship on the subject at this point, but does not explicitly indicate whether he understands this to be a building,[57] while Kee suggests that it does not refer to a building or a local organization but simply to a group.[58] Tellbe, in his general discussion of the use of συναγωγή in Acts, concludes that of the 19 references 16 clearly relate to buildings, but fails to indicate which ones he thinks do not.[59] In correspondence with him, he indicates that Acts 6.9, 9.2 and 13.43 may refer only to the gathering, nonetheless, he does not exclude the possibility that they were buildings and suggests, 'probably they refer both to the building and to the people in the building'.[60] This is the most likely solution: the use of συναγωγή does not necessarily require that we choose between the two options, both can be meant by the use of the word.

Given that it could be understood to be a congregation, it is interesting to note that Flesher is willing to accept Acts 6.9 as a building.[61] He has argued that in the first century there was a division within Palestine: in Judaea the 'Temple cult apparently held sway in this area and maintained a religious environment that prevented the synagogue from gaining a foothold in the area',[62] whereas in the areas north of Judaea the 'synagogue' flourished. Along with Acts 6.9 he allows the Theodotos synagogue as the only two references to synagogue buildings in Judaea. Further, he contends that both of these were for Diaspora Jews who had imported the practices of their local communities into Jerusalem, which explains their existence at this time.[63]

While the Theodotos inscription explicitly states that part of the synagogue building's function was for pilgrims to use when they visited Jerusalem, it should be acknowledged that it is at least possible that it, along with the 'synagogues' mentioned in Acts 6, was also used by Diaspora Jews permanently residing in Jerusalem. Nevertheless, the 'synagogues' of Acts 6 were used by Jews either from, or connected to, Asia Minor and North Africa, and it is likely that the practices within these 'synagogues' would have reflected some of those of this area. Also, it would seem likely that the language used within these 'synagogues' would

---

57 Witherington, *Acts*, pp. 253–57. His discussion appears to indicate he favours a building.

58 H.C. Kee, *To Every Nation under Heaven* (The New Testament in Context; Harrisburg: Trinity Press, 1997), p. 90, p. 317, n. 3.

59 M. Tellbe, *Paul Between Synagogue and State: Christians, Jews, and Civil Authorities in 1 Thessalonians, Romans and Philippians* (ConNT, 34; Stockholm: Almqvist & Wiksell, 2001), p. 220.

60 M. Tellbe, e-mail correspondence dated 28 January 2004.

61 P.V.M. Flesher, 'Palestinian Synagogues Before 70 C.E.: A Review of the Evidence', in *ASHAAD*, vol. 1, pp. 27–39 (32).

62 *Ibid.*, p. 30.

63 *Ibid.*, p. 39.

have been Greek. Scholars have suggested that Acts 6 and the Theodotos inscription could refer to the same building.[64] It is impossible to be certain on this issue, and, as suggested earlier, it is likely that Acts 6 refers to two groups, and both buildings and gatherings. It does, however, appear likely that the function of these 'synagogues' was similar.

It has been suggested in previous chapters that the model for the 'synagogue' in the Diaspora was often the voluntary association. If, as proposed, Diaspora practices influenced the 'synagogues' of Acts 6 then this may also have been evidenced in the style of architecture. The description of the various buildings of Theodotos' synagogue fits well with the evidence gathered from the Diaspora, and it seems likely that the 'synagogues' of the Freedmen would have been similar. Therefore, we should understand such buildings as providing a centre for this group, which may have provided them with a place to meet for communal meals and other gatherings as well as worship activities.

4.2.1.2. Acts 24.12 and 26.9-11[65]

Two other references to 'synagogues' in Jerusalem come in Paul's defence of himself, first before governor Felix and then Agrippa:

> And neither in the Temple nor in the synagogues nor anywhere in the city did they find me arguing with anyone or causing the onset of a crowd (καὶ οὔτε ἐν τῷ ἱερῷ εὗρόν με πρός τινα διαλεγόμενον ἢ ἐπίστασιν ποιοῦντα ὄχλου οὔτε ἐν ταῖς συναγωγαῖς οὔτε κατὰ τὴν πόλιν).[66]

> Indeed, I myself was convinced that I ought to do many things against the name of Jesus of Nazareth. And that is what I did in Jerusalem; with authority received from the chief priests, I not only locked up many of the saints in prison, but I also cast my vote against them when they were being condemned to death. By punishing them often in all the synagogues I tried to force them to blaspheme (καὶ κατὰ πάσας τὰς συναγωγὰς πολλάκις τιμωρῶν αὐτοὺς ἠνάγκαζον βλασφημεῖν); and since I was so furiously enraged at them, I pursued them even to foreign cities (εἰς τὰς ἔξω πόλεις).[67]

Of the first, Binder concludes that it is referring to buildings, as 'it would be awkward to refer to a crowd "in the gatherings" '.[68] It is difficult to see

---

64   Foakes Jackson and Lake, *The Beginnings of Christianity*, vol. 4, p. 68; Riesner, 'Synagogues in Jerusalem', p. 205. But see Runesson, *Origins*, pp. 228–29.

65   Acts 22.19 may also refer to 'synagogues' in Jerusalem.

66   Acts 24.12. Here I follow the translation of Barrett which is a better rendering than that of the NRSV.

67   Acts 26.9-11. Two other references presumably allude to 'synagogues' in Jerusalem: Lk. 20.46; Acts 15.21.

68   Binder, *Temple Courts*, p. 158, n. 9.

that this is a necessary conclusion; perhaps the 'gathering' would be just the right place to stir up a crowd. Similarly inconclusive is Riesner's argument that the connection of the temple with 'synagogues' suggests a correlation between two buildings.[69] In fact, this is an ascending tricolon where the temple, 'synagogues' and the city are the same kind of entities;[70] it is difficult to conclude from this that buildings are meant.[71] Again, in the second reference it is not possible, from the immediate context, to decide whether this refers to a gathering or a building. However, wider evidence would suggest that there were synagogue buildings in Jerusalem at this time and would have been included here.[72]

Within these verses Luke provides some useful additional information regarding what could happen within the 'synagogue'. Paul, as a follower of Jesus, states that he was not guilty of arguing or stirring up a crowd; he also acknowledges that in his earlier life he had punished the Christians, causing them to blaspheme. Dealing with the punishments first: that a 'synagogue' could be used for judgement in the Diaspora is attested in a decree dated to the middle of the first century BCE in which the people of Sardis 'may, in accordance with their accepted customs, come together and have a communal life and adjudicate suits among themselves'.[73] This could also take place in Palestine as elsewhere Paul recalls his acts of punishment: 'they themselves know that in every synagogue I imprisoned and beat (ἐγὼ ἤμην φυλακίζων καὶ δέρων κατὰ τὰς συναγωγάς) those

69   Riesner, 'Synagogues in Jerusalem,' p. 204.

70   F. Blass and A. Debrunner, *A Greek Grammar of the New Testament and Other Early Christian Literature* (trans. R.W. Funk; Cambridge: Cambridge University Press, 1961), 445.2.

71   Only in Jn 18.20 does the comparison of the Temple with the 'synagogue' suggest a building.

72   In his discussion of these two passages Flesher argues that as Lukan literary constructions they reflect a 'post-70 diaspora situation', 'Synagogues Before 70', p. 32. However, the fact that Luke composed these passages does not mean they do not reflect a historical reality. If Flesher is happy to accept that Acts 6.9 refers to a building, why then exclude the possibility that here also Luke is accurate and intends a building? Presumably, allowing that these buildings may reflect the situation in Jerusalem at the time of Paul might indicate that there were also *Judaean* groups of Jews using synagogue buildings at this time; in contrast to Flesher's view that this was limited to the practices of Diaspora Jews. I have argued above that Flesher is wrong to exclude the synagogue buildings of Masada and Herodium, to which can now be added the remains of the building at Jericho, Kiryat Sefer and Modi'in (+ Qumran?) These along with the synagogue building of Theodotos, combined with other references noted in Chapter 2, (e.g., the συναγωγαί of the Essenes alluded to by Philo, which, in all probability, existed in Jerusalem in this period, *Omn. Prob. Lib.*, 81–82) suggest that there were synagogue buildings in Judaea at this time. Therefore, it is possible, even likely, that Paul's 'synagogues of the Freedmen' were buildings; see the discussion above. Similarly, Paul's references to 'synagogues' in Acts 24 and 26 are likely to include buildings, but 'house-synagogues' or 'gatherings' may be included, and, as indicated above, the term συναγωγή may well carry both the meaning of building and gathering.

73   Josephus, *Ant.*, 14.260. Cf. *Ant.*, 14.235; Sus. 28.

who believed'.[74] In Chapters 2 and 3 above, both literary and archaeological evidence indicate that often the 'synagogue' was not a single
building but could be made up of various rooms attached to a larger main
meeting room. One of these rooms may have been used for carrying out
judicial or even custodial functions.[75]

Having been accused of being an 'agitator among all the Jews
throughout the world',[76] Paul narrows the parameters noting that he is
not guilty of rousing a crowd or arguing with those in Jerusalem, pointing
out that he has only been in the city for 12 days. Elsewhere Paul's teaching
in 'synagogues' often did lead to heated debate, and many of our sources
indicate that discussion was a quite normal part of the exchange.[77] As
discussed in Chapter 3, the architecture of several Palestinian buildings for
which we have sufficient remains have benches around the walls of the
structure. These would lend themselves to an open discussion rather than
a lecture or prolonged sermon being delivered where those present simply
listened without any input. As has been noted, we should not think back
with the more formal Christian or Jewish liturgy of the twenty-first
century when assessing worship practices in the early 'synagogue'. In
Palestine, open debate and discussion around the teaching given was an
integral part of the Sabbath gathering.[78] What is clear is that it is not this
open exchange or debate within the setting of a 'synagogue' that is meant
here, but rather sedition which is an appropriate charge to bring before
Governor Felix.

4.2.1.3. *Conclusion*

We must acknowledge that the evidence we have for 'synagogues' in
Judaea and specifically in Jerusalem is limited. Scholars who argue for a
minimalist position would question Eric Meyers' suggestion that 'by the
first century CE numerous synagogues existed in Jerusalem itself'.[79]
Rabbinic sources which suggest many first-century synagogue buildings
must be treated with scepticism, and the proposal that the presence of the
Jerusalem temple meant that such gatherings were unnecessary, may have

---

74   Acts 22.19. The form of the punishment is unknown, but the suggestion that it would
have been flogging seems likely, see, Witherington, *Acts*, p. 742; Fitzmyer, *Acts*, p. 758. Cf. 2
Cor. 11.24.

75   Cf. Josephus, *Life*, 276–303, the city βουλή meet in the προσευχή of Tiberias to
debate.

76   Acts 24.5.

77   See the discussion in Chapter 4, 2.7.

78   We have noted that within some Diaspora 'synagogues', which modelled themselves
on voluntary associations, this kind of open debate may have been less important.

79   E.M. Meyers, 'Ancient Synagogues: An Archaeological Introduction', in S. Fine (ed.),
Sacred Realm: The Emergence of the Synagogue in the Ancient World (New York: Yeshiva
University Museum, 1996), pp. 3–20 (22).

some merit, as the temple was being used for some of the things that the 'synagogue' was used for in other locations. Claußen, also acknowledging the effect of the temple, writes: 'The possibility remains of numerous, perhaps hundreds, of synagogue-meetings in the private houses of Jerusalem. The presence of the Temple up to the year 70 CE made particular synagogue-buildings appear far less necessary than in the Diaspora.'[80] However, there is sufficient information to suggest that purpose-built synagogues also existed. While it seems entirely likely that some groups of Jews would have met in homes, Claußen, in line with his general hypothesis, probably overestimates the place of house-synagogues in the city.

As has been shown in earlier chapters, 'synagogues' fulfilled a variety of purposes: the Theodotos synagogue building details some of the functions it was to be used for and consisted of more than one room. Where Jerusalem synagogue buildings are meant in Acts, it is likely that they too performed more than one role in their community, including a judicial function, and would have been used throughout the week. Although Paul describes the 'synagogue' as a place for interrogation and imprisonment, elsewhere Acts records that Paul had persecuted the Christians in Jerusalem taking both men and women to prison (φυλακή).[81] It may be that if Christians were discovered, the 'synagogues' were used temporarily to keep them in custody before removing them to prison.

As in other areas, the reading of the Torah, followed by teaching and discussion of it, would have been the central component of the Sabbath practices of these 'synagogues'. However, it was noted in Chapter 4 that there is less reference to prayer within Judaea and particularly Jerusalem. This may have been reflected in the practices of those using these 'synagogues', perhaps favouring the temple surrounds as the place to pray.

4.2.2. *Galilee*
4.2.2.1. *Introduction*

Previous research on synagogue buildings in the area of Galilee identified a development in the architectural style of buildings.[82] More recent scholarship has correctly noted that there was greater diversity in the architectural pattern of buildings in this area, while some go further:

> The archaeological finds known to us lead to a single conclusion, namely, prior to the third century synagogues did not exist as special structures, with external identifying signs, as in the third-century Galilean synagogues. The synagogues in which the *tannaim* prayed in the second century and even those used by the early *amoraim* were

---

80 Claußen, *Versammlung*, p. 98, (author's translation).
81 Acts 8.3.
82 See the discussion in Chapter 3, 1.2.

located in houses with the plan and façade of private homes. These buildings usually included one hall larger than the rest for study and prayer, and often had additional rooms which served the community. In terms later used to characterize the Christian community, one can say that this was a sort of 'religious community building' – *domus ecclesiae*.[83]

The Gospel of Luke refers to συναγωγαί in Galilee on four occasions. The first describes the start of Jesus' ministry: 'He began to teach in their synagogues (καὶ αὐτὸς ἐδίδασκεν ἐν ταῖς συναγωγαῖς αὐτῶν)'.[84] The second, to which we will return below, refers to Jesus in a 'synagogue' in Nazareth,[85] while the remaining two are references to a 'synagogue' in Capernaum to which we now turn.

4.2.2.2. *Capernaum*

The village of Capernaum was situated on the north-western shore of Lake Galilee around 10 km north of Tiberias and 5 km from the mouth of the Jordan, which marked the border between the areas controlled by Herod Antipas and Philip. Josephus records being taken to the village after falling from his horse and breaking his wrist: he calls Capernaum a κώμη, a small town or village.[86] In the first century it would have been a busy village as it was surrounded by fertile land, had an active fishing industry and sat near to important trading routes.[87] Indeed Meyers and Strange suggest a large centre with a population of between 12,000 and 15,000.[88] Recently, Richard Horsley has criticized these figures, correctly arguing that this is a grossly inflated estimate, and pointing out that it would seem highly unlikely that Capernaum would have a population one third that of Jerusalem, which Meyers and Strange put at between 37,000 and 44,000.[89]

---

83   Y. Tsafrir, 'On the Source of the Architectural Design of the Ancient Synagogues in Galilee: A New Appraisal', in *ASHAAD*, vol. 1 pp. 70–86 (79). See also Horsley, *Galilee: History, Politics, People*, p. 222; H.C. Kee, 'Early Christianity in the Galilee: Reassessing the Evidence from the Gospels', in L.I. Levine, *The Galilee in Late Antiquity* (Cambridge, MA: The Jewish Theological Seminary of America, 1992), pp. 3–22 (12). Although accepting that there might occasionally have been purpose-built synagogue complexes in the larger cities, Claußen also thinks that they are to be seen as the exception, *Versammlung*, p. 295.

84   Lk. 4.14-15.

85   Lk. 4.16-30.

86   Josephus, *Life*, 403.

87   J.C.H. Laughlin, 'Capernaum from Jesus' Time and After', *BARev* 19.5 (1993), pp. 54–61 (58); E.M. Meyers and J.F. Strange, *Archaeology, the Rabbis and Early Christianity* (London: SCM, 1981), p. 60. S. Loffreda points out that a study of the coins and vessels found at Capernaum indicates it was involved in trade with areas to the north of the village, i.e., Upper Galilee, Golan, Syria, Phoenicia, Asia Minor and Cyprus, *Recovering Capharnaum* (Jerusalem: Franciscan Printing Press, 2nd edn, 1993), p. 19.

88   Meyers and Strange, *Archaeology*, p. 58.

89   Horsley, *Archaeology, History, and Society in Galilee*, p. 114. For Meyers and Strange's estimate for Jerusalem see, *Archaeology*, p. 52.

More recent research on the size of Jerusalem estimates a figure around twice this by the mid-first century, arguing that Jerusalem was 'extremely densely populated' with over 50 people per 1,000 m².[90] Stanislao Loffreda, one of the archaeologists who excavated Capernaum, notes that the village occupied an area of approximately 60,000 m²,[91] which would suggest a population of 3,000 if the density were similar. However, he also points out: 'Walls were built without true foundations, and the one storey rooms could hardly reach more than 3 m in height'.[92] In contrast, many of Jerusalem's houses were built in two or three storeys[93] and so it would seem likely that in a rural village the population density would be significantly lower. Laughlin has suggested a figure of around 1,000 in the first century and this would seem plausible.[94] And so we have a relatively small village which, nevertheless, enjoyed a reasonable level of commercial activity.

The first reference to a 'synagogue' comes at the start of Jesus' ministry and describes him teaching and healing there:

> He went down to Capernaum, a city in Galilee, and was teaching them on the sabbath. They were astounded at his teaching, because he spoke with authority. In the synagogue there was a man who had the spirit of an unclean demon, and he cried out with a loud voice, 'Let us alone! What have you to do with us, Jesus of Nazareth? Have you come to destroy us? I know who you are, the Holy One of God.' But Jesus rebuked him, saying, 'Be silent, and come out of him!' When the demon had thrown him down before them, he came out of him without having done him any harm. They were all amazed and kept saying to one another, 'What kind of utterance is this? For with authority and power he commands the unclean spirits, and out they come!' And a report about him began to reach every place in the region.[95]

In the second, a centurion sent some Jewish elders (πρεσβύτεροι τῶν Ἰουδαίων) to ask Jesus to heal one of his slaves. In this passage the reference to a συναγωγή must mean a building as the centurion is said to have built (οἰκοδομέω) it for the Jews:

> When they came to Jesus, they appealed to him earnestly, saying, 'He is worthy of having you do this for him, for he loves our people, and it is he who built our synagogue for us (καὶ τὴν συναγωγὴν αὐτὸς ᾠκοδόμησεν ἡμῖν)'.[96]

---

90 W. Reinhardt, 'The Population Size of Jerusalem and the Numerical Growth of the Jerusalem Church', in Bauckham, *The Book of Acts*, pp. 237–65 (263).

91 Loffreda, *Recovering*, p. 18.

92 *Ibid.*, p. 20.

93 Reinhardt, 'Population Size of Jerusalem', p. 253.

94 Laughlin, 'Capernaum from Jesus' Time', p. 57.

95 Lk. 4.31-37.

96 Lk. 7.4-5, cf. Mk 1.21 and Jn 6.59.

Regarding the dating of the second passage, Kee and Horsley both take this to be a Lukan addition to Q as it is missing in the Matthean equivalent (Mt. 8.5-13).[97] Indeed, many commentators suggest that the simpler version found in Matthew is more likely to have been original.[98] However, it is also noted that Matthew often abbreviated material, and it seems unlikely that Luke would have altered his account so much without some basis in a source.[99] Binder takes this discussion one stage further, arguing that the reason for Matthew's omission is his hostility towards the Jewish 'synagogue' and any 'synagogue' official.[100] He points to Matthew's account of the healing of Jairus' daughter; where Luke follows Mark and accords Jairus the title ἀρχισυνάγωγος, Matthew simply refers to him as an ἄρχων. 'It is therefore likely that Matthew follows this same pattern in the centurion passage, omitting from Q a reference connecting Jesus to the synagogue in a positive way'.[101]

In my critique of McKay earlier in this chapter, I noted that one of the functions of historical research should be to construct an interpretation of what a 'synagogue' might look like in a particular geographical location. Here in Capernaum we have one of the few occasions when a reference to a 'synagogue' in the New Testament may gain some direct perspective from archaeological material. As was shown in Chapter 3, we have the remains of a building, dating to the first century, buried below another that was clearly a synagogue building in the fourth/fifth century. This leads Strange and Shanks to claim: 'The first-century Capernaum synagogue in which Jesus preached has probably been found'.[102] While we may want to be a little more cautious in our assessment, this is, nonetheless, a distinct possibility.

The dimensions of the first-century building were 24.2 m × 18.5 m externally and 22 m × 16.5 m internally. Given that other synagogue buildings in this period had benches around some or all of their walls, and that the later building at Capernaum also contained stone benches, it is likely that the earlier meeting room would also have had benches. Gamla and Masada had four tiers of benches while Herodium and Jericho had three. If we assume a similar arrangement in Capernaum, three tiers of stone benches running around three of its walls would mean that there

97   Kee, 'Early Christianity in the Galilee', p. 10; Horsley, *Galilee: History, Politics, People*, p. 225.

98   E.g., Fitzmyer, *Luke*, vol. 1, pp. 648–49.

99   Marshall, *Luke*, p. 278; Nolland, *Luke*, vol. 1, p. 314. McKay also thinks it unlikely that Luke would have created the whole concept of a benefactor, but is reflecting what he was aware of in his time, *Sabbath and Synagogue*, p. 164.

100   Binder, *Temple Courts*, p. 96, also pp. 72–73.

101   *Ibid.*, p. 96.

102   J.F. Strange and H. Shanks, 'Synagogue Where Jesus Preached Found at Capernaum', *BARev* 9.6 (1983), pp. 25–31 (25).

were approximately 157.5 m of benches, which would provide seating for 310 people in the building.[103] This large meeting hall would therefore have been capable of seating around a third of the population of the village.

	Whole complex	Meeting Hall	Internal m^2	Total m. of benches	Capacity[104]
Capernaum	24.2 × 18.5 m	22 × 16.5 m	363	157.5	310[105]
Gamla	25.5 × 17 m	19.6 × 15.1 m	320	184.3[106]	360[107]
Herodium	16.7 × 12.3 m	15.15 × 10.6 m	160.6	106.6	205
Masada	ca. 15 × 12 m	ca. 12.5 × 10.5 m	102.2	109.15	210[108]
Jericho	ca. 28 × 20 m	16.2 × 11 m	178.2	63.3	120[109]
Q Sefer	9.6 × 9.6 m	8.5 × ca. 8.5 m	72.2	21.5	34
Modi'in		10.5–11.5 × 8.6 m	ca. 94.6	56	105
K Qana		ca. 20 × 15 m			

Table 5.2 Comparison of the size and capacity of first-century Palestinian synagogue buildings.

A variety of people, both Jews and Gentiles, are recorded to have made contributions to synagogue buildings; therefore, Luke's presentation of the centurion as a benefactor to the Jewish community is quite possible. Michael White notes: 'The wording of this passage clearly has a ring of authenticity about it, as it incorporates the conventionalized honorific

103   See Table 5.2.

104   50 cm of space per person has been allowed. It is also assumed that there would be some 'dead' seating space, e.g., where benches meet in a corner, or where a pillar/column occupied some of the space, as at Jericho. It is also assumed that the benches would have been the sole area used for seating.

105   Obviously this is conjecture as we do not have any indication of benches in the earlier building; however, we have assumed a design similar to that of the other buildings with three tiers of benches on three walls. If the earlier synagogue building had two rows of double benches, as in the later building, then the seating capacity would have been around 176.

106   It is assumed that the walkway was also used as a fourth tier of benches, but it is possible that only three benches were used to sit on. There is another bench running along part of the eastern wall which may also have been used; it has not been included.

107   E.P. Sanders estimates 300, *Judaism: Practice and Belief 63 BCE – 66CE* (London: SCM Press, 1992), p. 200, while E. Netzer puts the figure at 430, 'Synagogue from the Hasmonean Period Recently Exposed in the Western Plain of Jericho', *IEJ* 49 (1999), pp. 203–21 (220).

108   E. Netzer estimates 250, *Masada – The Yigael Yadin Excavations 1963–1965, Final Reports, III: The Buildings: Stratigraphy and Architecture* (Jerusalem, Israel Exploration Society, 1991), p. 412.

109   This is very close to Netzer's estimate of 125, 'Synagogue from the Hasmonean Period', p. 220.

language commonly found in building inscriptions among both Jews and pagans'. However, he goes on to say that this reflects the time of Luke's writing, and that it is used 'as a sign of the success of the Christian movement'.[110] Nolland is a little more circumspect, pointing out that it is surprising that a centurion should have sufficient wealth to provide a synagogue building.[111] Here we should follow the suggestion of Marshall: rather than being responsible for the construction of the whole synagogue building he may have been a significant contributor,[112] and his openness to both Judaism and Christianity fits well with Luke's portrait of Gentiles as receptive to Christianity.[113]

Recently Ehud Netzer has suggested that the buildings at Gamla and Jericho 'reflect larger and grander synagogues that existed in the big cities: Jerusalem, Sepphoris, Tiberias, Caesarea, etc'.[114] Similarly, Claußen, who argues that the majority of gatherings would have taken place in homes, allows that there could have been an increasing number of special synagogue buildings with large congregations, particularly in Jerusalem and other large cities, but that, generally, such synagogue-complexes were not present in Judaea and Galilee in the first century CE.[115] However, the main meeting hall of the synagogue building at Capernaum is larger than both Gamla and Jericho and, surprisingly, existed in a village with a relatively small population. How is such a building to be understood?

If the structure recently found at Khirbet Qana is also a synagogue building, then Capernaum looks less of an oddity. Nevertheless, that such a village could build and maintain a sizeable structure may well have been due to benefaction of some sort, as Luke records. Further, if this building

---

110 White, *Social Origins*, p. 86.

111 Nolland, *Luke*, vol. 1, pp. 316–17.

112 Marshall, *Luke*, p. 280; also Levine, *Ancient Synagogue*, p. 49, n. 29.

113 Horsley suggests that 'any "centurion" in Capernaum would likely have been an officer of the Tetrarch or client-king', *Archaeology, History, and Society in Galilee*, p. 115; see also, M.A. Chancey, *Greco-Roman Culture and the Galilee of Jesus* (SNTSMS, 134; Cambridge: Cambridge University Press, 2005), pp. 50–56. However, Laughlin has discovered a second or third-century Roman bathhouse in Capernaum, below which was another building dating to the first century. The excavators were reluctant to destroy the remains of the later building so a full excavation of the earlier one has not been carried out. 'In general, however, the outline of the lower building is similar to the bathhouse above it. If this first-century building was also a bathhouse, then this may confirm the existence of the Roman centurion and garrison at Capernaum referred to in the Gospels', 'Capernaum from Jesus' Time', p. 57. See also Riesner, 'Synagogues in Jerusalem', pp. 203–04.

114 E. Netzer, 'The Synagogues from the Second Temple Period According to Archaeological Finds and in Light of the Literary Sources', in G.C. Bottini, L. Di Segne and L.D. Chrupcala (eds), *One Land – Many Cultures: Archaeological Studies in Honour of S. Loffreda* (Studium Biblicum Franciscanum Collectio Maior, 41; Jerusalem: Franciscan Printing Press, 2003), pp. 277–85 (282).

115 Claußen, *Versammlung*, p. 295. He does give a list of Palestinian synagogues that he takes to be buildings which includes Capernaum, *ibid.*, p. 294.

could exist in Capernaum then it would seem highly likely that other, larger, towns in the region may also have had synagogue buildings.[116] Again, these would have been the venue for a variety of functions but, nevertheless, would also have been used as the Sabbath meeting place. For Claußen to accept the first-century building at Capernaum as a synagogue building but not adequately deal with its size and the community in which it was found, skews his argument. Nonetheless, we need to be careful not to swing too much in the other direction and assume that every small village and town had a complex such as the one at Capernaum.

It would seem likely that the Capernaum synagogue building mentioned in Lk. 7.5 functioned as the main 'synagogue' of that community. As such, it would have had a role in the public life of the village. If that is the case, and it could accommodate around 300 people, how are we to understand its place within the village? Did two-thirds of the community not attend the 'synagogue' on the Sabbath? If we incorporate the recent arguments of Runesson and Claußen into our understanding of how such communities ought to be perceived, then it is highly likely that other 'synagogues' existed in Capernaum.[117] Josephus and Philo mention Essene communities living in the cities of Palestine,[118] and if such a group existed in Capernaum then they, as well as other interpretive communities, would have gathered as 'semi-public synagogues', as Runesson describes them,[119] in smaller buildings or private homes. Although I have cautioned against the view that women had no part to play in the 'synagogue' gatherings, Jewish society was, nevertheless, undoubtedly patriarchal in nature. Therefore, it is also likely that many of the women and children did not attend 'synagogue' gatherings.[120] Finally, we should not assume that all Jews regularly attended the 'synagogue' on the Sabbath,[121] and note that in Capernaum there would also have been a non-Jewish element to the population, for example, the possible Roman garrison. Neither should we assume a modern western-church model where church starts at

---

116 Cf. Josephus' mention of the προσευχή in nearby Tiberias, *Life*, 279–80. R.A. Horsley excludes the evidence from Josephus of buildings at Dora, Caesarea and Tiberias classifying them as Hellenistic cities, 'Synagogues in Galilee and the Gospels', in H.C. Kee and L.H. Cohick (eds), *Evolution of the Synagogue: Problems and Progress*, (Harrisburg: Trinity Press, 1999), pp. 46–69 (54).

117 See Runesson, *Origins*, pp. 354–61.

118 Philo, *Omn. Prob. Lib.*, 76, 85–87; *Hypoth.*, 11.1; Josephus, *War*, 2.124-27.

119 Runesson, *Origins*, pp. 223–31; p. 360 n. 399.

120 For a discussion of the role of Jewish women see T. Ilan, *Jewish Women in Greco-Roman Palestine* (Peabody: Hendrickson, 1996). For a discussion of women specifically in the 'synagogue' see B.J. Brooten, *Women Leaders in the Ancient Synagogue: Inscriptional Evidence and Background Issues* (BJS, 36; Atlanta: Scholars Press, 1982); Levine, *Ancient Synagogue*, pp. 471–90.

121 Cf. Philo's condemnation of Jews who fail to observe the Sabbath and circumcision laws, *Abr.*, 89–93.

11am and finishes at 12.15pm. There may well have been more fluidity with people coming and going throughout the gathering.

4.2.3. *Palestinian Worship Practices*
4.2.3.1. *Introduction*

In the summary of the minimalists' position at the beginning of this chapter, it was noted that, for them, the author of Luke-Acts has incorporated the style of 'synagogue' worship that existed at his time of writing and in his place of writing. McKay argues: 'No one worshipped in synagogues on the sabbath in first-century Palestine, so Jesus could not have attended a service there on the sabbath'.[122] In Chapter 4 we sought to identify some of the practices which took place in the first-century 'synagogue' and also to address the geographical dimension to this debate. Whether the 'synagogue' would have been perceived as sacred, whether some form of cleansing was necessary before entering the 'synagogue', as well as identifying practices that were carried out which would have been considered worship, were all assessed. Although we should not view the first-century 'synagogue' as a homogeneous entity, there were, nonetheless, areas of similarity in the practices of diverse groups. In particular, it has been noted that certain activities within Palestine should be identified as worship and that communal prayer was not confined to the Diaspora as some have proposed. With this background we are now able to compare the data gathered with Luke's presentation of practices carried out within the 'synagogue'.

4.2.3.2. *Luke-Acts*

Perhaps the most obvious place to begin the comparison of Luke-Acts' presentation of the 'synagogue' and that of our other sources is its association with the Sabbath. As has been noted in earlier chapters, a variety of sources indicate that the Jews gathered together on the Sabbath. The close connection we have seen between the 'synagogues' and the Sabbath continues when we examine Luke-Acts.[123] In the Gospel, Jesus is portrayed teaching in the 'synagogue' on the Sabbath;[124] likewise Paul in his missionary journeys often goes to the 'synagogue' on the Sabbath, usually as his first point of contact in a city,[125] and among the early Christians there were those who continued to meet on the Sabbath.[126]

In Acts 15.21 Luke records: 'For in every city, for generations past, Moses has had those who proclaim him, for he has been read aloud every

---

122 McKay, 'From Evidence to Edifice', p. 197.
123 Lk. 4.16, 31-33; 6.6; 13.10; Acts 13.14; 15.21; 17.10; 18.4.
124 Lk. 4.16, 31; 6.6; 13.10.
125 Acts 13.14; 17.1-2; 18.4.
126 Col. 2.16, cf. Rom. 14.5-6; Gal. 4.10.

sabbath in the synagogues (Μωϋσῆς γὰρ ἐκ γενεῶν ἀρχαίων κατὰ πόλιν τοὺς κηρύσσοντας αὐτὸν ἔχει ἐν ταῖς συναγωγαῖς κατὰ πᾶν σάββατον ἀναγινωσκόμενος)'.[127] The reading of the Torah on the Sabbath is attested here, as in other sources, and that it had its origins in antiquity echoes the account of Josephus.[128] 'Those who proclaim him' are likely to be the ones who read the Scripture, although κηρύσσω may indicate more than just reading and could include the preaching/teaching that took place along with the reading, and which is again attested elsewhere. However, as well as this focus on Scripture reading, Luke-Acts provides us with some additional details which add to our understanding of practices within the 'synagogue'.

4.2.3.3. *Luke 4.16-30*

In their accounts of Jesus teaching in Nazareth, Matthew and Mark tell us simply that he taught in the 'synagogue' (διδάσκειν ἐν τῇ συναγωγῇ).[129] However, Luke gives some further information:

> When he came to Nazareth, where he had been brought up, he went to the synagogue on the sabbath day, as was his custom (καὶ εἰσῆλθεν κατὰ τὸ εἰωθὸς αὐτῷ ἐν τῇ ἡμέρᾳ τῶν σαββάτων εἰς τὴν συναγωγήν). He stood up to read, and the scroll of the prophet Isaiah was given to him. He unrolled the scroll and found the place where it was written: 'The Spirit of the Lord is upon me, because he has anointed me to bring good news to the poor. He has sent me to proclaim release to the captives and recovery of sight to the blind, to let the oppressed go free, to proclaim the year of the Lord's favour.' And he rolled up the scroll, gave it back to the attendant, and sat down. The eyes of all in the synagogue were fixed on him. Then he began to say to them, 'Today this scripture has been fulfilled in your hearing.'[130]

A great deal of scholarly literature exists on the structure of this passage, and on Luke's possible source(s).[131] The beginning of the account bears similarities to Mk 6.1 and many scholars argue that much of the material in 4.16-30 is Lukan addition to Mk 6.1-6.[132] Bovon disagrees: 'The Markan passage is only distantly related to our pericope, and it appears in another context. Luke is familiar with it, but is probably not using it as his

---

127 Acts 15.21.

128 Josephus, *Apion*, 2.175. The Jews are also described as 'hearers of the law', Rom. 2.13, cf. Josephus, *Ant.*, 5.107; Jas 1.22-23; *Sib. Or.*, 3.70.

129 Mk 6.2; Mt. 13.54.

130 Lk. 4.16-21.

131 For a detailed bibliography see Nolland, *Luke*, vol. 1, pp. 188–90.

132 Fitzmyer, *Luke*, vol. 1, p. 527; C.F. Evans, *Saint Luke* (London: SCM Press, 1990), pp. 266–67. For a summary of the various possibilities see D.L. Bock, *Luke* (BECNT, 2 vols; Grand Rapids: Baker Books, 1994–96), vol. 1, pp. 396–97.

model here'.[133] Schürmann suggests that Luke is drawing on Q for his material;[134] others suggest another source.[135] Verse 23 indicates that the passage is not in its original position, and Luke certainly places his account at the start of Jesus' ministry in order to lay out many of the themes to be followed; indeed, scholars argue that it is programmatic for the whole of Luke-Acts.[136] Many of these themes are particularly Lukan which might suggest a free composition;[137] however, there is linguistic evidence within the passage that Luke is using a source, for example, Ναζαρά in an Aramaic form where Luke normally uses Ναζαρέθ; βιβλίον rather than βίβλιος which Luke uses consistently elsewhere.[138] It seems likely that as well as adding his own material, Luke either had available to him an account of Jesus' teaching in the Nazareth 'synagogue' which contained greater detail than that used by Mark, or that Mark chose to abbreviate his source. This being the case, the source Luke uses must obviously predate his work, although by how much we cannot be certain.

There are several interesting details in this account. First, Jesus reads from the Prophets, in contrast to our other references where the Torah is mentioned. However, there is no reason to suggest that the Torah reading had not already taken place. Rabbinic evidence would suggest that this is quite likely, as the Torah reading appears to have been broken down among a number of readers, with the final reader going on to read from the Prophets, the *hafterah*.[139] We should note also that Luke follows the

---

133   F. Bovon, *Luke 1* (Hermeneia; Minneapolis: Fortress Press, 2002), p. 150.

134   H. Schürmann, *Das Lukasevangelium* (HTKNT, 3; 2 vols; Freiburg: Herder, 1969), vol. 1, pp. 227–28.

135   Nolland notes the passage seems to have some difficult transitions in thought and that different sources appear to have been welded together. He suggests that had this been a free composition by Luke it would have contained more obvious unity; therefore, some form of Lukan editing is the most likely solution, *Luke*, vol. 1, p. 192. See also, Marshall, *Luke*, pp. 179–80; Bovon, *Luke*, p. 151; Bock, *Luke*, vol. 1, p. 397.

136   J.T. Sanders, *The Jews in Luke-Acts* (London: SCM Press, 1987), pp. 164–68; Marshall, *Luke*, pp. 177–78; Nolland, *Luke*, vol. 1, p. 195; Bovon, *Luke*, p. 152.

137   P.F. Esler, *Community and Gospel in Luke-Acts: The Social and Political Motivations of Lucan Theology* (SNTSMS, 57; Cambridge: Cambridge University Press, 1987), pp. 164–67.

138   Nolland, Luke, vol. 1, p. 192. See also the comments of Schürmann on τρέφω, *Das Lukasevangelium*, vol. 1, p. 227.

139   See L.H. Schiffman, 'The Early History of Public Reading of the Torah', in S. Fine (ed.), *Jews, Christians, and Polytheists in the Ancient Synagogue* (New York: Routledge, 1999), pp. 44–56 (53). The Mishnah reports that, on a Sabbath, seven people should make the reading from the Torah (*m. Meg.* 4.20); a person should read a minimum of three verses (*m. Meg.* 4.4); if it is being translated he should read only one verse at a time (*m. Meg.* 4.4); the person who starts the reading and the one that ends the reading from the Torah say a blessing (*m. Meg.* 4.2); the person who reads the final reading from the prophets, also recites the *Shema*, blessings and then goes before the ark and says a blessing – a minor and others may not do this (*m. Meg.* 4.5).

Septuagint in his reporting of the passage Jesus read, which is understandable given that he was writing in Greek. However, it is unlikely that the Greek text would have been used in a setting such as Nazareth, where Aramaic would have been the vernacular. In the previous chapter the presence of a translation of the scripture reading was discussed, and it is likely that a targum would have been delivered alongside Jesus' reading of the Scripture. Additionally, we should note that the teaching given by Jesus was also based on the prophetic reading, at least as Luke records it.

The second piece of information Luke provides is that Jesus unrolled the scroll and found (εὑρίσκω) the verses, which may suggest he had some freedom to choose the passage that he read. As has been noted above, the previous presumption that a single fixed lectionary cycle existed in the first century CE has now largely been discounted, and even if there was one, it is more likely to have related to the reading of the Torah rather than the Prophets. That Jesus would have had some freedom to choose the passage from which he wished to preach therefore seems to be a possibility.[140] It should be noted that the passage he supposedly reads is actually an amalgam of two texts from Isa. 61.1-2 and 58.6.[141] Are we to assume that Jesus had the freedom to do this? This seems unlikely.[142] Alternatively, i) Luke, or more likely his source, may have joined two readings made by Jesus on separate occasions;[143] ii) Jesus could have read Isaiah 61 and added a commentary from Isaiah 58;[144] iii) this could reflect the use of

---

140 But see the caution of M.D. Goulder, *The Evangelists' Calendar: A Lectionary Explanation of the Development of Scripture* (London: SPCK, 1978), pp. 5–6.

141 The linking of texts by terms used in both, *gezerah shavah*, is a principal of interpretation found in various rabbinic sources (see, G. Stemberger, *Introduction to the Talmud and Midrash* [trans. M. Bockmuehl; Edinburgh: T&T Clark, 2nd edn, 1996], pp. 18–19), so it is possible that *gezerah shavah* is being employed here, see the discussion in Bock, *Luke*, vol. 1, pp. 404–405. James A. Sanders points out that Isaiah 61 with its message of release from captivity was a popular passage in first-century Judaism and would have been readily understood by Jesus' audience, 'Isaiah in Luke', in C.A. Evans and J.A. Sanders (eds), *Luke and Scripture: The Function of Sacred Tradition in Luke-Acts* (Minneapolis: Fortress, 1993), pp. 14–25 (22–23); *idem*, 'From Isaiah 61 to Luke 4,' in J. Neusner (ed.), *Christianity, Judaism and Other Greco-Roman Cults: Studies for Morton Smith at Sixty* (SJLA, 12; Leiden: Brill, 1975), pp. 75–106 (89–92). Sanders also suggests that the connection between the passages is therefore ἄφεσις ('Isaiah in Luke', p. 21). Although the connection of ἄφεσις works with the LXX version of Isaiah 58 and 61, if, as suggested, the reading was made in Hebrew, no such correlation exists as different terms are used. The connection would therefore have been made by Luke (or his source) rather than Jesus.

142 See, C. Perrot, 'Luc 4, 16–30 et la lecture biblique de l'ancienne synagogue', *RevScRel* 47 (1973), pp. 324–37 (327).

143 See Max Turner's helpful discussion, *Power from on High: The Spirit in Israel's Restoration and Witness in Luke-Acts* (JPTSup, 9; Sheffield: Sheffield Academic Press, 2000), pp. 215–26.

144 Bock, *Luke*, vol. 1, p. 411.

these verses by the church of Luke's time. Given that Luke used source material here, perhaps the first option is most likely.

Third, Jesus stands up to read from the scroll, but then sits down to expound, sitting being regarded as the posture of a teacher.[145] With the survey of the archaeological data to aid us, it is worth considering where Jesus might have stood and sat in a Palestinian synagogue building and we will return to this below. Fourth, there was an attendant (ὑπηρέτης)[146] present who took the scroll from Jesus; presumably he had also given it to him in the first place. We have evidence of just such a person, albeit in Egypt, in a προσευχή. In a papyrus dated to the second half of the second century BCE, several officers of a Jewish σύνοδος are mentioned, including ἀρχυπηρέται.[147] Even if we allow that Luke may have transposed a title used in Diaspora communities, it is clear that a variety of titles existed in the first century for particular positions within the 'synagogue', although exactly what their roles were is less certain.[148] Where the scroll would have been kept is also worth considering. Although niches at Gamla and Jericho have been proposed as repositories for the scrolls, it is difficult to be certain about either. Strange suggests that wooden furniture existed in which the scrolls were kept, and that such furniture is likely to have reflected the best craftsmanship.[149] The Torah ark is mentioned in the Mishnah and, by the third century CE, we have depictions of what appear to be small wooden Torah shrines on inscriptions from the catacombs of Rome.[150] Strange concludes: 'If the ark exists around 200 C.E., it is because it fulfils a ritual need. If that need exists in the first century, then it seems reasonable that the ark also existed

---

145   See C. Schneider, 'Κάθημαι, καθίζω, καθέζομαι', *TDNT*, vol. 3, p. 443.

146   Kee argues that it is wrong to think of this as a technical term for a 'synagogue' official, rather it refers 'simply to one who follows instructions. Further, even if Luke did intend it in this way he is using it anachronistically, reflecting his time of writing', 'Early Christianity in the Galilee', pp. 13–14. However, ὑπηρέτης is often used in the New Testament to signify an 'officer' or 'official' of the Jewish authorities, e.g., Jn 18.12. See also the discussion in Burtchaell, *From Synagogue to Church*, pp. 246–49, and K.H. Rengstorf, 'ὑπηρέτης, ὑπηρετέω', *TDNT*, vol. 8, p. 540.

147   *CPJ*, 138. Presumably as well as ἀρχυπηρέται, there must have been ὑπηρέται, see Oster, 'Supposed Anachronism', p. 202. Claußen suggests that this may reflect a greater degree of institutionalization in Egyptian communities, *Versammlung*, p. 291.

148   See A.D. Clarke, *Serve the Community of the Church: Christians as Leaders and Ministers* (Grand Rapids: Eerdmans, 2000), pp. 126–38; T. Rajak and D. Noy, 'Archisynagogoi: Office, Title and Social Status in the Greco-Jewish Synagogue', *JRS* 83 (1993), pp. 75–93; Claußen, *Versammlung*, pp. 256–93.

149   J.F. Strange, 'Archaeology and Ancient Synagogues up to about 200 C. E.', in B. Olsson and M. Zetterholm (eds), *The Ancient Synagogue: From its Origins to 200 C.E.: Papers Presented at an International Conference at Lund University, October 14–17, 2001* (*ConNT*, 39; Stockholm: Almqvist & Wiksell, 2003), pp. 37–62 (55 n. 37). See also, Perrot, 'Luc 4, 16–30', p. 326.

150   See *JIWE* 2, 11, 185, 164, 167, 187, 195, see also plate 7.

then'.[151] The problem is that we have no evidence of any such early Torah shrines in the first century. Binder suggests that it is more likely that the scrolls were kept in the niches, noted above, which would have had a drape to cover them.[152] While Binder is correct to highlight our lack of evidence for wooden furniture, we should not completely rule out their existence. As has been noted, the reading of the Torah was the most important element of Sabbath practice. Given the status of the Torah scrolls, it is likely that they were kept in a special place and not all the archaeological remains examined in Chapter 3 had niches. That a simple wooden cupboard or box would have been used seems highly likely.

As well as certain scholars of first-century 'synagogues', there are those with an interest in historical Jesus studies that are sceptical of Luke's portrayal of this 'synagogue' service. For Funk and Hoover the only words that may be authentic are: 'The truth is, no prophet is welcome on his home turf', which get a pink rating.[153] In his *The Historical Jesus*, Crossan does not refer to this passage at all, presumably because he thinks it has no factual content.[154] However, in his more recent work he does include our passage, writing:

> Luke also presumes that a tiny hamlet like Nazareth had both a synagogue building and scrolls of scripture. The first presumption is most unlikely and, as noted above, no evidence for a first-century synagogue building was discovered at Nazareth. The second presupposition is questionable; scrolls were mostly an urban privilege.[155]

Crossan is correct when he points out that no archaeological remains of a first-century synagogue building have been found at Nazareth,[156] but, as has been shown in earlier chapters, this is far from conclusive evidence. Synagogue buildings from the first-century period are difficult to identify as there are few with special characteristics to mark them out. Also, while the description of Nazareth as a 'tiny hamlet' may bring to mind only a

---

151   Strange, 'Archaeology and Ancient Synagogues', p. 55.

152   D.D. Binder, 'The Origins of the Synagogue: An Evaluation', in Olsson and Zetterholm, *The Ancient Synagogue*, pp. 113-81 (121, n. 9).

153   R.W. Funk and R.W. Hoover, *The Five Gospels: the Search for the Authentic Words of Jesus* (New York: Macmillan, 1993), pp. 279–80.

154   J.D. Crossan, *The Historical Jesus: The Life of a Mediterranean Jewish Peasant* (Edinburgh: T&T Clark, 1991).

155   Crossan and Reed, *Excavating Jesus*, pp. 30–32. See also J.T. Sanders: 'We are not dealing here with any real synagogue sermon that the real Jesus preached in the real Nazareth, but rather with a narrative that Luke has constructed for a purpose', *The Jews in Luke-Acts* (London: SCM Press, 1987), p. 166.

156   There is some evidence of a synagogue building, but it cannot be dated back to the first century, V. Tzaferis, 'Nazareth', *NEAEHL*, vol. 3, p. 1104.

few houses, Crossan and Reed propose a population of 200–400.[157] Although we should tend towards the upper figure,[158] they are correct in their assessment that Nazareth was a fairly small settlement. Nevertheless, the recent identification of buildings which appear to have been for communal use, possibly as synagogue buildings, at Khirbet Qana, Qiryat Sefer and Modi'in, along with the synagogue building at Capernaum, point towards the possibility that even in relatively small villages some form of synagogue building existed. As to the availability of scrolls; although our evidence is limited, there is a clear understanding in various first-century sources that the Scriptures were read on the Sabbath, and that this was a practice carried out widely.[159]

Having argued that the reference to a 'synagogue' in Luke 4 may well relate to a building, we can now return to the question of where Jesus might have stood and sat. As noted in Chapter 3, the evidence we have of first-century Palestinian synagogue architecture shows tiered stone benches around the walls of the building. It was suggested that such an arrangement was either to focus on the central part of the building between the benches, or was to facilitate easy discussion between those present. That the central component of the Sabbath gathering was the reading of Scripture, and that Jesus stood to do so indicates that the central area would be the most likely place for the reading to have taken place. Having read, Jesus then sat down. Where is he likely to have sat? Philo recounts that the Essenes have a particular seating arrangement where the older members of the group sit in rows above the younger ones,[160] and both Matthew and Luke mention that there are πρωτοκαθε-δρία, 'best seats', in the συναγωγή. In Masada there is a single bench on one of the walls of the synagogue building, at Gamla there is a single bench above the other tiers on one wall and at Jericho there is evidence of a single bench before the addition of the *triclinium*. In the other Palestinian buildings that we have sufficient evidence for, there are no separate benches. Where these single benches existed, it seems likely that they would have been for leaders of the communities, setting them apart from the rest of the assembly, rather than for the person teaching. Where there was no separate bench, it may be that a particular level was more desirable.[161] Jesus does not appear to have a role of leadership within the community; indeed the people, noting his background, are amazed at the way he teaches. In all likelihood he resumed his position on one of the

---

157   Crossan and Reed, *Excavating Jesus*, p. 32. Note that the figure they then go on to use is 200, see p. 37.

158   See Horsley, *Galilee: History, Politics, People*, p. 193.

159   E.g., Acts 15.21; Josephus, *Ant.*, 2.175; Philo, *Spec. Leg.*, 2.62. See also Chapter 4, 2 above.

160   Philo, *Omn. Prob. Lib.*, 81–82.

161   See the discussion in Strange, 'Archaeology and Ancient Synagogues', pp. 52–54.

tiered benches and taught from there, after which there would normally have been a discussion. However, according to Luke, after Jesus had finished teaching, the people are so incensed that they physically remove him from the town.

The account of Jesus' teaching in the synagogue building of Nazareth fits well with the picture we have built of first-century 'synagogue' practice.[162] Reading of Scripture is widely attested, and could be carried out by a variety of people. Agreement or disagreement with what is said which caused some discussion and debate is also found elsewhere.[163] The greater formality or institutionalization that the minimalists see in this passage is largely absent, and the description Luke gives, while adding certain details to our understanding, is in line with our other sources. Some elements of Luke's account do need to be questioned: for example, the term ὑπηρέτης may not have been used in Palestine (although the role would most likely have existed); another is the splicing together of two sections from Isaiah in Jesus' reading. Nevertheless, generally Luke's account accords with the sources gathered in Chapter 4.

The problem lies not in what Luke records, but in the additional formalities that commentators have assumed would have accompanied Jesus' teaching. Here we have to tread a fine line: on the one hand it is highly likely that other elements of this 'synagogue' service did exist but are not recorded, on the other we need to be very careful how we attempt to fill these gaps. While Luke edits what Jesus would have said,[164] and keeps to the areas in which Jesus is involved in order to have him centre stage, other elements would, undoubtedly, have been present, but Luke fails to inform us of them. Most commentators have either directly used rabbinic evidence to illuminate these missing details (e.g., *m. Meg.* 3–4; *m. Ber.* 2), or have relied on works such as Schürer, or Strack and Billerbeck, who themselves focus on the rabbinic material.[165] As has been discussed above, this is fraught with problems.

---

162 Even McKay allows: 'This description shows only slight developments from the reading and expounding of the scriptures described by Philo and Josephus for Sabbath gatherings, namely, the addition of an attendant and a clearer statement of the standing posture of the reader, followed by the teacher seating himself to speak to the already seated listeners', *Sabbath and Synagogue*, p. 165.

163 Philo, *Somn.*, 2.117; Josephus, *Life*, 276f.

164 Asher Finkel tries to reconstruct the sermon that Jesus preaches, 'Jesus' Preaching in the Synagogue on the Sabbath (Luke 4.16-28)', in C.A. Evans and W.R. Stegner (eds), *The Gospels and the Scripture of Israel* (Sheffield, Sheffield Academic Press, 1994).

165 E.g., Marshall, *Luke*, p. 181; Fitzmyer, *Luke*, vol. 1, p. 531. Bock does make explicit his reasons for using the Mishnah, *Luke*, vol. 1, p. 403, n. 18.

4.3. *Diaspora*
4.3.1. *Philippi*

In Acts 16, there is another intriguing reference to a meeting of Jews on the Sabbath. Paul and his companions travelled to Philippi and Luke informs us: 'On the sabbath day we went outside the gate by the river, where we supposed there was a place of prayer (οὗ ἐνομίζομεν προσευχὴν εἶναι); and we sat down and spoke to the women who had gathered there'.[166] This is the only time in Acts that a Sabbath meeting place is described as a προσευχή, so why does Luke use this term rather than συναγωγή?

4.3.1.1. *Προσευχή as a Place of Prayer*

The main argument against understanding the προσευχή as a building is that Philippi was a Roman colony and therefore there would have been a very small Jewish population. Consequently, there was no synagogue building and the Jews came down to the river to purify themselves and then to pray at the προσευχή, the place of prayer.[167] There is certainly evidence that Philippi was a strongly Roman city: it became a Roman colony in 42 BCE after it was the site of a battle where Brutus and Cassius were defeated by Antony and Octavian. After this victory, a group of Roman veterans were settled in Philippi with a second group of colonists arriving in 31 BCE at which time the city was accorded the *ius Italicum*, meaning that its citizens had the same rights as those of an Italian city.[168] The total number of veterans who settled in Philippi is uncertain, probably around 20–30 per cent of the population, with all citizens of the city also being Roman citizens.[169] The strength of the Roman influence in Philippi can clearly be seen from the widespread use of Latin which was the official language of the city.[170]

In his commentary, Bruce argues: 'At Philippi, however, there does not

---

166   Acts 16.13.

167   Fitzmyer, *Acts*, p. 585; G.D. Fee, *Paul's Letter to the Philippians* (NICNT; Grand Rapids: Eerdmans, 1995), p. 27.

168   C. Koukouli-Chrysantaki, 'Colonia Iulia Augusta Philippensis', in C. Bakirtzes and H. Koester (eds), *Philippi at the Time of Paul and after His Death* (Pennsylvania: Trinity Press, 1998), pp. 5–35 (8). B. Levick points out that 'at Philippi a double settlement ensured the vigour of the Italian element', *Roman Colonies in Southern Asia Minor* (Oxford: Oxford University Press, 1967), p. 197.

169   Tellbe, *Paul Between Synagogue and State*, pp. 213–14; P. Oakes, *Philippians: From People to Letter* (SNTSMS, 110; Cambridge: Cambridge University Press, 2001), p. 52. Note the alarm of the magistrates who realized that they had condemned a Roman citizen, Acts 16.38-40.

170   Levick reports that of the 421 inscriptions found in Philippi, only 60 are in Greek and twice as many tombstones are in Latin than Greek, *Roman Colonies*, p. 161. Paul also uses a Latin form when addressing the Philippians as Φιλιππήσιοι, see G.F. Hawthorne, *Philippians* (WBC, 43; Dallas: Word Books, 2002), p. 203.

appear to have been a regular synagogue. That can only mean that there were very few resident Jews; had there been ten Jewish men, they would have sufficed to constitute a synagogue'.[171] Hemer suggests that as Philippi was a Roman colony and not a centre of commerce this was a reason that there were few Jews.[172] It would appear that some of these suggestions are built on the evidence of later sources and others on false stereotypes of the Jews. Philippi lay on the busy Via Egnatia; there was a large agricultural industry in the surrounding area as well as precious metal mines,[173] and Jews are known to have been residents of other cities in the area. The view that the Jewish population was very small may be built on incorrect assumptions. Witherington adds another possible explanation for the Jews meeting outside the city; he thinks it likely that foreign cults, particularly small ones, were not allowed to meet within its bounds.[174]

4.3.1.2. Προσευχή as a Building

Some see virtually no difference between the words used here by Luke and argue that he is merely using two terms for the same establishment.[175] Hengel, pointing to the fact that προσευχή is used of Diaspora buildings, suggests that Luke is using a written source from the Diaspora and hence the terminology.[176] This passage is the first of the 'we' sections in Acts and there is much scholarly debate about the origin and function of these passages. It seems likely that Luke is here incorporating his own journal notes leaving the 'we' to indicate his association with Paul in these events.[177] However, this does not offer a solution to the identity of the προσευχή.

---

171   Bruce here is assuming that the regulations of *m. Sanh.* 1.6 and *m. Abot* 3.6 would have been in force at the time, *Acts*, p. 310.

172   Hemer, *Book of Acts*, p. 114.

173   Witherington, *Acts*, p. 488.

174   *Ibid.*, p. 490.

175   Schürer, *HJP*, vol. 2, p. 445. See also Levine, *Ancient Synagogue*, pp. 109, 293; R. Pesch, *Die Apostelgeschichte* (EKKNT, 5; 2 vols.; Zurich: Benziger, 1986), vol. 2, pp. 104–105; Brooten, *Women Leaders*, pp. 139–40; Johnson, *Acts*, p. 292; Binder, *Temple Courts*, pp. 290–92; Runesson, *Origins*, p. 353.

176   Hengel, *Proseuche und Synagoge*, p. 175. Also F.G. Hüttenmeister, "Synagoge' und 'Proseuche' bei Josephus und in anderen antiken Quellen', in D.A. Koch and H. Lichtenberger (eds), *Begegnungen zwischen Christentum und Judentum in Antike und Mittelalter* (Göttingen: Vandenhoeck & Ruprecht, 1993), pp. 163–81 (168–69); Binder, *Temple Courts*, p. 291.

177   For a discussion of the 'we' passages in Acts see, S.M. Praeder, 'The Problem of First Person Narration in Acts', *NovT* 39 (1987), pp. 193–218; S.E. Porter, 'The "We" Passsages', in D.W.J. Gill and C. Gempf (eds), *The Book of Acts in its Graeco-Roman Setting* (*TBAFCS*, vol. 2), pp. 545–74; Fitzmyer, *Acts*, pp. 98–103; Witherington, *Acts*, pp. 480–86.

Against the view that there was a relatively small Jewish population in Philippi at this time, Mattila argues that Phil. 3.1-10 suggests 'a reasonably influential Jewish community'.[178] But it is by no means clear that Paul is there arguing against an existing Jewish group in Philippi at this time; rather it indicates 'Paul's expectation that sooner or later they would make their way to Philippi as they have to other Pauline centers',[179] or perhaps that they are itinerant and have visited Philippi. Brooten, who also sees this gathering as 'genuine synagogue worship',[180] maintains that the tendency among scholars to identify the gathering at Philippi as not an actual 'synagogue' service, 'but rather some sort of outdoor prayer meeting',[181] comes from the fact that only women are mentioned as being present. If that is the case, she correctly notes, this is a circular argument: women are assumed not to be present at 'synagogue' gatherings and therefore, if a text reports women being present, it cannot be genuine 'synagogue' worship.[182] Indeed, as McKay points out, these verses do not prohibit men being present, they only indicate that Paul spoke to women.[183]

We should note that, in the Diaspora, it is quite possible that women were able to be part of a gathering on a Sabbath; this does not need to be explained by proposing that the προσευχή was a 'house which was used on a regular basis by the women',[184] or that there were separate meeting times for men and women,[185] or that the women were gathered to prepare food to be eaten later.[186] Luke-Acts provides us with other examples of

178 S.L. Mattila, 'Where Women Sat in Ancient Synagogues: The Archaeological Evidence in Context', in J.S. Kloppenborg and S.G. Wilson (eds), *Voluntary Associations in the Graeco-Roman World* (New York: Routledge, 1996), pp. 266–86 (275).

179 Fee, *Paul's Letter to the Philippians*, p. 290 n. 18; M. Bockmuehl, *The Epistle to the Philippians* (BNTC; London: A. & C. Black, 1997), pp. 183–84.

180 Brooten, *Women Leaders*, p. 140.

181 *Ibid.*, p. 139.

182 So Rudolf Pesch, who supposes a building but assumes the women were gathered outside, *Apostelgeschichte*, vol. 2, p. 105. For a very thorough and clear presentation of a feminist perspective on Lydia see I.R. Reimer, *Women in the Acts of the Apostles: A Feminist Liberation Perspective* (Minneapolis: Fortress Press, 1995), pp. 71–149. For her arguments that the προσευχή should be understood as a synagogue building see esp. pp. 71–92.

183 McKay, *Sabbath and Synagogue*, p. 170.

184 So B. Blue, 'Acts and the House Church', in Gill and Gempf, *Book of Acts*, pp. 119-222 (152–53, n. 130). Binder is right to ask if this was the case why does Paul return on another occasion, (Acts 16.16)? *Temple Courts*, p. 291, n. 115. Eckey proposes that it was a small prayer house and that there were no Jewish males in the city, *Die Apostelgeschichte*, vol. 2, p. 361.

185 So Binder, *Temple Courts*, p. 291.

186 A. Runesson, 'Water and Worship: Ostia and the Ritual Bath in the Diaspora Synagogue', in B. Olsson, D. Mitternacht and O. Brandt (eds), *The Synagogue of Ancient Ostia and the Jews of Rome: Interdisciplinary Studies* (Stockholm: Paul Åströms Förlag, 2001), pp. 115-29 (123, n. 79).

women being present in a 'synagogue': in Lk. 13.10-17 Jesus heals a woman in a 'synagogue'; in Thessalonica 'a great many of the devout Greeks and not a few of the leading women' are persuaded by Paul in the 'synagogue';[187] and Apollos is corrected by Priscilla and Aquila after they hear him teaching in a 'synagogue' in Ephesus.[188] Outside the New Testament there is also evidence of women being present and possibly having a role in the proceedings of the 'synagogue'. In a decree, quoted by Josephus, the Jews of Sardis are granted a place 'in which they may gather together with their wives and children and offer their ancestral prayers and sacrifices to God'.[189] So the fact that women are present at this προσευχή, again does not aid our understanding of the term.

4.3.1.3. *Conclusion*

As indicated above, we would argue that this section is taken from Luke's own reminiscences of events in Philippi, probably using an earlier written source. The fact that Luke uses προσευχή here in contrast to συναγωγή, which he uses throughout the rest of Acts, suggests that he either intends to indicate a different type of gathering, or is using exactly the correct terminology for this particular city. It should be noted that in connection with Philippi, the most often cited evidence in favour of a building is a decree quoted by Josephus which mentions προσευχαί near to the sea in Halicarnassus. Binder writes:

> As was the case with the synagogues at Halicarnassus, which were apparently built near the sea, the synagogue at Philippi was also said to have been located near a body of water. Because the text indicates that Paul and his entourage expected to find a synagogue there, such site placement was probably customary for synagogues in the diaspora.[190]

I have shown elsewhere that this decree allows prayers to be made at the shore rather than prayer-houses to be built,[191] and a similar expression of worship appears to have taken place among the Jews of Alexandria who met at the shore, which Philo indicates was a pure place.[192] In Chapter 4 it was shown that sanctity was an important part of the activities

---

187   Acts 17.4.

188   Acts 18.26.

189   Josephus, *Ant.*, 14.260. See also the arguments of Brooten, that women could hold positions of some importance within 'synagogues', *Women Leaders, passim,* although whether these positions were functional rather than honorific has been questioned, see Rajak and Noy, 'Archisynagogoi', p. 87.

190   Binder, *Temple Courts*, p. 291. See also Claußen, *Versammlung*, p. 118; Reimer, *Women in the Acts of the Apostles*, p. 86; Runesson, 'Water and Worship', p. 123.

191   Catto, 'Does προσευχὰς ποιεῖσθαι', pp. 159–68.

192   See Chapter 4, 2.2.1. Also, P.W. van der Horst, *Philo's Flaccus: The First Pogrom* (Philo of Alexandria Commentary Series, 2; Leiden: Brill, 2003), p. 204.

surrounding the Sabbath and it was argued that in the Diaspora the dominant means of purification was by washing or sprinkling the hands. The translators of the Septuagint are reported to have 'washed their hands in the sea in the course of their prayers to God',[193] and it would seem likely that gathering at places near to water allowed the Jews to purify themselves and pray. Witherington's suggestion that the group of women mentioned would have assembled 'to recite the Shema, to pray the Shemoneh Esreh, and to read from the Law and Prophets and perhaps discuss its meaning, to hear from a teacher, and to receive a final blessing'[194] is unlikely. This is not because it is only a group of women that are meeting, but rather because, as has been shown above, it is difficult to find evidence for some of these elements in more formalized structures and so it would seem unlikely in this more informal gathering. Although the Torah reading has been shown to be the most dominant practice associated with Sabbath gatherings, whether such a reading would have taken place in Philippi is questionable. Would a relatively small Diaspora community have had access to a Torah scroll? The practicalities of using a sacred scroll in such an environment are also questionable. It may be that the meeting beside the river was purely for purification and prayer which might also explain Luke's use of προσευχή. Further, the use of νομίζω in Acts 16.13 shows that Luke supposes that there were frequently such places for meeting near water.

Although the small size of the Jewish population in Philippi may be exaggerated, it would, nevertheless, appear likely that the community was not in a position to provide a purpose-built synagogue in which to meet on the Sabbath. One question remains: I have shown above that if a Jewish community did not have the resources to provide a purpose-built structure they may well have met in homes, that is, house-synagogues, so why is this not the case in Philippi? Could it be that the Jewish population really was only a few women and therefore this was the only option available to them, or, as Witherington proposes, that as a small religious group they were forced to meet outside the city? One further possibility that follows from the suggestion that the activities at the river were limited to prayer and purification, is that the Torah reading and teaching then took place later, perhaps in a home.

4.3.2. *Pisidian Antioch*

Pisidian Antioch was actually in Phrygia; many Antiochs existed at this time, including two in Phrygia, this one is so designated as it is close to the border of Pisidia.[195] It occupied an important strategic position and,

---

193　*Ep. Arist.*, 305.
194　Witherington, *Acts*, p. 491.
195　See Strabo, *Geography*, 12.3.31; 12.8.14.

consequently, was established as a Roman colony in 25 BCE.[196] In the city there was a temple to Men Askaenos which pre-dated the Roman colonization,[197] and, by the time of Paul and Barnabas' visit, there was also a temple to the emperor which dominated the centre of the city and could be seen from miles away.[198] Antioch covered an area of around 115 acres and had a population of 6,000–10,000.[199]

When Paul and Barnabas arrived in Pisidian Antioch we are informed that they went to the συναγωγή on the Sabbath, where they were invited to address those present. Then, as Paul and Barnabas were in the process of leaving, the people asked them to return the following Sabbath. At this point the text reads: 'λυθείσης δὲ τῆς συναγωγῆς' which the NRSV translates as: 'when the meeting of the synagogue broke up'.[200] Howard Kee observes:

> Translators of this passage feel obliged to render the Greek as 'the meeting of the synagogue broke up', apparently assuming that the omission of the explicit reference to the synagogue would imply that a seismic disturbance had wrecked the building.[201]

He is correct to note the problem; however, surely it is the inclusion of 'the meeting' that militates against understanding this as referring to an earthquake! We have here a clear use of συναγωγή indicating a 'gathering'. So if used in this way here, does the other reference to a συναγωγή in Antioch also refer to a gathering rather than a building? We will return to this below.

As Paul and Barnabas left the 'synagogue' some of the Jews and proselytes followed them. We are then informed that 'the next sabbath almost the whole city gathered to hear the word of the Lord',[202] which Fitzmyer puts down to Lukan hyperbole.[203] I mentioned in the introduction to this chapter that Fitzmyer appears to forget his previous discussion of the possible understandings of συναγωγή when he writes: 'One wonders how the "whole town" could have fitted into the synagogue'.[204]

---

196   Levick, *Roman Colonies*, p. 35.

197   S. Mitchell and M. Waelkens, *Pisidian Antioch: The Site and its Monuments* (London: Duckworth, 1998), pp. 37–90. According to Strabo it had considerable land and temple slaves, *Geography*, 12.8.14. For a discussion of the cult of Men see, E.N. Lane, 'Men: A Neglected Cult of Roman Asia Minor', *ANRW*, II.18.3, pp. 2161–74.

198   S. Mitchell, *Anatolia: Land, Men, and Gods in Asia Minor* (2 vols; Oxford: Clarendon Press, 1993), vol. 1, pp. 104–107; Mitchell and Waelkens, *Pisidian Antioch*, pp. 113–73.

199   These figures are based on a comparison of similar sized cities and the population density known from Pompeii, see Levick, *Roman Colonies*, pp. 93–94.

200   Acts 13.43.

201   Kee, 'Defining', p. 491.

202   Acts 13.44.

203   Fitzmyer, *Acts*, p. 520. See also, Haenchen, *Acts*, pp. 413–14.

204   Fitzmyer, *Acts*, p. 520.

Besides my earlier criticism, it is important to note that there is, in fact, no explicit reference to the fact that the group gathered in a synagogue building. It may indeed be that the implication is that this meeting took place in the synagogue building, and that this should be understood as hyperbole.[205] However, we should at least acknowledge the possibility that on this occasion the group was so large that the 'gathering' met elsewhere, in the agora for example, particularly as Luke has just used συναγωγή in this manner.

Finally, Luke provides us with details of how opposition to Paul was gathered: 'But the Jews incited the devout women of high standing and the leading men of the city, and stirred up persecution against Paul and Barnabas, and drove them out of their region'.[206] It would appear that the Jews of Antioch were in a position to influence the judgment of those in authority. The women are described as σεβόμεναι, presumably indicating that they attended the 'synagogue'.[207] Whether they themselves were in positions of authority in the city, or simply influenced their husbands is not clear. From Josephus we learn that at the end of the third century BCE Antiochus III moved 2,000 Jewish families into Phrygia and Lydia following a rebellion in the region, and Cicero records that a large amount of temple tax was taken by the Romans in Asia, which would indicate some wealth in the Jewish communities.[208] Further light on the importance and influence of the Jews in this region can be gained from an inscription from Acmonia, approximately 130 km from Pisidian Antioch. There a non-Jew, Julia Severa, acted as benefactor to the Jewish population of the city and donated a synagogue building.[209] Therefore, it seems likely that Pisidian Antioch had a sizeable and well established Jewish population which was capable of supporting a synagogue building.

Given this background, when Paul and his companions 'went into the synagogue and sat down (εἰσελθόντες εἰς τὴν συναγωγὴν ... ἐκάθισαν)'[210] we should understand this to be a building. However, as they left, it is the 'gathering' that is described as breaking up, not the building, and further, it is possible that the gathering on the following Sabbath did not take place in the synagogue building.

---

205   Certainly Luke regularly uses πᾶς for effect, see P. Trebilco, *The Early Christians in Ephesus from Paul to Ignatius* (WUNT, 166; Tübingen: Mohr Siebeck, 2004), p. 137, n. 147.

206   Acts 13.50.

207   Probably as God-fearers rather than proselytes, see the discussion in I. Levinskaya, *The Book of Acts in its Diaspora Setting* (TBAFCS, vol. 5), pp. 122–24.

208   Josephus, *Ant.*, 12.147-53; Cicero, *Flac.*, 67–68.

209   See Chapter 3, 2.4.1.

210   Acts 13.14.

4.3.3. *Diaspora Worship Practices*

As well as providing us with the only clear use of συναγωγή for a 'gathering', Luke's account of events at Pisidian Antioch also gives us details of what happened in the 'synagogue' in this Diaspora community. The account is very similar to that of Luke 4:

> And on the sabbath day they went into the synagogue (συναγωγή) and sat down. After the reading of the law and the prophets, the officials of the synagogue sent them a message, saying, 'Brothers, if you have any word of exhortation for the people, give it.' So Paul stood up and with a gesture began to speak.[211]

We then have Luke's account of Paul's first sermon in Acts, after which the people ask them to return on the following Sabbath. Whether the sermon of Paul is entirely a Lukan composition is not important to our discussion. What matters here is whether Luke is presenting a 'synagogue' setting which reasonably accurately represents what may have taken place in Pisidian Antioch.

The first thing to note is that on this occasion we have a reading from both the Torah and the Prophets.[212] After this, Paul and Barnabas are encouraged to teach, this invitation coming from οἱ ἀρχισυνάγωγοι. Our sources have shown that the person who read needed no particular qualification; however, the one who went on to teach should be suitably competent, and Paul may have fulfilled such a requirement because of his training. Luke gives an intriguing aside when he writes: 'Paul stood up and with a gesture began to speak (ἀναστὰς δὲ Παῦλος καὶ κατασείσας τῇ χειρὶ εἶπεν)'. Of this Barrett remarks: 'It suggests a Greek rhetor rather than a synagogue preacher'.[213] Given that Pisidian Antioch was a cosmopolitan Graeco-Roman city and that the Jewish population was significant and influential, combined with the evidence of a synagogue building in nearby Acmonia which had a non-Jewish benefactor, perhaps the aside gives us further insight into the 'synagogue' gathering. I have shown in earlier chapters that often Jewish populations would integrate practices found in other groups, for example, voluntary associations. It may be that Paul is deliberately using a particular mannerism that is familiar to this group of Jews.

The most notable difference between this passage and that in Luke 4 is the posture taken to teach. In Luke 4 Jesus sits to teach while here Paul stands. Runesson suggests three possible reasons for this: i) Luke was not interested in the details of his accounts; ii) he did not know of one set pattern for teaching; iii) he is describing accurately two different practices,

---

211 Acts 13.14-16.
212 Note that in v. 27 Paul says that the Prophets are read every Sabbath.
213 Barrett, *Acts*, vol. 1, p. 629.

one from the Diaspora and one from Palestine. He suggests the last is the most likely, particularly in light of Philo's report of the pose for teaching in a Diaspora 'synagogue' setting.[214] Another possibility is that the larger synagogue building in Pisidian Antioch required that Paul stood up simply to be seen and heard. Here again we may have slight differences in the practice of particular communities.

5. *Conclusion*

In Chapter 1 it was noted that the first-century 'synagogue' did not operate like a modern franchise business: the size of the village or city, the place that the Jewish population occupied in the local socio-economic milieu, and buildings in the vicinity will all help us build a more accurate picture of how we should understand a particular reference to a συναγωγή. Whether we should perceive it as a building, a gathering, or both, must be considered. Where a building is meant, what the architecture of such a building might have looked like ought to be thought through. Similarly, Luke's reference to a προσευχή will be better understood in light of the totality of available data rather than just the Egyptian inscriptions relating to προσευχαί buildings. Consideration of these areas will also assist in understanding how a 'synagogue' may have functioned in a particular location: if it was the main building within a locality then its importance in the community will need to be considered; however, if it is more likely that a gathering took place in a domestic setting then this must have had an impact on how functions such as worship were carried out. This more nuanced approach has been the goal of this chapter. Therefore, having discussed references in Luke-Acts from Judea, Galilee, Phrygia and Macedonia we can now make the following observations:

1. Buildings: a detailed analysis of the relative size and seating capacity of all the potential first-century Palestinian synagogue sites helps us create a picture of how these buildings should be understood within their communities. Focusing on the building at Capernaum, we could begin to assess how this structure may have been used within the community; who might have attended; whether this increased the likelihood of other 'synagogues' in the city, etc. If, with Runesson, we assume that it functioned as the public synagogue building then this will further aid our perception of its role.

    In contrast to Atkinson, it has been argued that when Paul or

214   Philo, *Spec. Leg.*, 2.62, Runesson, *Origins*, p. 219. Oster incorrectly uses this reference to show that the account in Luke 4 is accurate, 'Supposed Anachronism', p. 201.

Jesus enters a 'synagogue' we should not immediately think of a building such as the one at Gamla. Although we consider that often a building will be meant, this will not always be the case and only a thorough understanding of the particular context will allow us to be more precise. We must take the literary and archaeological evidence for a particular area or community and combine it with more general 'synagogue' research to establish what the historical reality might have looked like. Here it would be tempting to use the definition of the minimalist Heather McKay: 'descriptions of doors, entering, seats, or of arson, threatened or perpetrated, will be regarded as literary evidence of a building in the mind of an author writing about assemblies of Jews'.[215] This would at least allow us to identify some of Luke's references clearly as buildings.[216] However, is such a definition really justified, is it not possible to enter a 'gathering' and to have demarcated seating in a setting that does not require a building?

It is proposed that the incident in Antioch probably did take place within a building, at least in Paul and Barnabas' first encounter in the city. The Jews had some influence and, in view of the other architecture in the city, combined with the Julia Severa inscription from Acmonia, may well have had a building resembling that of a voluntary association – we could think in terms of a building similar to that at Ostia. Clearly the situation in Nazareth is different. If the Jews met in a building then it would have been something simpler; however, *pace* Claußen and White's general hypothesis, we do not need to automatically think of modified domestic space. The presence of public buildings in nearby villages means that the possibility of a synagogue building should not be discounted. Nevertheless, if the 'synagogues' at Antioch and Nazareth were buildings, the architectural style would have been different. Generally the plan within Palestinian buildings made the centre of the meeting hall the focus, either to allow someone to address the group from a central position or to facilitate discussion among the group. Although there is less archaeological evidence in the Diaspora, such a focus appears less likely.

2. Terminology: It has been shown that there were a wide variety of terms used of the Jewish gathering(place)s in the first century of this era. In light of this, Luke's almost exclusive use of the term συναγωγή appears strange, particularly as it has been noted that he often uses the correct local terminology for officials or geographical details elsewhere. Therefore, in this regard he may be seen as inaccurate: he simply does not reflect the various terminology

---

215   McKay, 'From Evidence to Edifice', p. 190.
216   E.g., a reference to seats in Lk. 11.43, and of entering the 'synagogue' at Iconium, Acts 14.1.

which is likely to have been used in the towns and cities he recounts. However, the minimalist's charge that he is anachronistic when he uses συναγωγή of a building has been shown to be wrong, as evidence exists that it could be used in this way in the first half of the first century CE.

Luke appears deliberately to choose προσευχή in Acts 16 to indicate something other than a συναγωγή, and it has been argued that this should be understood as a place of prayer rather than a building. On at least one occasion he uses συναγωγή for the gathered community rather than some kind of institution or building. However, it is not clear whether he uses it in this way in any of his other references; it is likely that on occasions it carries both the meaning of a building and a gathering.

3.   The contexts of the two accounts of 'synagogue' worship in Luke-Acts are quite different. One takes place in a small rural village in Galilee, the other in a large Roman colony in the Diaspora. As we read the accounts there are clearly similarities between them, and the areas of difference are not immense. Nevertheless, certain details might indicate that Luke knew of some variation in pattern and style of worship that existed between the two areas. We have shown that there is sufficient evidence from other contemporaneous sources to indicate that Luke may well be presenting a reasonably accurate picture of what went on within these two gatherings. From these accounts it is not possible to argue that Luke is transposing a scene from a later Diaspora setting. There is also sufficient detail, although tantalizingly sparse, to indicate possible differences in certain areas of practice within these two gatherings.

Given the fact that Luke's accounts are focused on the teaching of both Jesus and Paul, the ancillary activities that went on around are of minor importance to him. However, with the evidence brought in the previous chapters, we can speculate a little on what may also have taken place:

1.   Ritual cleansing: It has been shown that ritual purity was a matter of concern to first-century Jews, and that they saw purity and 'synagogue' practice as connected.[217] It has been argued that some form of action to bring about purity was likely when someone entered a 'synagogue', but how this happened in any particular locality differed. Many of the Palestinian synagogue buildings, including those in Galilee, were either close to a source of natural water, or had *miqwaoth* near to them. In the Diaspora there is no evidence of *miqwaoth*, but again buildings were often built close to natural water, or had other facilities for providing water. In

217   See Chapter 4, 2.3.

Pisidian Antioch we have evidence of troughs and pools being used for ritual washing,[218] and we know of water facilities at the Ostian synagogue building. If, as has been suggested, the synagogue building in Pisidian Antioch had similarities to voluntary associations or pagan temples, it is likely that they would have included some form of water receptacle for washing at the entrance. Those entering would have dipped their hands and washed or sprinkled themselves to bring about cleansing.

2. Prayer/hymn singing: We have seen that communal prayer in the 'synagogue' was a practice to be found both in Palestine and in the Diaspora; not the formalized prayers of the 18 benedictions, but possibly including the *Shema*. In some communities we have evidence of embryonic elements of prayers such as the *Qedushah* which became part of the more formal liturgy of a later period. It is highly likely that different communities developed their liturgies at different rates, and there would have been greater or less formality depending on the situation of a particular 'synagogue'. Further, we cannot make simple lines of demarcation between the Diaspora and Palestine; the picture is more variegated.

3. Other functions: It has been shown that the first-century 'synagogue' performed many functions, particularly if there was a synagogue building. This is also the case in Luke-Acts with Sabbath worship, heated discussion, exorcism, interrogation of Christians, judgement, and imprisonment all recorded. In Chapter 4 it was argued that communal dining would have been an important part of Jewish life and that there is evidence of its association with the Sabbath. The building at Ostia provides physical data on how such a meal may have taken place within a synagogue building setting, as can the building in Jericho. Although there is evidence for such meals in a variety of geographical locations, it was argued that, particularly within Graeco-Roman settings, Jewish communities modelled some of their practices on the communal dining seen around them. Further, a false division between the sacred and communal activities of voluntary associations or pagan temples should be avoided as the communal meal formed part of the worship of the group.[219] As in Ostia, in Pisidian Antioch we have evidence of other religious groups having buildings that functioned

---

218   There were four water fountains at the entrance to the imperial sanctuary, Mitchell and Waelkens, *Pisidian Antioch*, pp. 150–51, and stone basins in the temple of Men, *ibid.*, pp. 78–79; D.W.J. Gill, 'Acts and Roman Religion: Religion in a Local Setting', in Gill and Gempf, *Book of Acts*, p. 89.

219   See the comments of Mitchell and Waelkens: 'Religious acts of ritual or devotion, narrowly defined, comprised only a small part of the activity of any Greek religious centre, whether it was a small shrine or a major sanctuary. Other aspects of community worship were more conspicuous and equally significant, and the most important of these involved banqueting', *Pisidian Antioch*, p. 83.

as banqueting halls and it may be that some form of *triclinium* adjoined the synagogue building there.

A further difference that may have existed between a setting such as Nazareth and Pisidian Antioch is the role of women. There is evidence that women played a more active part in day-to-day life in Asia Minor than in Palestine;[220] decrees allowing sacred rites to be observed and prayers to be made included both Jewish men and women[221] and such involvement is reflected in the God-fearing women of Acts 13.

Clearly some of what is included in these last paragraphs is a reconstruction. However, it is built on the evidence gathered in the previous chapters. As indicated above, purely to footnote the undisputed data that we possess is insufficient in a work such as this. Some of these suggestions are built on material that continues to be the focus of scholarly debate and as such it may be that future archaeological evidence will shed further light on the subject;[222] nonetheless, such conjecture is well founded in the current state of research

220   S.B. Pomeroy, *Goddesses, Whores, Wives, and Slaves: Women in Classical Antiquity* (New York: Schocken Books, 1975), pp. 125–27.

221   Josephus, *Ant.*, 14.256-61.

222   See especially the ongoing archaeological work of L.M. White on the Ostian synagogue building.

Chapter 6

CONCLUSION

The purpose of this book has been twofold. First, the relevant primary and secondary source material was assessed to evaluate the form and function of the 'synagogue' in the first-century period. Second, we compared that material to the presentation of the 'synagogue' in Luke-Acts, using it to inform our exegesis of texts better. While the literary evidence has been reassessed in detail, a particular focus of this work has been the available archaeological evidence. New discoveries are aiding the discussion of first-century Judaism generally, and 'synagogue' studies have benefited from a number of reasonably recent finds. The continued investigation of these sites, along with others that will undoubtedly be proposed, will further aid our understanding of first-century 'synagogues' and, at times, give us the framework to comprehend better the literary evidence.

In recent scholarly debate it has become customary to talk of Judaisms rather than Judaism. To what extent the belief and practice of all first-century Jews should be conceived as being the same has been the topic of much debate. While not directly interacting with this discussion, some of the issues raised are similar to those covered in this study. When we read a text that mentions a συναγωγή are we to think of something with a clearly defined form, the functions of which were universally understood? Or should we, in fact, highlight that the Jewish meeting(place)s evidenced great diversity and that this diversity extended to the practices of various Jewish communities?

What has been argued for here is, to some extent, a tightrope walk between these two positions. It has been shown that the position of a previous generation of scholars who perceived the 'synagogue' as a monolithic entity and translated various terms with the English 'synagogue' is untenable. Similarly, using evidence from much later sources to envision the worship practice of these first-century communities was commonplace, but is no longer acceptable. However, the shortcomings in the arguments of the minimalists have also been highlighted throughout our discussion. In our critique of the debate between the minimalists and maximalists, it was argued that too often those involved fail to recognize the strengths of the others' arguments.

The variegation both in synagogue building style and worship practice of Jewish communities, and the assimilation of practices of the culture in which they found themselves have been highlighted. At the same time, false understandings of what might constitute worship in a first-century setting have also been critiqued. It has been argued that differences in practice existed between Palestinian and Diaspora communities, but that this should not be understood simply as geographical demarcation: it is possible to find a Diaspora style 'synagogue' even within Jerusalem. The similarity in style of architecture within Palestinian synagogue buildings would have facilitated an easy exchange of ideas following the reading and teaching from the Torah. The influence of voluntary associations on Diaspora 'synagogues' was noted and the building at Ostia allowed a comparison with other guild buildings in the city. Of particular interest here was the associated dining facility, and it was argued that there would have been sacred elements associated with communal meals.

Having described the current situation as akin to a tightrope walk, if we wanted to fall off the tightrope onto one side then it should be on that of greater commonality. There is sufficient evidence of practice that united Jews: in a wide range of places and in various Jewish groups the reading and teaching of the Torah is highlighted. In addition, it was shown that while no fixed liturgy can be argued for in the first century, there is evidence that common biblical themes were used to influence the flow of worship, and that elements that became part of a more fixed later liturgy are evidenced in the first-century period. Communal prayer/hymn singing was also shown to have existed at this time both in the Diaspora and in Palestine.

The application of these arguments to the text of Luke-Acts highlighted the problems associated with the recent arguments over Luke's presentation of the 'synagogue'. Further, it has allowed a more detailed understanding of Luke's references to a συναγωγή or προσευχή. The necessarily limited scope of this study has meant that we have not been able to interact fully with all the material which might be explored in Luke-Acts, for example, we have not discussed the 'synagogues' at Corinth or in Syria. However, by focusing on disputed texts, or passages that deal with worship practices most fully, and integrating the potential for geographical diversity, we have laid the parameters for future investigation.

As well as the continued integration of archaeological evidence into 'synagogue' research, this study also highlights other areas of potential investigation. The influence of the surrounding culture and the socio-economic position of a Jewish community would, it has been argued, influence the place in which they met and to a lesser extent, the way in which they worshipped. Similar arguments can and should be applied to the worship of the early Christian community. Too often it is assumed that Paul's exchange with the church in Corinth should be seen as normative for all gatherings of the early Christian community. Further, to what extent was Christianity influenced by its Jewish roots? How great an influence was the 'synagogue' on the worship practices of early Christians? Finally, as has been noted earlier, this study illuminates one of the important first-century Jewish institutions and as such provides good background material to understanding the social setting for historical Jesus research. Further nuancing of the arguments will allow us to gain a clearer picture of Palestine in Jesus' day.

BIBLIOGRAPHY

Primary Sources and Translations

The Babylonian Talmud (ed. I. Epstein; 17 vols; London: Soncino Press, 1935–48).

Cassius Dio (trans. E. Cary; LCL; 9 vols; Cambridge, Mass.: Harvard University Press, 1914–27).

Cicero (trans. C. MacDonald; LCL; Cambridge, Mass.: Harvard University Press, 1977).

Corpus Papyrorum Judaicarum (ed. V.A. Tcherikover and A. Fuks; 3 vols; Cambridge, Mass.: Harvard University Press, 1957–1960).

The Dead Sea Scrolls: Study Edition (trans. F.G. Martínez and E.J.C. Tigchelaar; 2 vols; Leiden: Brill, 1997–98).

The Complete Dead Sea Scrolls in English (trans. G. Vermes; London: Penguin Books, 4th edn, 1995).

The Holy Bible (NIV; London: Hodder and Stoughton, 1984).

The Holy Bible (NRSV; Nashville: Thomas Nelson, 1989).

The Jerusalem Talmud (ed. H.W. Guggenheimer; Studia Judaica: Forschungen zur Wissenschaft des Judentums 18–20. Berlin: Walter de Gruyter, 2000–).

Josephus (trans. H.St.J. Thackery *et al.*; LCL; 10 vols; Cambridge, Mass.: Harvard University Press, 1926–65).

Juvenal (trans. G.G. Ramsay; LCL; London: Heinemann, 1918).

The Mishnah (trans. J. Neusner; New Haven: Yale University Press, 1988).

The Mishnah (trans. H. Danby; London: Oxford University Press, 1933).

Novum Testamentum Graece (ed. B. Aland *et al.*; Stuttgart: Deutsche Bibelgesellschaft, 27th edn, 1993).

Parry, D.W. and E. Qimron, *The Great Scroll (1QIsaa): A New Edition* (STDJ, 32; Leiden: Brill, 1999).

Philo (trans. F.H. Colson, G.H. Whitaker and R. Marcus; LCL; 10 vols; Cambridge, Mass.: Harvard University Press, 1929–53).

Seneca (trans. F.J. Miller; LCL; 5 vols; London: Heinemann, 1917–25).

Sokoloff, M., *The Targum to Job from Qumran Cave XI* (Ramat-Gan: Bar-Ilan University, 1974).

Tacitus (trans. C.H. Moore and J. Jackson; LCL; 5 vols; Cambridge, Mass.: Harvard University Press, 1914–70).

The Tosefta (trans. J. Neusner; 2 vols; Peabody, Mass.: Hendrickson, 2002).

Übersetzung des Talmud Yerushalmi (ed. M. Hengel *et al.*; Tübingen: Mohr Siebeck, 1976–).

DJD XV (E. Ulrich *et al.*; Oxford: Clarendon Press, 1997).

Zulueta, F. de, *The Institutes of Gaius* (2 vols; Oxford: Clarendon Press, 1946).

Secondary Sources

Albright, W.F., 'A Biblical Fragment from the Maccabean Age: The Nash Papyrus', *JBL* 56 (1937): 145–76.

Alexander, P.S., 'Rabbinic Judaism and the New Testament', *ZNW* 74 (1983): 237–46.

Applebaum, S., *Jews and Greeks in Ancient Cyrene* (SJLA, 28; Leiden: Brill, 1979).

Atkinson, K., 'On Further Defining the First-Century CE Synagogue: Fact or Fiction? A Rejoinder to H.C. Kee', *NTS* 43 (1997): 491–502.

Avi-Yonah, M., 'The Foundation of Tiberias', *IEJ* 1 (1950–51): 160–69.

——'When did Judea become a Consular Province?', *IEJ* 23 (1973): 209–13.

——'Ancient Syngogues', in J. Gutmann (ed.), *The Synagogue: Studies in Origins, Archaeology and Architecture* (New York: KTAV, 1975), pp. 95–109.

——'Some Comments on the Capernaum Excavations', in L. I. Levine (ed.), *Ancient Synagogues Revealed* (Jerusalem: Israel Exploration Society, 1981), pp. 60–62.

Bachmann, H. and W.A. Slaby, *Computer-Konkordanz Zum Novum Testamentum Graece* (Berlin: Walter De Gruyter, 1980).

Barclay, J.M.G., *Jews in the Mediterranean Diaspora from Alexander to Trajan (323 BCE-117 CE)* (Edinburgh: T&T Clark, 1996).

Barrett, C.K., *Acts* (ICC; 2 vols; Edinburgh: T&T Clark, 1994–98).

Bartlett, J.R., *The First and Second Books of the Maccabees* (Cambridge: Cambridge University Press, 1973).

Beckwith, R., 'The Daily and Weekly Worship of the Primitive Church', *EvQ* 56 (1984): 65–80.

——*Daily and Weekly Worship: Jewish to Christian* (Alcuin/GROW Liturgical Study 1; Bramcote: Grove Books, 1987).

——*Calendar and Chronology, Jewish and Christian: Biblical, Intertestamental and Patristic Studies* (Leiden: Brill, 1996).

Bernard, J.H., *The Pastoral Epistles* (Cambridge: Cambridge University Press, 1906).

Bickerman, E.J., 'The Civic Prayer for Jerusalem', *HTR* 55 (1962): 163–85.

Bilde, P., *Flavius Josephus between Jerusalem and Rome: His Life, his Works, and their Importance* (JSPSup, 2; Sheffield: JSOT Press, 1988).

Binder, D.D., *Into the Temple Courts: The Place of the Synagogues in the Second Temple Period* (SBLDS, 169; Atlanta: SBL, 1999).

——'The Origins of the Synagogue: An Evaluation', in B. Olsson, and M. Zetterholm (eds), *The Ancient Synagogue: From its Origins to 200 C.E.: Papers Presented at an International Conference at Lund University, October 14–17, 2001* (*ConNT*, 39; Stockholm: Almqvist and Wiksell, 2003), pp. 118–31.

Blass, F. and A. Debrunner, *A Greek Grammar of the New Testament and Other Early Christian Literature* (trans. R.W. Funk; Cambridge: Cambridge University Press, 1961).

Bloedhorn, H. and G. Hüttenmeister, 'The Synagogue', in W. Horbury, W. D. Davies and J. Sturdy (eds), in *CHJ*, 3, pp. 267–97.

Blue, B., 'Acts and the House Church', in D.W.J. Gill and C. Gempf (eds), *The Book of Acts in its Graeco-Roman Setting* (*TBAFCS*, vol. 2; Grand Rapids: Eerdmans, 1994), pp. 119–222.

Bock, D.L., *Luke* (BECNT, 2 vols; Grand Rapids: Baker Books, 1994–96).

Bockmuehl, M., *The Epistle to the Philippians* (BNTC; London: A. & C. Black, 1997).

Borgen, P., K. Fuglseth and R. Skarsten (eds), *The Philo Index* (Grand Rapids: Eerdmans, 2000).

Bovon, F., *Luke 1* (Hermeneia; Minneapolis: Fortress Press, 2002).

Bremmer, J.N., *Greek Religion* (Oxford: Oxford University Press, 1994).

Brooten, B.J., *Women Leaders in the Ancient Synagogue: Inscriptional Evidence and Background Issues* (BJS, 36; Atlanta: Scholars Press, 1982).

Bruce, F.F., *The Book of the Acts* (NICNT; Grand Rapids: Eerdmans, rev. edn, 1988).

Bruneau, P., *Recherches sur les cultes de Délos a l'époque hellénistique et a l'époque impérial* (Bibliothèque des écoles françaises d'Athènes et de Rome, 217; Paris: E. De Boccard, 1970).

——' "Les Israélites de Délos" et la juiverie délienne', *Bulletin de Correspondance Hellénique* 106 (1982): 465–504.

Bruneau, P. and J. Ducat, *Guide de Délos* (Paris: E. de Boccard, 2nd edn, 1966).

Buckert, W., *Greek Religion: Archaic and Classical* (trans. J. Raffan; Oxford: Blackwell, 1985).

Burtchaell, J.T., *From Synagogue to Church: Public Services and Offices in the Earliest Christian Communities* (Cambridge: Cambridge University Press, 1992).

Campbell, R.M., '*Parashiyyot* and their Implications for Dating the Fragment-Targums', in P. V. M. Flesher (ed.), *Targum and Scripture: Studies in Aramaic Translation and Interpretation* (SAIS, 2; Leiden: Brill, 2002), pp. 105–14.

Catto, S.K., 'Does προσευχὰς ποιεῖσθαι, in Josephus' *Antiquities of the Jews* 14.257-8, Mean "Build Places of Prayer"?', *JSJ* 35 (2004): 159–68.

Chancey, M.A., *Greco-Roman Culture and the Galilee of Jesus* (SNTSMS, 134; Cambridge: Cambridge University Press, 2005).

Charlesworth, J., *Jesus within Judaism: New Light from Exciting Archaeological Discoveries* (London: SPCK, 1989).

Chazon, E.G., '4QDibham: Liturgy or Literature?', *RevQ* 15 (1992): 447–55.

——'On the Special Character of Sabbath Prayer: New Data from Qumran', *Journal of Jewish Music and Liturgy* 115 (1992/3): 1–21.

Chen, D., 'The Design of the Ancient Synagogues in Judea: Masada and Herodium', *BASOR* 239 (1980): 37–40.

Chiat, M.J.S., *Handbook of Synagogue Architecture* (BJS, 29; Chico: Scholars Press, 1982).

Clarke, A.D., *Serve the Community of the Church: Christians as Leaders and Ministers* (Grand Rapids: Eerdmans, 2000).

Claußen, C., *Versammlung, Gemeinde, Synagoge: Das hellenistisch-jüdische Umfeld der frühchristlichen Gemeinden* (SUNT, 27; Göttingen: Vandenhoeck & Ruprecht, 2002).

——'Meeting, Community, Synagogue – Different Frameworks of Ancient Jewish Congregations in the Diaspora', in B. Olsson, and M. Zetterholm (eds), *The Ancient Synagogue: From its Origins to 200 C.E.: Papers Presented at an International Conference at Lund University, October 14–17, 2001* (ConNT, 39; Stockholm: Almqvist and Wiksell, 2003), pp. 144–67.

Cohen, S.J.D., 'Pagan and Christian Evidence on the Ancient Synagogue', in L.I. Levine (ed.), *The Synagogue in Late Antiquity* (Philadelphia: The American Schools of Oriental Research, 1987), pp. 159–81.

——*From the Maccabees to the Mishnah* (Philadelphia: Westminster Press, 1987).

——'The Temple and the Synagogue', in *CHJ*, 3, pp. 298–325.

Collins, J.J., 'Sibylline Oracles', in J.H. Charlesworth (ed.), *The Old Testament Pseudepigrapha* (2 vols; New York: Doubleday, 1983), vol. 1, pp. 317–472.

——*Daniel: A Commentary on the Book of Daniel* (Hermeneia; Minneapolis: Fortress Press, 1993).

Conzelmann, H., *Acts of the Apostles* (trans. J. Limburg *et al.*; Philadelphia: Fortress Press, 1987).

Corbo, V.C., 'L'Herodion di Giabal Fureidis: Relazione Preliminare della Terza e Quarta Campagna di Scavi Archeologici', *Liber Annuus* 17 (1967): 65–121.

——'Gébel Fureidis (Hérodium)', *RB* 75 (1968): 424–28.

——'Resti Della Sinagoga del Primo Secolo a Cafarnao', *Studia Hierosolymitana III* (1982): 314–57.

——*Herodion I: Gli Edifici della Reggia-Fortezza* (Jerusalem: Studium Biblicum Franciscanum, 1989).

Courtney, E., *A Commentary on the Satires of Juvenal* (London: The Athlone Press, 1980).

Crossan, J.D., *The Historical Jesus: The Life of a Mediterranean Jewish Peasant* (Edinburgh: T&T Clark, 1991).

Crossan, J.D. and J.L. Reed, *Excavating Jesus: Beneath the Stones, Behind the Texts* (London: SPCK, 2001).

Croy, N.C., *3 Maccabees* (Septuagint Commentary Series; Leiden:Brill, 2006).

Davids, P.H., *The Epistle of James* (NIGTC; Grand Rapids: Eerdmans, 1982).

Davies, P., 'A Note on I Macc. III. 46', *JTS* 23 (1972): 117–21.

Davila, J.R., *Liturgical Works* (Eerdmans Commentaries on the Dead Sea Scrolls, 6; Grand Rapids: Eerdmans, 2000).

Deissmann, G.A., *Light from the Ancient East: The New Testament Illustrated by Recently Discovered Texts of the Graeco-Roman World* (London: Hodder and Stoughton, 1910).

Dibelius, M., *A Commentary on the Epistle of James* (trans. M.A. Williams; Hermeneia; Philadelphia: Fortress Press, rev. edn, 1976).

Dibelius, M. and H. Conzelmann, *A Commentary on the Pastoral Epistles* (trans. P. Buttolph and A. Yarbro; Philadelphia: Fortress, 1972).

Dion, P.E., 'Synagogues et Temples dans L'Égypte Hellénistique', *ScEs* 29 (1977): 45–75.

Eckey, W., *Die Apostelgeschichte: der Weg des Evangeliums von Jerusalem nach Rom* (2 vols; Neukirchener-Vluyn: Neukirchener, 2000).

Edwards, D.R., 'Jews and Christians at Ancient Chersonesus: The Transformation of Jewish Public Space', in H.C. Kee and L.H. Cohick (eds), *Evolution of the Synagogue* (Harrisburg: Trinity Press, 1999), pp. 158–73.

——'Khirbet Qana: from Jewish Village to Christian Pilgrim Site', in J.H. Humphrey (ed.), *The Roman and Byzantine Near East*, vol. 3 (Journal of Roman Archaeology Supplementary Series, 49; Portsmouth, Rhode Island: JRA, 2002), pp. 101–32.

Elbogen, I., *Jewish Liturgy: A Comprehensive History* (trans. R.P. Scheindlin; Philadelphia: The Jewish Publication Society, 1993).

Eshel, E., 'Prayer in Qumran and the Synagogue', in B. Ego, A. Lange and P. Pilhofer (eds), *Gemeinde ohne Tempel, Community without Temple: Zur Substituierung und Transformation des Jerusalemer Tempels und seines Kults im Alten Testament, antiken Judentum und frühen Christentum* (WUNT, 118; Tübingen: Mohr Siebeck, 1999), pp. 323–34.

Esler, P.F., *Community and Gospel in Luke-Acts: The Social and Political Motivations of Lucan Theology* (SNTSMS, 57; Cambridge: Cambridge University Press, 1987).

——*Conflict and Identity in Romans: The Social Setting of Paul's Letter* (Minneapolis: Fortress Press, 2003).

Evans, C.F., *Saint Luke* (London: SCM Press, 1990).

Falk, D.K., 'Jewish Prayer Literature and the Jerusalem Church', in R. Bauckham (ed.), *The Book of Acts in its Palestinian Setting* (*TBAFCS*, vol. 4; Grand Rapids: Eerdmans, 1995), pp. 267–301.

——*Daily, Sabbath, and Festival Prayers in the Dead Sea Scrolls* (STDJ, 27; Leiden: Brill, 1998).

——'Prayer in the Qumran Texts', in *CHJ*, 3, pp. 852–76.

Fee, G.D., *Paul's Letter to the Philippians* (NICNT; Grand Rapids: Eerdmans, 1995).

Feldman, L.H., *Josephus and Modern Scholarship (1937–1980)* (Berlin: Walter de Gruyter, 1984).

——'Diaspora Synagogues: New Light from Inscriptions and Papyri', in S. Fine (ed.), *Sacred Realm: The Emergence of the Synagogue in the Ancient World* (New York: Yeshiva University Museum, 1996), pp. 48–66.

Fine, S., *Sacred Realm: The Emergence of the Synagogue in the Ancient World* (New York: Yeshiva University Museum, 1996).

——'From Meeting House to Sacred Realm: Holiness and the Ancient Synagogue', in S. Fine (ed.), *Sacred Realm: The Emergence of the Synagogue in the Ancient World* (New York: Yeshiva University Museum, 1996), pp. 21–47.

——*This Holy Place: On the Sanctity of the Synagogue During the Greco-Roman Period* (Notre Dame: Notre Dame Press, 1997).

——(ed.), *Jews, Christians, and Polytheists in the Ancient Synagogue* (New York: Routledge, 1999).

Finkel, A., 'Jesus' Preaching in the Synagogue on the Sabbath (Luke 4.16-28)', in C.A. Evans and W.R. Stegner (eds), *The Gospels and the Scripture of Israel* (Sheffield, Sheffield Academic Press, 1994), pp. 325–41.

Fitzgerald, G.M., 'Notes on Recent Discoveries', *PEFQS* 53 (1921), 175–86.

Fitzmyer, J.A., *The Gospel According to Luke* (AB, 28; 2 vols; New York: Doubleday, 1970–85).

——*The Acts of the Apostles* (AB, 31; New York: Doubleday, 1998).

Fleischer, E., 'On the Beginnings of Obligatory Jewish Prayer', *Tarbiz* 59 (1990): 397–425, (Hebrew).

——'Rejoinder to Dr Reif's Remarks', *Tarbiz* 60 (1991), viii-ix, (English Summaries).

Flesher. P.V.M., 'Palestinian Synagogues Before 70 C.E.: A Review of the Evidence', in *ASHAAD*, vol. 1, pp. 27–39.

Foakes Jackson F.J. and K. Lake, *The Beginnings of Christianity* (5 vols; London: Macmillan and Co., 1933).

Foerster, G., 'Notes on Recent Excavations at Capernaum (Review Article)', *IEJ* 21 (1971): 207–11. Reprinted in L.I. Levine (ed.), *Ancient Synagogues Revealed* (Jerusalem: Israel Exploration Society, 1981), pp. 57–59.

——'The Synagogues at Masada and Herodium', in L.I. Levine (ed.), *Ancient Synagogues Revealed* (Jerusalem: Israel Exploration Society, 1981) , pp. 24–29.

——'Herodium,' in *NEAEHL*, vol. 2, pp. 618–21.

——'Dating Synagogues with a "Basilical" Plan and Apse', in *ASHAAD*, vol. 1, pp. 87–94

Fraser, P.M., *Ptolemaic Alexandria* (2 vols; Oxford: Clarendon Press, 1972).

Freyne, S., *Galilee from Alexander the Great to Hadrian 323 B.C. E. to 135 C.E.: A Study of Second Temple Judaism* (Notre Dame: University of Notre Dame Press, 1980).

Funk, R.W. and R.W. Hoover, *The Five Gospels: the Search for the Authentic Words of Jesus* (New York: Macmillan, 1993).

Gerhardsson, B., *The Shema in the New Testament: Deut 6.4-5 in Significant Passages* (Lund: Nova Press, 1996).

Gibson, E.L., *The Jewish Manumission Inscriptions of the Bosporus Kingdom* (TSAJ, 75; Tübingen: Mohr Siebeck, 1999).

Gill, D.W.J., 'Acts and Roman Religion: Religion in a Local Setting', in D.W.J. Gill and C. Gempf (eds), *The Book of Acts in its Graeco-Roman Setting* (*TBAFCS*, vol. 2; Grand Rapids: Eerdmans, 1994), pp. 79–92.

Goodenough, E.R., *Jewish Symbols in the Greco-Roman Period* (Bollingen Series 37; 13 vols; New York: Pantheon Books, 1953–68).

——'Sacred Space in Diaspora Judaism' in B. Isaac and A. Oppenheimer (eds), *Studies on the Jewish Diaspora in the Hellenistic and Roman Periods* (Te'uda, 12; Tel-Aviv: Ramot, 1996), pp. 1–16.

Goodman, M., 'Sacred Space in Diaspora Judaism', in B. Isaac and A. Oppenheimer (eds), *Studies on the Jewish Diaspora in the Hellenistic and Roman Periods* (Te'uda, 12; Tel-Aviv: Ramot, 1996), pp. 1–16.

Görtz-Wrisberg, I. von., 'A Sabbath Service in Ostia: What Do We Know about the Ancient Synagogal Service?' in B. Olsson, D. Mitternacht and O. Brandt (eds), *The Synagogue of Ancient Ostia and the Jews of Rome: Interdisciplinary Studies* (Stockholm: Paul Åströms Förlag, 2001), pp. 167–202.

Goulder, M., *The Evangelists' Calendar: A Lectionary Explanation of the Development of Scripture* (London: SPCK, 1978).

Grabbe, L.L., 'Synagogues in Pre-70 Palestine: A Re-assessment', *JTS* 39 (1988): 401–410.

Green, J.B., *The Gospel of Luke* (NICNT; Grand Rapids: Eerdmans, 1997).

Griffiths, J.G., 'Egypt and the Rise of the Synagogue', *JTS* 38 (1987): 1–15.

——'The Legacy of Egypt in Judaism', in *CHJ*, 3, pp. 1025–51.

Gundry, R., *Matthew: A Commentary on His Handbook for a Mixed Church under Persecution* (Grand Rapids: Eerdmans, 2nd edn, 1994).

Gutmann, J. (ed.), *The Synagogue: Studies in Origins, Archaeology and Architecture* (The Library of Biblical Studies; New York: KTAV, 1975).

——(ed.), *Ancient Synagogues: The State of Research* (BJS, 22; Chico: Scholars Press, 1981).

Gutman, S., 'The Synagogue at Gamla', in L.I. Levine (ed.), *Ancient Synagogues Revealed* (Jerusalem: Israel Exploration Society, 1981), pp. 30–34.

——'Gamala', in *NEAEHL*, vol. 2, pp. 459–62.

Hachlili, R., 'The Origin of the Synagogue: A Re-assessment', *JSJ* 28 (1997): 34–47.

——*Ancient Jewish Art and Archaeology in the Diaspora* (Leiden: Brill, 1998).

Haenchen, E., *The Acts of the Apostles* (Oxford: Blackwell, 1971).

Harland, P.A., *Associations, Synagogues and Congregations: Claiming a Place in Ancient Mediterranean Society* (Minneapolis: Fortress, 2003).

Harrington, D.J., 'Pseudo-Philo', in J.H. Charlesworth (ed.), *Old Testament Pseudepigrapha* (2 vols; New York: Doubleday, 1985), vol. 2, pp. 297–377.

Harrington, H.K., *The Impurity Systems of Qumran and the Rabbis: Biblical Foundations* (SBLDS, 143; Atlanta: Scholars Press, 1993).

Hatch E. and H.A. Redpath, *A Conconrdance to the Septuagint and the Other Greek Versions of the Old Testament* (Grand Rapids: Baker, 2nd edn, 1998).

Hawthorne, G.F., *Philippians* (WBC, 43; Dallas: Word Books, 2002).

Heinemann, J., *Prayer in the Talmud: Forms and Patterns* (SJ, 9; Berlin: Walter De Gruyter, 1977).

Hemer, C.J., *The Book of Acts in the Setting of Hellenistic History* (ed. C.H. Gempf; WUNT, 49; Tübingen: Mohr Siebeck, 1989).

Hengel, M., 'Proseuche und Synagoge: Jüdische Gemeinde, Gotteshaus und Gottesdienst in der Diaspora und in Palästina', in G. Jeremias, H.W. Kuhn and H. Stegemann (eds), *Tradition und Glaube. Das frühe Christentum in seiner Umwelt. Festgabe für Karl Georg Kuhn zum 65. Geburtstag* (Göttingen: Vandenhoeck und Ruprecht, 1971), pp. 157–83. Reprinted in, J. Gutmann (ed.), *The Synagogue: Studies in Origins, Archaeology and Architecture* (The Library of Biblical Studies; New York: KTAV, 1975), pp. 27–54.

——*Judaism and Hellenism: Studies in their Encounter in Palestine During the Early Hellenistic Period* (2 vols; London: SCM Press, 1974).

Hermansen, G., *Ostia: Aspects of Roman City Life* (Edmonton: University of Alberta Press, 1982).

Hoenig, S.B., 'The Ancient City Square: The Forerunner of the Synagogue', *ANRW* II.19.1, 448–76.

Hoppe, L.J., *The Synagogues and Churches of Ancient Palestine* (Collegeville, Minnesota: The Liturgical Press, 1994).

Horbury, W., 'Herod's Temple and "Herod Days"', in W. Horbury (ed.), *Templum Amicitiae: Essays on the Second Temple Presented to Ernst Bammel* (JSNTSup, 48; Sheffield: JSOT Press, 1991), pp. 103–49.

——*Jews and Christians in Contact and Controversy* (Edinburgh: T&T Clark, 1998).

——'Women in the Synagogue', in *CHJ*, 3, pp. 358–401.

Horsley, R.A., *Galilee: History, Politics, People* (Valley Forge: Trinity, 1995).

——*Archaeology, History, and Society in Galilee: The Social Context of Jesus and the Rabbis* (Valley Forge: Trinity, 1996).

——'Synagogues in Galilee and the Gospels', in H.C. Kee and L.H. Cohick (eds), *Evolution of the Synagogue* (Harrisburg: Trinity Press, 1999), pp. 46–69.

Horst, P.W. van der., 'Was the Synagogue a Place of Sabbath Worship Before 70 CE?', in S. Fine (ed.), *Jews, Christians, and Polytheists in the Ancient Synagogue* (New York: Routledge, 1999), pp. 18–43.

——*Philo's Flaccus: The First Pogrom* (Philo of Alexandria Commentary Series, 2; Leiden: Brill, 2003).

Hurtado, L.W., *At the Origins of Christian Worship: The Context and Character of Earliest Christian Devotion* (Grand Rapids: Eerdmans, 1999).

Hüttenmeister, F.G., 'Synagoge und Proseuche bei Josephus und in anderen antiken Quellen', in D.A. Koch and H. Lichtenberger (eds) *Begegnungen zwischen Christentum und Judentum in Antike und Mittelalter* (Festschrift H. Schreckenberg; Göttingen: Vandenhoeck and Ruprecht, 1993), pp. 163–81.

Ilan, T., *Jewish Women in Greco-Roman Palestine* (Peabody: Hendrickson, 1996).

Instone-Brewer, D., *Traditions of the Rabbis from the Era of the New Testament*, vol. 1, *Prayer and Agriculture* (Grand Rapids: Eerdmans, 2004).

Jacobson, H., *A Commentary on Pseudo-Philo's Liber Antiquitatum Biblicarum* (AGJU, 31; Leiden: Brill, 1996).

Jervell, J., *Die Apostelgeschichte* (KEK, 3; Göttingen: Vandenhoeck and Ruprecht, 1998).

Johnson, L.T., *The Acts of the Apostles* (Minnesota: Liturgical Press, 1992).

Kant, L.H., 'Jewish Inscriptions in Greek and Latin', *ANRW* II.20.2, 671–713.

Kasher, A., 'Synagogues as "Houses of Prayer" and "Holy Places" in the Jewish Communities of Hellenistic and Roman Egypt', in *ASHAAD*, vol. 1, pp. 205–20.

Kee, H.C., 'The Transformation of the Synagogue after 70 C.E.: Its Import for Early Christianity', *NTS* 36 (1990): 1–24.

——'Early Christianity in the Galilee: Reassessing the Evidence from the Gospels', in L.I. Levine (ed.), *The Galilee in Late Antiquity* (Cambridge, MA: The Jewish Theological Seminary of America, 1992), pp. 3–22.

——'The Changing Meaning of Synagogue: A Response to Richard Oster', *NTS* 40 (1994), pp. 281–83.

——'Defining the First-Century CE Synagogue: Problems and Progress', *NTS* 41 (1995): 481–500. Reprinted in, H.C. Kee and L.H. Cohick (eds), *Evolution of the Synagogue* (Harrisburg: Trinity Press, 1999), pp. 7–26.

——*To Every Nation under Heaven* (The New Testament in Context; Harrisburg: Trinity Press, 1997.

Kimelman, R., 'The Šĕmaʿ and its Blessings: The realization of God's Kingship', in L.I. Levine (ed.), *The Synagogue in Late Antiquity* (Philadelphia: The American Schools of Oriental Research, 1987), pp. 73–86.

Klinghardt, M., *Gemeinschaftsmahl und Mahlgemeinschaft: Soziologie und Liturgie frühchristlicher Mahlfeiern* (Texte und Arbeiten zum neutestamentlichen Zeitalter, 13; Tübingen: Francke Verlag, 1996).

Kloppenborg Verbin, J.S., 'Dating Theodotos (CIJ II 1404)', *JJS* 51 (2000): 243–80.

Knight, G.W., *The Pastoral Epistles: A Commentary on the Greek Text* (NIGTC; Grand Rapids: Eerdmans, 1992).

Koester, H., 'Paul and Philippi: The Evidence from Early Christian Literature', in C. Bakirtzes and H. Koester (eds), *Philippi at the Time of Paul and after His Death* (Pennsylvania: Trinity Press, 1998), pp. 49–65.

Kohl, H. and C. Watzinger, *Antike Synagogen in Galiläa* (Leipzig: Heinrichs, 1916).

Koukouli-Chrysantaki, C., 'Colonia Iulia Augusta Philippensis', in C. Bakirtzes and H. Koester (eds), *Philippi at the Time of Paul and after His Death* (Pennsylvania: Trinity Press, 1998), pp. 5–35.

Kraabel, A.T., 'New Evidence of the Samaritan Diaspora has been Found on Delos', *BA* 47 (March 1984): 44–46.

——'The Diaspora Synagogue: Archaeological and Epigraphic Evidence since Sukenik', *ANRW* II.19.1, 477–510. Reprinted in, *ASHAAD*, vol. 1, pp. 95–126.

Lampe, P., *From Paul to Valentinus: Christians at Rome in the First Two Centuries* (Minneapolis, Fortress Press, 2003).

Lane, E.N., 'Men: A Neglected Cult of Roman Asia Minor', *ANRW* II.18.3, 2161–74.

Laughlin, J.C.H., 'Capernaum from Jesus' Time and After', *BARev* 19.5 (1993): 54–61.

Leon, H.J., *The Jews of Ancient Rome* (updated edn, C.A. Osiek,; Peabody: Hendrickson, 1995).

Leonhardt, J., *Jewish Worship in Philo of Alexandria* (TSAJ, 84; Tübingen: Mohr Siebeck, 2001).

Levick, B., *Roman Colonies in Southern Asia Minor* (Oxford: Oxford University Press, 1967).

Levine, L.I., 'Ancient Synagogues – A Historical Introduction', in L.I. Levine (ed.), *Ancient Synagogues Revealed* (Jerusalem: Israel Exploration Society, 1981), pp. 1–10.

——'The Second Temple Synagogue: The Formative Years', in. L.I. Levine (ed.), *The Synagogue in Late Antiquity* (Philadelphia: The American Schools of Oriental Research, 1987), pp. 7–31.

——'The Nature and Origin of the Palestinian Synagogue', *JBL* 115 (1996): 425–48.

——*Judaism and Hellenism in Antiquity* (Seattle: University of Washington Press, 1998).

——*The Ancient Synagogue: The First Thousand Years* (New Haven: Yale University Press, 2000).

——'The First-Century Synagogue: New Perspectives', *STK* 77 (2001): 22–30.

——'The First Century C.E. Synagogue in Historical Perspective', in B. Olsson, and M. Zetterholm (eds), *The Ancient Synagogue: From its Origins to 200 C.E.: Papers Presented at an International Conference at Lund University, October 14–17, 2001* (*ConNT*, 39; Stockholm: Almqvist and Wiksell, 2003), pp. 1–24.

Levinskaya, I., 'A Jewish or Gentile Prayer House? The Meaning of ΠΡΟΣΕΥΧΗ', *TynBul* 41 (1990): 154–59.
——*The Book of Acts in Its Diaspora Setting* (*TBAFCS*, vol. 5; Eerdmans: Grand Rapids, 1996).
Loffreda, S., 'The Late Chronology of the Synagogue of Capernaum', in L.I. Levine (ed.), *Ancient Synagogues Revealed* (Jerusalem: Israel Exploration Society, 1981), pp. 52–56.
——'Ceramica Ellenisticco-Romana nel Sottosuolo della Sinagoga di Cafarnao', *Studia Hierosolymitana III* (1982): 273–313.
——'Capernaum', in *NEAEHL*, vol. 1, pp. 291–95.
——*Recovering Capharnaum* (Jerusalem: Franciscan Printing Press, 2nd edn, 1993).
McKay, H.A., 'From Evidence to Edifice: Four Fallacies about the Sabbath', in R.P. Carroll (ed.), *Text as Pretext: Essays in Honour of Robert Davidson* (JSOTSup, 138; Sheffield: JSOT Press, 1992), pp. 179–99.
——*Sabbath and Synagogue: The Question of Sabbath Worship in Ancient Judaism* (Religion in the Graeco-Roman World, 122; Leiden: Brill, 1994).
——'Ancient Synagogues: The Continuing Dialectic Between Two Major Views', *Currents in Research: Biblical Studies* 6 (1998): 103–42.
——'Who or What were Synagogues: The People, the Building or the Function (unpublished paper, SBL Annual Meeting, San Francisco, November 1997).
MacLennan, R.S., 'In Search of the Jewish Diaspora: A First-Century Synagogue in Crimea?', *BARev* 22.2 (1996): 44–51, 69.
MacMullen, R., *Paganism in the Roman Empire* (New Haven: Yale University Press, 1981).
Magen, Y., Y. Zionit and O. Sirkis, 'Qiryat-Sefer, a Jewish Village and Synagogue dating to the Second Temple Period', *Qadmoniot* 33 (1999): 25–32, (Hebrew).
Ma'oz, U.T., 'The Synagogue of Gamla and the Typology of Second-Temple Synagogues', in L.I. Levine (ed.), *Ancient Synagogues Revealed* (Jerusalem: Israel Exploration Society, 1981), pp. 35–41.
——'The Synagogue that wasn't in the Hasmonean Palace in Jericho: A Response to an Article by Ehud Netzer, Ya'akov Kalman and Rachel Loris (Qadmoniot 32, 1998, 17–24)', *Qadmoniot* 32 (1998): 120–21, (Hebrew).
——'The Synagogue at Capernaum: A Radical Solution', in J.H. Humphrey (ed.), *The Roman and Byzantine Near East*, vol. 2 (Journal of Roman Archaeology Supplementary Series, 31; Portsmouth, Rhode Island: JRA, 1999), pp. 137–48.
——'Gamla – Old and New, Comments on an Article by D. Syon and Z. Yavor', *Quamoniot* 34 (2001): 130, (Hebrew).

Marshall, I.H., *The Gospel of Luke* (NIGTC; Grand Rapids: Eerdmans, 1978).

——'How far did the Early Christians Worship God?', *Churchman* 99 (1985): 216–29.

——'Military', in J.B. Green, S. McKnight and I.H. Marshall (eds), *Dictionary of Jesus and the Gospels* (Leicester: IVP, 1992), pp. 548–49.

——*The Pastoral Epistles* (ICC; Edinburgh: T&T Clark, 1999).

Martin, M.J., 'Philo's Interest in the Synagogue', *ANES* 37 (2000): 215–23.

——'Interpreting the Theodotos Inscription: Some Reflections on a First Century Jerusalem Synagogue Inscription and E.P. Sanders' "Common Judaism"', *ANES* 39 (2002): 160–81.

Martin, R.P. and P.H. Davids (eds), *Dictionary of the Later New Testament and its Developments* (Leicester: IVP, 1997).

Maser, P., 'Synagoge und Ekklesia: Erwägungen zur Frühgeschichte des Kirchenbaus', in D.A. Koch and H. Lichtenberger (eds), *Begegnungen zwischen Christentum und Judentum in Antike und Mittelalter* (Festschrift H. Schreckenberg; Göttingen: Vandenhoeck and Ruprecht, 1993), pp. 271–92.

Mason, S., *Flavius Josephus: Life of Josephus* (Leiden: Brill, 2001).

Mattila, S.L., 'Where Women Sat in Ancient Synagogues', in J.S. Kloppenborg and S.G. Wilson (eds), *Voluntary Associations in the Graeco-Roman World* (New York: Routledge, 1996), pp. 266–86.

Mazur, B.D., *Studies on Jewry in Greece* (Athens, Printing Office Hestia, 1935).

Meiggs, R., *Roman Ostia* (Oxford: Clarendon Press, 2nd edn, 1973).

Mendels, D., 'Pseudo-Philo's *Biblical Antiquities*, the "Fourth Philosophy," and the Political Messianism of the First Century CE', in J.H. Charlesworth (ed.), *The Messiah: Developments in Earliest Judaism and Christianity* (Minneapolis: Fortress Press, 1992), pp. 261–75.

Meyers, E.M., 'Ancient Synagogues: An Archaeological Introduction', in S. Fine (ed.), *Sacred Realm: The Emergence of the Synagogue in the Ancient World* (New York: Yeshiva University Museum, 1996), 3–20.

——'Synagogues', in *ABD*, vol. 6, pp. 251–60.

Meyers, E.M. and M. Chancey, 'How Jewish was Sepphoris in Jesus' Time?', *BARev* 26.4 (2000): 19–33, 61.

Meyers, E.M. and A.T. Kraabel, 'Archaeology, Iconography, and Nonliterary Written Remains', in R.A. Kraft and G.W.E. Nickelsburg (eds), *Early Judaism and its Modern Interpreters* (Society of Biblical Literature Centennial Publications; Philadelphia: Fortress Press, 1986), pp. 175–210.

Meyers, E.M. and J.F. Strange, *Archaeology, the Rabbis and Early Christianity* (London: SCM, 1981).

Miller, S.S., 'On the Number of Synagogues in the Cities of 'Erez Israel', *JJS* 49 (1998): 51–66.

Mitchell, S., *Anatolia: Land, Men, and Gods in Asia Minor* (2 vols; Oxford: Clarendon Press, 1993).

Mitchell, S. and M. Waelkens, *Pisidian Antioch: The Site and its Monuments* (London: Duckworth, 1998).

Modrzejewski, J.M., *The Jews of Egypt from Rameses II to Emperor Hadrian* (trans. R. Cornman; Edinburgh: T&T Clark, 1995).

Moehring, H.R., 'The *Acta Pro Judaeis* in the Antiquities of Flavius Josephus: A Study in Hellenistic and Modern Apologetic Historiography', in J. Neusner (ed.), *Christianity, Judaism and other Greco-Roman Cults* (SJLA, 12; 4 vols; Leiden: Brill, 1975), vol. 3, pp. 133–57.

Moo, D.J., *The Letter of James* (TNTC; Grand Rapids: Eerdmans, 1985).

Morris, L., *The Gospel According to Matthew* (Grand Rapids: Eerdmans, 1992).

——'The Saints and the Synagogue', in M.J. Wilkins and T. Paige (eds), *Worship, Theology and Ministry in the Early Church: Essays in Honor of Ralph P. Martin* (JSNTSup, 87; Sheffield: JSOT Press, 1992), pp. 39–52.

Mounce, W.D., *Pastoral Epistles* (WBC, 46; Nashville: Nelson, 2000).

Nanos, M., *The Mystery of Romans: The Jewish Context of Paul's Letter* (Minneapolis: Fortress Press, 1996).

Netzer, E., *Masada – The Yigael Yadin Excavations 1963–1965, Final Reports, III: The Buildings: Stratigraphy and Architecture* (Jerusalem: Israel Exploration Society, 1991).

——'Synagogue from the Hasmonean Period Recently Exposed in the Western Plain of Jericho', *IEJ* 49 (1999): 203–21.

——'Eine Synagoge aus hasmonäischer Zeit', *Antike Welt* 5 (2000): 477–84.

——'A Hasmonean Period Synagogue in Jericho: A Response to a Review by Uri Tzvi Ma'oz (Qadmoniot 118)', *Qadmoniot* 33 (2000): 69–70, (Hebrew).

——'The Synagogues from the Second Temple Period According to Archaeological Finds and in Light of the Literary Sources', in G.C. Bottini, L. Di Segni and D. Chrupcala (eds), *One Land – Many Cultures: Archaeological Studies in Honour of S. Loffreda* (Studium Biblicum Franciscanum Collectio Maior, 41; Jerusalem: Franciscan Printing Press, 2003), pp. 277–85.

Neusner, J., 'The Use of the Later Rabbinic Evidence for the Study of First-Century Pharisaism', in W.S. Green (ed.), *Aproaches to Ancient Judaism: Theory and Practice* (BJS, 1; Missoula: Scholars Press, 1978), pp. 215–25.

——*Formative Judaism: Religious, Historical, and Literary Studies* (BJS, 37; Chico: Scholars Press, 1982).

Nitzan, B., *Qumran Prayer and Religious Poetry* (STDJ, 12; Leiden: Brill, 1994).

Nolland, J., *Luke* (WBC, 35; 3 vols; Dallas: Word Books, 1989–93).

Noy, D., 'A Jewish Place of Prayer in Roman Egypt', *JTS* 43 (1992): 118–22.

Oakes, P., *Philippians: From People to Letter* (SNTSMS, 110; Cambridge: Cambridge University Press, 2001).

Oesterley, W.O.E., *The Jewish Background of the Christian Liturgy* (Oxford: Oxford University Press, 1925).

Olsson, B., 'The Origins of the Synagogue: An Evaluation', in B. Olsson and M. Zetterholm (eds), *The Ancient Synagogue: From its Origins to 200 C.E.: Papers Presented at an International Conference at Lund University, October 14–17, 2001* (ConNT, 39; Stockholm: Almqvist and Wiksell, 2003), pp. 132–38.

Olsson, B., D. Mitternacht and O. Brandt (eds), *The Synagogue of Ancient Ostia and the Jews of Rome: Interdisciplinary Studies* (Stockholm: Paul Åströms Förlag, 2001).

Onn, A. and S. Weksler-Bdolach, 'Umm-Al-Umdan Ruins: A Jewish Village and a Synagogue Dating to the Second Temple in Modi'in', *Qadmoniot* 38 (2005), pp. 107–16, (Hebrew).

Oster, R.E., 'Supposed Anachronism in Luke-Acts' Use of ΣΥΝΑΓΩΓΗ', *NTS* 39 (1993), pp. 178–208.

Patrich, J., 'Corbo's Excavations at Herodium: A Review Article', *IEJ* 42 (1992): 241–45.

Perrot, C., 'Luc 4, 16–30 et la lecture biblique de l'ancienne synagogue', *RevScRel* 47 (1973): 324–37.

——'The Reading of the Bible in the Ancient Synagogue', in M.J. Mulder (ed.), *Mikra: Text, Translation, Reading & Interpretation of the Hebrew Bible in Ancient Judaism & Early Christianity* (CRINT; Assen: van Gorcum, 1988), pp. 137–59.

Pervo, R., *Profit with Delight: The Literary Genre of the Acts of the Apostles* (Philadelphia: Fortress, 1987).

Pesch, R., *Die Apostelgeschichte* (EKKNT, 5; 2 vols; Zurich: Benziger, 1986).

Petuchowski, J.J., 'The Liturgy of the Synagogue', in J.J. Petuchowski and M. Brocke (eds), *The Lord's Prayer and Jewish Liturgy* (London: Burns and Oates, 1978), pp. 45–57.

Plassart, A., 'La Synagogue Juive de Délos', *RB* 11 (1914): 522–34.

Poirier, J.C., 'Purity beyond the Temple in the Second Temple Era', *JBL* 122 (2003): 247–65.

Pomeroy, S.B., *Goddesses, Whores, Wives, and Slaves: Women in Classical Antiquity* (New York: Schocken Books, 1975).

Porter, S.E., 'The "We" Passsages', in D.W.J. Gill, and C. Gempf (eds), *The Book of Acts in its Graeco-Roman Setting* (*TBAFCS*, vol. 2; Grand Rapids: Eerdmans, 1994), pp. 545–74.

Praeder, S.M., 'The Problem of First Person Narration in Acts', *NovT* 39 (1987): 193–218.

Pummer, R., 'Samaritan Synagogues and Jewish Synagogues: Similarities and Differences', in S. Fine (ed.), *Jews, Christians, and Polytheists in the Ancient Synagogue* (New York: Routledge, 1999), pp. 118–60.

Pucci Ben Zeev, M., 'Caesar and Jewish Law', *RB* 102 (1995): 28–37.

——'Who Wrote a Letter Concerning Delian Jews?', *RB* 103 (1996): 237–43.

——*Jewish Rights in the Roman World: The Greek and Roman Documents Quoted by Josephus Flavius* (TSAJ, 74; Tübingen: Mohr Siebeck, 1998).

Rajak, T., *Josephus: The Historian and His Society* (London: Duckworth, 1983).

——'Jews as Benefactors', in B. Isaac and A. Oppenheimer (eds), *Studies on the Jewish Diaspora in the Hellenistic and Roman Periods* (Te'uda, 12; Tel-Aviv: Ramot, 1996), pp. 17–38.

——'The Synagogue within the Greco-Roman City', in S. Fine (ed.), *Jews, Christians, and Polytheists in the Ancient Synagogue* (New York: Routledge, 1999), pp. 161–73.

Rajak, T. and D. Noy, 'Archisynagogoi: Office, Title and Social Status in the Greco-Jewish Synagogue', *JRS* 83 (1993): 75–93.

Rapinchuk, M., 'The Galilee and Jesus in Recent Research', *Currents in Biblical Research* 2 (2004): 197–222.

Rapuano, Y., 'The Hasmonean Period "Synagogue" at Jericho and the "Council Chamber" Building at Qumran', *IEJ* 51 (2001): 48–56.

Reich, R., 'The Hot Bath-House (*balneum*), the Miqweh and the Jewish Community in the Second Temple Period', *JJS* 39 (1988): 102–107.

——'Two Possible *Miqwa'ot* on the Temple Mount', *IEJ* 39 (1989): 63–65.

——'The Synagogue and the *Miqweh* in Eretz-Israel in the Second-Temple, Mishnaic, and Talmudic Periods', in *ASHAAD*, vol 1., pp. 289–97.

Reif, S.C., *Judaism and Hebrew Prayer: New Perspectives on Jewish Liturgical History* (Cambridge: Cambridge University Press, 1993).

——'Jewish Liturgy in the Second Temple Period: Some Methodological Considerations', in *Proceedings of the 11th World Congress of Jewish Studies, Jerusalem, June 22–29, 1993* (Jerusalem: Magnes Press, 1994), pp. 1–8.

——'Sabbath and Synagogue' (review) *JTS* 46 (1995): 610–12.

——'Prayer in the Qumran Texts', in *CHJ*, 3, pp. 852–76.

——'The Early Liturgy of the Synagogue', in *CHJ*, 326–57.

Reimer, I.R., *Women in the Acts of the Apostles: A Feminist Liberation Perspective* (Minneapolis: Fortress Press, 1995).

Reinhardt, W., 'The Population Size of Jerusalem and the Numerical Growth of the Jerusalem Church', in R. Bauckham (ed.), *The Book of Acts in its Palestinian Setting* (*TBAFCS*, vol. 4, Grand Rapids: Eerdmans, 1995), pp. 237–65.

Rengstorf, K.H. (ed.), *A Complete Concordance to Flavius Josephus* (4 vols; Leiden: Brill, 1973–1983).

Reynolds, J.M., 'Inscriptions', in J.A. Lloyd (ed.), *Excavations at Sidi Khrebish Benghazi (Berenice)*, vol. 1, *Buildings, Coins, Inscriptions, Architectural Decoration* (Supplements to Libya Antiqua, 5; Hertford: Stephen Austin and Sons, 1977), pp. 233–54.

Richardson, P., 'Early Synagogues as Collegia in the Diaspora and Palestine', in J.S. Kloppenborg and S.G. Wilson (eds) *Voluntary Associations in the Graeco-Roman World* (New York: Routledge, 1996), pp. 90–109.

——'Augustan-Era Synagogues in Rome', in K.P. Donfried and P. Richardson (eds), *Judaism and Christianity in First-Century Rome* (Grand Rapids: Eerdmans, 1998), pp. 17–29.

——'An Architectural Case for Synagogues as Associations', in B. Olsson and M. Zetterholm (eds), *The Ancient Synagogue: From its Origins to 200 C.E.: Papers Presented at an International Conference at Lund University, October 14–17, 2001* (*ConNT*, 39; Stockholm: Almqvist and Wiksell, 2003), pp. 90–117.

——*Building Jewish in the Roman East* (Waco: Baylor University Press, 2004).

Riesner, R., 'Archaeology and Geography', in J.B. Green, S. McKnight and I.H. Marshall (eds), *Dictionary of Jesus and the Gospels* (Leicester: IVP, 1992), pp. 33–46.

——'Synagogues in Jerusalem', in R. Bauckham (ed.), *The Book of Acts in its Palestinian Setting* (*TBAFCS*, vol. 4; Grand Rapids: Eerdmans, 1995), pp. 179–211.

Robinson, G.L., 'Where Archaeological Investigation left off in Palestine and Assyria', *AJA* 21 (1917): 84.

Runesson, A., 'The Oldest Original Synagogue Building in the Diaspora: A response to L. Michael White', *HTR* 92 (1999): 409–33.

——*The Origins of the Synagogue: A Socio-Historical Study* (*ConNT*, 37; Stockholm: Almqvist and Wiksell, 2001).

——'The Synagogue at Ancient Ostia: The Building and its History From the First to the Fifth Century', in B. Olsson, D. Mitternacht and O. Brandt (eds), *The Synagogue of Ancient Ostia and the Jews of Rome: Interdisciplinary Studies* (Stockholm: Paul Åströms Förlag, 2001), pp. 29–99.

——'Water and Worship: Ostia and the Ritual Bath in the Diaspora

Synagogue', in B. Olsson, D. Mitternacht and O. Brandt (eds), *The Synagogue of Ancient Ostia and the Jews of Rome: Interdisciplinary Studies* (Stockholm: Paul Åströms Förlag, 2001), pp. 115–29.

——'A Monumental Synagogue from the First Century: The Case of Ostia', *JSJ* 33 (2002) 171–220.

Runesson, A., B. Olsson and D.D. Binder, *The Ancient Synagogue: A Source Book* (Leiden: Brill, 2007: forthcoming).

Rutgers, L.V., 'Diaspora Synagogues: Synagogue Archaeology in the Greco-Roman World', in S. Fine (ed.), *Sacred Realm: The Emergence of the Synagogue in the Ancient World* (New York: Yeshiva University Museum, 1996), pp. 67–95.

Safrai, Z., 'The Communal Functions of the Synagogue in the Land of Israel in the Rabbinic Period', in *ASHAAD*, vol. 1, pp. 81–204.

Sanders, E.P., *Jewish Law from Jesus to the Mishnah: Five Studies* (London: SCM Press, 1990).

——*Judaism: Practice and Belief 63 BCE – 66CE* (London: SCM Press, 1992).

——'Common Judaism and the Synagogue in the First Century', in S. Fine (ed.), *Jews, Christians, and Polytheists in the Ancient Synagogue* (New York: Routledge, 1999), pp. 1–17.

Sanders, J.A., 'From Isaiah 61 to Luke 4', in J. Neusner (ed.), *Christianity, Judaism and Other Greco-Roman Cults: Studies for Morton Smith at Sixty* (SJLA, 12; Leiden: Brill, 1975), pp. 75–106.

——'Isaiah in Luke', in C.A. Evans and J.A. Sanders (eds), *Luke and Scripture: The Function of Sacred Tradition in Luke-Acts* (Minneapolis: Fortress, 1993), pp. 14–25.

Sanders, J.T., *The Jews in Luke-Acts* (London: SCM Press, 1987).

Sarason, R.S., 'The "Intersections" of Qumran and Rabbinic Judaism: The Case of Prayer Texts and Liturgies', *DSD* 8 (2001): 169–81.

Schiffman, L.H., 'The Dead Sea Scrolls and the Early History of Jewish Liturgy', in L.I. Levine (ed.), *The Synagogue in Late Antiquity* (Philadelphia: The American Schools of Oriental Research, 1987), pp. 33–48.

——'The Early History of Public Reading of the Torah', in S. Fine (ed.), *Jews, Christians, and Polytheists in the Ancient Synagogue* (New York: Routledge, 1999), pp. 44–56.

Schneider, C., 'Κάθημαι, καθίζω, καθέζομαι', *TDNT*, vol. 3, p. 433.

Schürmann, H., *Das Lukasevangelium* (HTKNT, 3; 2 vols; Freiburg: Herder, 1969).

Schrage, W., 'συναγωγή', *TDNT*, vol. 7, pp. 797–841.

Seager, A.R., 'Ancient Synagogue Architecture: An Overview', in J. Gutmann (ed.), *Ancient Synagogues: The State of Research* (BJS, 22; Chico: Scholars Press, 1981), pp. 39–47.

Seager, A.R. and A.T. Kraabel, 'The Synagogue and the Jewish

Community', in G.M.A. Hanfmann (ed.), *Sardis from Prehistoric to Roman Times: Results of the Archaeological Exploration of Sardis 1958–1975* (Cambridge, Mass.: Harvard University Press, 1983), pp. 168–90.

Shanks, H., *Judaism in Stone: The Archaeology of Ancient Synagogues* (New York: Harper and Row, 1979).

Sheppard, A.R.R., 'Jews, Christians and Heretics in Acmonia and Eumeneia', *AnSt* 29 (1979) 169–80.

Shiloh, Y., *Excavations at the City of David*, Vol. 1, *Interim Report of the First Five Seasons, 1978–82* (Jerusalem: Hebrew University of Jerusalem, 1984).

Shinan, A., 'Synagogues in the Land of Israel: The Literature of the Ancient Synagogue and Synagogue Archaeology', in S. Fine (ed.), *Sacred Realm: The Emergence of the Synagogue in the Ancient World* (New York: Yeshiva University Museum, 1996), pp. 130–52.

Smallwood, E.M., *The Jews under Roman Rule: From Pompey to Diocletian* (SJLA, 20; Leiden: Brill, 1976).

Smith, D.E., *From Symposium to Eucharist: The Banquet in the Early Christian World* (Minneapolis: Fortress Press, 2003).

Squarciapino, M.F., 'La sinagoga di Ostia', *Bullettino d'arte* 46 (1961): 326–37.

——'La sinagoga recentemente scoperta ad Ostia', *Rendiconti: Atti della Pontificia Accademia Romana di Archeologia*, ser. 3, 34 (1961–62): 119–32.

——'Die Synagoge von Ostia Antica', *Raggi: Zeitschrift für Kunstgeschichte und Archäologie* 4 (1962): 1–8.

——'The Synagogue at Ostia', *Archaeology* 16 (1963): 194–203.

——'The Most Ancient Synagogue known from Monumental Remains: The Newly Discovered Ostia Synagogue and its First and Fourth Century A.D. Phases', *The Illustrated London News* (28 September 1963): 468–71.

Stacey, D., 'Was there a Synagogue in Hasmonean Jericho?', Cited 8 October 2004. Online: http://www.bibleinterp.com/articles/ Hasmonean_Jericho.htm.

Stemberger, G., *Introduction to the Talmud and Midrash* (trans. M. Bockmuehl; Edinburgh: T&T Clark, 2nd edn, 1996).

Steudel, A., 'The House of Prostration CD xi 21 – xii 1 – Duplicates of the Temple', *RevQ* 61 (1993): 49–68.

Strange, J.F., 'Ancient Texts, Archaeology as Text, and the Problem of the First-Century Synagogue', in H.C. Kee and L.H. Cohick (eds), *Evolution of the Synagogue: Problems and Progress* (Harrisburg: Trinity Press, 1999), pp. 27–45.

——'Archaeology and Ancient Synagogues up to about 200 C. E.', in B. Olsson and M. Zetterholm (eds) *The Ancient Synagogue: From its*

Origins to 200 C.E.: Papers Presented at an International Conference at Lund University, October 14–17, 2001 (*ConNT*, 39; Stockholm: Almqvist and Wiksell, 2003), pp. 37–62.

Strange, J.F. and H. Shanks, 'Synagogue Where Jesus Preached Found at Capernaum', *BARev* 9.6 (1983): 25–31.

Sukenik, E.L., *Ancient Synagogues in Palestine and Greece* (London: Oxford University Press, 1934).

Syon, D., 'Gamla: Portrait of a Rebellion', *BARev* 18.1 (1992): 20–37.

Syon, D. and Z. Yavor, 'Gamla – Old and New', *Qadmoniot* 34 (2001): 2–33, (Hebrew).

Talmon, S., *The World of Qumran from Within: Collected Studies* (Jerusalem: Magnes Press, 1989).

Taylor, J.E. and P.R. Davies, 'The So-Called Therapeutae of De Vita Contemplativa', *HTR* 91 (1998): 3–24.

Tellbe, M., *Paul Between Synagogue and State: Christians, Jews, and Civil Authorities in 1 Thessalonians, Romans and Philippians* (*ConNT*, 34; Stockholm: Almqvist and Wiksell, 2001).

Tomson, P.J., 'Sabbath and Synagogue' (review) *JSJ* 28 (1997): 342–43.

Tracey, R., 'Jewish Renovation of an Amphitheatre', in G.H.R. Horsley (ed.), *New Documents Illustrating Early Christianity: A Review of the Greek Inscriptions and Papyri Published in 1979* (Grand Rapids: Eerdmans, 1987), pp. 202–209.

Trebilco, P.R., *Jewish Communities in Asia Minor* (SNTSMS, 69; Cambridge: Cambridge University Press, 1991).

——'Diaspora Judaism', in R.P. Martin and P.H. Davids (eds), *Dictionary of the Later New Testament and its Developments* (Leicester: IVP, 1997), pp. 287–300.

——*The Early Christians in Ephesus from Paul to Ignatius* (WUNT, 166; Tübingen: Mohr Siebeck, 2004).

Tsafrir, Y., 'The Synagogue at Capernaum and Meroth and the Dating of the Galilean Synagogue', in J.H. Humphrey (ed.), *The Roman and Byzantine Near East* (Journal of Roman Archaeology Supplementary Series, 14; Ann Arbor, Michigan: Cushing-Malloy, 1995), pp. 151–61.

——'On the Source of the Architectural Design of the Ancient Synagogues in Galilee: A New Appraisal', in *ASHAAD*, vol. 1, pp. 70–86.

Turner, M., *Power from on High: The Spirit in Israel's Restoration and Witness in Luke-Acts* (JPTSup, 9; Sheffield: Sheffield Academic Press, 2000).

Tzaferis, V., 'Nazareth', in *NEAEHL*, vol. 3, pp. 113–16.

VanderKam, J.C., *The Book of Jubilees* (Sheffield: Sheffield Academic Press, 2001).

Vaux, R. de., *Archaeology and the Dead Sea Scrolls, The Schweich*

Lectures of the British Academy (Oxford: Oxford Universtiy Press, 1959).

Vermes, G., *Post-Biblical Jewish Studies* (SJLA, 8; Leiden: Brill, 1975).

Vincent, L.H., 'Découverte de la "synagogue des affranchis" à Jérusalem' *RB* 30 (1921): 247–77.

Weill, R. *RB* 11 (1914): 280.

——*La Cité De David: Compte rendu des fouilles executes, à Jérusalem, sur le site de la ville primitive. Campagne de 1913–1914* (Paris: Paul Geuthner, 1920).

White, L.M., 'The Delos Synagogue Revisited: Recent Fieldwork in the Graeco-Roman Diaspora', *HTR* 80 (1987): 133–60.

——*The Social Origins of Christian Architecture* (HTS, 42; 2 vols; Valley Forge: Trinity Press, 1990–97).

——'Synagogue and Society in Imperial Ostia: Archaeology and Epigraphic Evidence', *HTR* 90 (1997): 23–58.

——'Reading the Ostia Synagogue: A Reply to A. Runesson', *HTR* 92 (1999): 435–64.

Wilcox, M., 'The God-Fearers in Acts – A Reconsideration', *JSNT* 13 (1981): 102–22.

Wintermute, O.S., 'Jubilees', in J.H. Charlesworth (ed.), *Old Testament Pseudepigrapha* (2 vols; New York: Doubleday, 1985), vol. 2, pp. 35–142.

Witherington, B., *The Acts of the Apostles: A Socio-Rhetorical Commentary* (Grand Rapids: Eerdmans, 1998).

Wright, B.G., 'Jewish Ritual Baths – Interpreting the Digs and the Texts: Some Issues in the Social History of Second Temple Judaism', in N.A. Silberman and D. Small (eds), *The Archaeology of Israel: Constructing the Past, Interpreting the Present* (JSOTSup, 237; Sheffield: Sheffield Academic Press, 1997), pp. 190–214.

Yadin, Y., 'The Excavation of Masada 1963/64, Preliminary Report', *IEJ* 15 (1965): 1–120 + plates.

——'The Synagogue at Masada', in L.I. Levine (ed.), *Ancient Synagogues Revealed* (Jerusalem: Israel Exploration Society, 1981), pp. 19–23.

York, A.D., 'The Dating of Targumic Literature', *JSJ* 5 (1974): 49–62.

Ziegler, K. and W. Sontheimer, *Der Kleine Pauly: Lexikon der Antike* (5 vols; Munich: Alfred Druckenmüller, 1972).

INDEX